So You Want to Be a

Financial Planner

Your Guide to a New Career

Nancy Langdon Jones, CFP®

So You Want to Be a Financial Planner
Your Guide to a New Career

First Printing September 2001
Second Printing December 2001
Third Printing December 2002, Revised

Nancy Langdon Jones, CFP®
http://www.nancybooks.com
nancy@nljones.com

AdvisorWorks
http://www.advisorworks.com
1153 Bordeaux Drive, Suite 109
Sunnyvale, CA 94089
info@advisorworks.com

Cover design by Peter W. Johnson, Jr.

ISBN 0-9714436-3-7
$55

Printed in the United States of America.

Dedicated to the future of the Financial Planning profession
and to those who will help shape it.

CONTENTS

CHAPTER ONE   **1**

Why?

A brief overview of the industry and thought-provoking questions potential financial planners need to ask themselves before embarking upon a career in the financial services industry.

CHAPTER TWO   **11**

Back to School

The importance of the CFP® credential, finding the right school, how to study, what to expect, sample questions from the comprehensive test, where to go for help and the importance of finding a mentor.

CHAPTER THREE   **37**

Who's the Boss?

From Wirehouses to Sole Proprietorships, Banks, Broker/Dealers and Insurance Companies: what to ask, what to avoid, and what it takes to be on your own. Who can help and how to get paid.

CHAPTER FOUR   **69**

The Dreaded Regulatory Stuff

Keep out of trouble with the many and various powers that be by correctly setting up the practice, keeping proper records and playing by the rules right from the beginning. Legal, compliance and ethics authorities provide straightforward pointers on how to run a responsible business.

Setting Up Shop

The software, the hardware, the network and other resources, plus tips on putting a professional financial planning office together, and a shopping list with start-up items. Advice from the best on what's needed to start. Dealing with clients and staff, vendors and brokers, media and mentors.

Marketing 101

Tips from those who have been there and done that: The marketing tools that got them started and what they wish they had done differently. They know what works, and share their expertise so new planners can jump-start their careers.

From Plotter to Planner in Less Than Five Years

Blow by blow narratives from planners who have been in the industry five years or less, and how they made the transition. First-hand accounts detailing obstacles and triumphs encountered as new practices were dreamed about, created and flourish in today's exciting financial planning community.

CHAPTER EIGHT

Get a Life!

Financial Planners tend to be type "A" personalities (aka workaholics). There are lots of diverse activities planners can participate in during the normal course of business, but it's crucial to keep balance. This chapter will explore ways to keep that balance, in spite of 60-hour workweeks.

APPENDICES

ACKNOWLEDGMENTS

There is no way this eBook could have been written without the help of an incredible number of generous, supportive individuals. There is likewise no way I could possibly thank all those involved! There are some, however, without whose affectionate nitpicking and nagging I could never have succeeded.

Bob Veres, my mentor and Dutch Uncle. Thank you for sticking with me.

Tim Bennett and **Robin Vaccai-Yess**, editors extraordinaire, whose shrewd sense of humor and clever quips kept me from committing hara-kiri in spite of ruthless admonitions and scrupulous content revisions. Thank you for keeping me on track.

Peter W. Johnson, Jr., distributor and co-publisher, always there with a graphic…or a safety net. Thanks to you and AdvisorWorks, I have not only survived, but thrive on Amazon! Thank you for that soothing voice that was always there for me.

I am grateful also for:

My Clients, who have welcomed me into their lives and shared their dreams with me.

The Nazrudin Project, kindred spirits all, but especially the NazLA group, Brent, Eric, Gordon, Jane, Jim, Joel, Ray and Ronnie, who continue to challenge and forge the holistic, psychological aspects of this profession within an empathetic environment.

Ronnie, my wonderful paraplanner, who diligently dealt with the back office, providing the vital time and resource link between client and book, smoothing the future path for both.

Jim Emmerson, a career changer who will soon be a colleague, and has given so much of his time as a skilled webmaster for both nljones.com and nancysbooks.com.

Mike Heryford, Lieutenant, U.S. Navy Supply Corps and **Carleton W. Moten**, for their eagle eyes and relentless proofreading.

Claude, my wonderful husband of 30 years, who lovingly fed me and carried me off to bed when he knew I'd had enough…and begrudged not the time I stole from us.

You, the future financial planners, who courageously posted questions and revealed dreams on the Financial Planning Interactive discussion boards.

My **friends** and **colleagues**, who generously shared stories, knowledge and information and unselfishly gave of their time and wisdom, so that the profession might grow stronger.

…and **Beth**.

FOREWORD

Chances are, if you've come across this book, you're interested in becoming a part of the financial planning profession. But before you jump in, you're asking yourself some very good, very basic, very important questions.

How hard will it be to become a planning professional? What hurdles and hoops will I have to get past?

If I get past them, what will I spend my days doing, and what difference will I be able to make in peoples' lives?

Can I make a living at financial planning?

Is this something I'll enjoy doing for the rest of my life?

Before you get to Nancy's answers to these questions and more, let me give you a quick "big picture" summary of what you're getting into, what planners do, where they typically come from and what they think of their lives and careers.

Financial planning started as a revolution against the Old Way of doing things. The Old Way was to sell people things (investments, life insurance, sometimes coins and diamonds) whether the customer needed them or not. A small handful of salespeople decided that, instead of working in the best interests of this or that large investment firm, they'd start working for their clients.

This guerrilla movement spread, slowly and quietly at first, until finally it matured into a new profession, called financial planning.

Yes, there are still stockbrokers and life insurance agents who care more about selling you something than about improving your life, and there probably always will be. But if you want to become a financial planner today, the professional culture demands that your first goal is to make people better investors, and improve their lives.

This, I think, is a big reason why financial planning was recently selected as the best and most fulfilling profession in the United States. Another reason is that finally, after many years of struggling to find its place in the world economy, financial planning is now a relatively prosperous career. You can make good money at it, because what people want more than anything else from a financial professional is objective advice, from somebody who sincerely wants them to prosper from it.

Today, there are many different types of planner, just as there are many different specialties in medicine, law and accounting. And, since the profession is still relatively new, it is constantly reinventing its business models and structures. You can find excellent practitioners who are compensated by commissions through affiliation with a broker-dealer, and excellent planners who work only for fees paid directly by their clients, or who are paid directly out of their client portfolios. I think that within 10 years, the great majority of planners will have given up their commission revenue--in some cases, with the encouragement of their broker-dealers.

What does a planning office look like? Typically, it will include at least one "principal"--the owner or founder of the firm, who deals directly with its clients. One of the recent trends in the planning profession is for two or more independent offices to merge, and suddenly where there was one senior planner, now there are three or four.

The senior planner's work is often supported by a less experienced professional who does much of the analytical work on each client's financial situation, putting into the computer the client's income and net worth, insurance coverage, financial goals, current investments and a host of other things that relate to our financial lives. This "casewriting professional" will perform all the basic analyses, using spreadsheets or professional software. The issues are at the same time straightforward and complex. Can this person retire in 12 years based on the size and composition of the investment portfolio, and based on how much is being saved and invested each year? Is this person paying too much in taxes? Is there a will, an estate plan, powers of attorneys, life, health, disability, auto and property-casualty insurance?

In many cases, these casewriters are "planners in training," and often are "partners in training" as well. They're working on their CERTIFIED FINANCIAL PLANNER™ (CFP®) designation, and one day expect to have clients of their own--at which point they will hire their own casewriter, who helps and supports their work with clients.

The typical office also includes people who schedule appointments, send out correspondence and answer the phone, and sometimes others who work with the trading desk of the clearing firm or who tend the computer interfaces.

What does the planner do? The planner offers several important services:

1) S/he helps clients organize their financial lives. This, in many cases, is a huge undertaking. People typically buy investments on a whim, they have no idea what they need to save and invest to meet their retirement and other goals, their insurance coverage is an overlapping hodgepodge and the whole nether world of wills and powers of attorney is an ugly mystery better put off until death or (preferably) sometime thereafter. (If you aspire to do this for people, you will need to become educated in the raw basics of financial planning.)

2) The planner helps people change their behavior. Every investor tends to panic when the market goes down, and there is a strong tendency to buy during euphoric highs. Many people don't save enough to fund their future goals; others, who survived the depths of the Depression, have more than they'll ever need and cannot manage to spend money for their own enjoyment. They need advice and counsel from somebody who they respect, and will not change their behavior unless the advisor can earn that respect. (This may be the defining "talent" of a planning professional; when casewriters are watched for partner potential, the first thing you look for is the ability to handle a client meeting and get clients moving in more efficient, personally beneficial directions.)

3) Increasingly, financial planners help people define their deepest and most personal goals, and serve as a general contractor to help them build a better and more fulfilling life. This is where the planning profession is going; it is the logical endpoint of the journey that began when a handful of rebels decided to stop selling and start serving their clients. (As you gain life experience, and as you spend time with successful people who are able to afford to hire a planner, you learn how to provide this most valuable service for others.)

All of the planning firms that I know started small. Originally, most planners were career-changers; insurance agents, stockbrokers or accountants who wanted to broaden their service offer.

Alternatively, people moved into the field with little or no financial training. The founder of the company has an interest in investments, takes night classes while maintaining his/her day job. Then, still working a day job, the planner began offering financial advice, for not much money, to friends, relatives and acquaintances. Over time, they referred friends, and the advisor began raising fees just enough to make ends meet. At that point, s/he would decide to offer financial planning full-time, sometimes in a home office, sometimes in rented facilities.

The client list would grow slowly until suddenly, one day, it seemed like there was more business coming in the door than could be handled. Then the advisor would face the usual issues of managing business growth: hiring people, making the usual mistakes and counting the usual small successes of any small business. Chances are, if you talk to even the most successful advisors today, they still feel as if they're running a struggling small business instead of the dominant planning firm in their market.

Today, people are getting into the business through a different route, gaining a college or certificate education in planning, and then joining one of these established firms as the person who handles trades or a casewriter for one of the senior planners. Eventually, this person will take on clients of his own, and works toward the day when he becomes a partner or buys out the firm from a retiring founder.

Planners who have done this for years tell me that there isn't another profession on the planet that lets you share more personally in the personal growth and success of other people. In this respect, it is tremendously rewarding and fulfilling.

But it also requires a great deal of attention to detail, and a willingness to study and learn the nuances of investments and portfolio development, tax and estate planning, how to structure charitable contributions and evaluate insurance contracts and a million other details that most people find tedious and (as a consequence) are willing to pay handsomely if somebody would just take them off their backs.

In addition, it requires the ability to communicate effectively with people, to let them know what you know, and to show them that you care about them and their lives, families and future. It requires listening skills, and a certain dose of psychology. You deal with successful people from all walks of life.

Finally, financial planners in the future will be increasingly expected to become exemplars of the successful, fulfilling life they preach. That means taking the time to understand what you, yourself, want out of life, and pursuing your own goals with the same passion that you expect from your best clients. Planners all over the country are pioneering business arrangements that allow them to cross-country ski in the evenings from their back porch, or take yearly vacation trips, sometimes with two or three of their favorite clients, or cut back on their lifestyle expenditures so that they can afford to reduce their work hours and have more time for relationships, art and music or smelling the flowers that most of us hardly notice in our hectic push to get ahead of the rat race.

If this interests you, if you have these capabilities within you, then the profession needs you. The truth is, there just are not enough financial advisors in this world to handle the need for their services. I once divided the number of households by the number of financial planners in each state in the country, and found that there are many thousands of unserved households for each planning office in virtually every part of this country. I don't know of any successful practitioner who can handle more than 200 clients at once, so the market is going to be bigger than the profession for years to come.

In fact, one area of quiet concern in the profession is that middle-income people are not being served by the planning profession today, because most advisors can hardly keep up with the wealthy clients who knock on their doors. Many firms that I'm in contact with have all but closed their doors to new business.

This is, in other words, a wide-open field.

Elsewhere in this book, you'll read that I was "kind enough" to encourage Nancy Langdon Jones to write the book you are now reading. The truth is, I welcome this book purely out of self-interest. Once people in the early stages of entering the planning profession become aware of my newsletter and web service, they would come to me with basic questions. Each year, I get many hundreds of requests from people who want to know how, step-by-step, they can become a financial planning professional. Often, I would send them away with some encouragement and general advice--and feel like I hadn't given them nearly what they asked for.

On the financial planning discussion boards, I've seen Nancy answer many of these same requests with a deft touch, drawing from her own experience and the experience of many others she has talked with over the years. But, again, in a single post, off the top of your head, you can only offer so much advice. What people really needed was a "how to" manual.

Now--finally--we have it. Finally, when people call with those difficult questions, I have a place I can send them, a resource I can recommend without qualification.

If I haven't discouraged you from pursuing a career in financial planning, then let me get out of the way and let Nancy answer your important questions in more detail. If you're attracted to this profession, chances are you have a wonderful life mission to fulfill, and this is a great place to get started. In my view, there is nothing more precious in this world than a financial planner in training who will someday change peoples' lives for the better.

Best of luck in all you undertake.

Robert N. Veres
Publisher, Inside Information
http://www.bobveres.com

INTRODUCTION

This eBook was written to be read on a computer with access to the Internet. There are over a hundred links for websites you can visit to acquire additional information. My decision to publish in electronic format rather than in traditional print was two-fold:

We live in an era where technology is changing the way we work, play, and think on a daily basis. During the year it took me to write this book, the evolution in the financial planning profession astounded me! In Appendix B I recommend four very good books to help you "get started". Two of them were published in 2000, and another in 2001. All were outdated before they hit the streets. By ePublishing, new editions of **So You Want to Be a Financial Planner** will be available within days of major industry events.

It is important to me that **So You Want to Be a Financial Planner** be interactive. I want to hear about your successes, and about your frustrations. I hope you'll share your experiences with education, Broker/Dealers, software, business plans and anything else that's on your mind. I anticipate an annual update, where I will incorporate stories of new planners, new resources and new trends. It is only with your participation that **So You Want to Be a Financial Planner** can become the definitive tool to developing a successful career in financial planning.

Please join me at the Financial Planning Interactive website http://www.financial-planning.com/wwwboard5/.

Nancy's Network, is a forum where readers can share current information about schools, study materials, broker/dealers, interviews, complaints, internship and employment opportunities, problems making a transition, etc. Benefits of membership include free downloads of updated editions of "So You Want to Be a Financial Planner", access to the Nancy's Network Directory and discussion, plus notification of new products or services to help beginning planners. The cost is a one-time set-up fee of $30. If you're interested in subscribing to the network, please visit www.nancysbooks.com and sign up!

Bookmark these sites and let me, and others, know what's on your mind!

IMPORTANT NOTE:

Purchase of this book in Print Format entitles the purchaser to a free download so that the book may be read on a PC with Internet connection. To obtain the free download, please send an e-mail explaining where you obtained the print version (i.e. Amazon, Trader's Library, etc.) to nancy@nancysbooks.com and request your free copy of the current PDF file. Please be certain you have at least 2 MG of storage on your e-mail server before receiving the PDF file.

XIV

Chapter One

Why?

Once upon a time, I was giving an after-dinner speech to a group of Nurse Practitioners, on the importance of understanding the family's finances. When it was over, one woman sat in the back of the room until it cleared, then came up and told me she appreciated what I had said.

"My husband has been after me for years to take a more active role in our money," she began, "but I'm simply not interested. He enjoys doing the investments and does a good job. What I hate is his insistence that I sit down with him every month for a few minutes while he explains the brokerage statements and goes over the income and expenses. The worst time is when I have to go to the tax accountant once a year and listen while they tell me where the numbers on the tax form come from before I have to sign the darned return!

"I'm going home now and tell him that the next time he wants to explain it to me I really will pay attention," she continued. "Now I know it's because he loves me that he wants me to understand what we're doing."

It felt good to know that even one person had heard what I had to say that night. It was a couple of years later, however, that the full impact hit me. I had forgotten about the incident when the Nurse Practitioner telephoned to tell me her husband had been killed in an accident six months earlier.

"Since his death, I've received dozens of calls from financial sales people wanting to 'take care of me,'" she explained, "just like you said I might. But I know right where everything is. I manage the bills, watch the stocks, and call the accountant every now and then. I haven't made any big changes. Now that the shock is easing, I'm ready to talk with you about making plans for the rest of my life."

The night I spoke to the Nurse Practitioners, I made a difference. That is why I am a financial planner.

The 2001 edition of *Jobs Rated Almanac* put Financial Planning at the top of its list for the following reasons:

    1. Make lots of money: Of course, if you sell lots of stuff. You can do that in any industry, if you're a good salesperson!

    2. Set your own hours: Uh huh. No problem, if you don't mind 60-80 hour workweeks.

    3. Low stress. Oh, sure. Dealing with other people's money and lives has always been low stress, particularly in today's economic climate.

Financial Planning is not a way to get rich quick, unless your definition of riches is the reward deemed from the knowledge you have made a difference for the better, in the life of your client.

Years after I had started to practice as a financial planner, a friend invited me to a meeting of the Nazrudin[1] Project, an unstructured, leaderless association of sorts, still in its infancy at the time. I sat back and observed while several people I recognized as leaders in the profession discussed how they truly loved what they did, and found such joy in their vocation that they would gladly do it for nothing, save the fact they had to put food on their own table. I had felt that way for years, yet would never admit it for fear of appearing silly, or worse, unprofessional. But here were well-known practitioners with exemplary practices, feeling just as I felt.

In those few hours, listening to the echoes around me, I realized for the first time that financial planning is a very specific career choice completely misunderstood by nearly everyone – including many of those who call themselves financial planners.

I am convinced the financial planning profession is not only in its infancy, but that the world *ain't seen nuthin' yet!*[2]

It is my conviction, and also the belief of literally hundreds of my colleagues, that financial planners will one day soon be engaged not just for investment and tax advice, but for helping clients achieve a comfortable current and future lifestyle.

On the bus to the airport from FPA's Retreat 2001 in Tampa, I talked with Roy Diliberto, CFP®, CLU, ChFC, and then Chair of the FPA Board of Directors Executive Committee. He made a most profound observation about the profession:

"Financial Planning," Roy said, "is **looking at the future and bringing it back into the present while you can still do something about it**."

Whoa. That can't be right! The FPA Chair defining the profession in such esoteric, holistic language?

"We're so young we don't have models yet," he continued. "I'm frustrated over it! The profession was born out of the insurance industry. We tried to build our practices by going out and selling like the insurance companies, but it didn't work. People coming into the profession just have to become part of the infrastructure, gain experience, and work their way up."

---

[1] Nazrudin is an experience, not a definition. Annual membership in Nazrudin is $50.00. If you are interested in joining, contact Leena Dwiggins at SoleSupportSrv@aol.com to learn where to send your check. Be sure to include your name, mailing address, telephone number, fax number and e-mail address. Once your payment is received, you will receive further instructions on accessing the group's conversations on yahoo. If you need more information, please email Carol Nowka at: nowka@hamilton.net.

[2] Al Jolson

"The compleat[3] financial planner," according to David Brand[4], who participated in a discussion on the Nazrudin website, "understands who the client is, what s/he values, and respects where s/he is in life's journey. Sometimes, gently expanding an interest or awareness in a client's life is all that can and should be done. Financial planners have a unique opportunity to apply these 'life-enhancing' skills in their practice. They are requisite skills for any professional who wishes to excel in their craft."

For years, I've been opening my complimentary meetings by asking the prospect before me, "Why are you here?" If the response is something like, "We're looking for a better return on our investments," I cringe. Then I tell them to go talk to a stockbroker – or get another stockbroker if they don't think the current one is making enough money for them. It disturbs me when people are unclear on the concept; yet, even I have an awful time explaining exactly what a financial planner does. We do so many things, but I want to make this perfectly clear:

FINANCIAL PLANNING IS NOT ABOUT MONEY!

FINANCIAL PLANNING IS ABOUT LIFE...

ABOUT DREAMS...and how to achieve them.

Sure, investments, taxes, budgets, money stuff is involved. However, the operative word here is **life**, as in, "What do you want to do with it?"

One of the briefest encounters I have ever had with a potential client was also one I found most rewarding.

Awhile back, I talked with a corporate executive who had been offered a "golden parachute" if he took early retirement. Over the phone, he told me in no uncertain terms that he was accepting the deal. His accountant and attorney had both said it was an outstanding offer. Everything fit precisely into his budget, and he was only calling because someone told him to "run it by a financial planner."

Nevertheless, he informed me there was nothing I could say to change his mind. I told him my fee and arranged the appointment.

He and his wife arrived hauling a file box filled with pension information. I greeted them and walked them back to my conference room, asking if they'd like coffee. They would. I left to get it, shaking my head, wondering why I had agreed to meet with these people who

---

[3] com·pleat (kəm-plēt′) adj.
Of or characterized by a highly developed or wide-ranging skill or proficiency: "The compleat speechwriter... comes to anonymity from Harvard Law" (Israel Shenker).
Being an outstanding example of a kind; quintessential: "Here was the compleat modern misfit: the very air appeared to poison him; his every step looked treacherous and hard won" (Stephen Schiff).
[4] David Brand has over 20 years experience as executive manager of non-profit professional associations. Most recently, he was executive director of the Financial Planning Association. David holds a Law Degree, as well as a Masters Degree in Public Administration.

had already made up their mind. I felt not only redundant, but also a little irritated that it was late and I wasn't enjoying dinner with my husband.

When I returned with the coffee, just to break the ice I asked, "Well…what will you be doing when you retire?" We all just sat there. She took a sip of the coffee. I smiled and shuffled papers. The big box sat unopened on the floor. Minutes passed after which he reached into his back pocket, and wrote out a check for my fee.

"I'm not going to retire," he said as he slid the check across the table to me. "I have nothing to do in retirement." His wife sighed with relief. It turned out their entire life revolved around his clients. He golfed with them, networked with them, supported them, and entertained them. I had asked the right question.

He had expertly evaluated all the money stuff. But he hadn't considered the life stuff! At first, I felt guilty for taking an hour's pay for only ten minutes of interface. When I reflected on this encounter in the scheme of things, however, it became incredibly clear to me. My client had paid me for invaluable advice. He thought he was coming to me about the money. He already knew about the money. His CPA had calculated the taxes. His attorney had considered the impact on his estate. His pension administrator had evaluated the cash flow implications. But nobody had put the picture together. No one had asked the client what he wanted to do with his life.

Before getting too far into this chapter, it's best to define what we're talking about here: **Financial Planning**. After all, this is a book about how to become a *Financial Planner* to presumably do *Financial Planning*. Simple enough, right? Wrong. Sit down while I explain the difficulty I had in finding a definition to put with either of these terms.

The CFP Board of Standards[5] spells out the six steps a financial planner needs to follow in order to complete a financial planning engagement. It looks like this:

The Financial Planning Process

- Establish and define the client-planner relationship
- Gather client data including goals
- Analyze and evaluate the client's financial status
- Develop and present financial planning recommendations and/or alternatives
- Implement the financial planning recommendations
- Monitor the financial planning recommendations

Notice that this is a *process*, not a definition. Financial planners know what it is that they do, but I challenge anyone to come up with a universal definition of exactly what *Financial Planning* is. Save your energy. There isn't any such thing. Yet.

---

[5] http://www.cfp-board.org

The **only** "definition" of *Financial Planner* I could find came from the InvestorWords[6] website, and looks like this:

"Financial Planner: An investment professional who helps individuals set and achieve their long-term financial goals, through investments, tax planning, asset allocation, risk management, retirement planning, and estate planning."

Tip of the iceberg. Well, maybe back in the olden days, more than twenty years ago, when *Financial Planning* was just beginning to emerge from its insurance wrapped cocoon, financial planning might have been defined so narrowly. Today, you will find, if you have read Bob Veres'[7] comments in the Foreword, that it has grown to mean much more than a rudimentary "Financial Planner = Investment Professional".

Bob adds, "…improve their lives." **Improve their lives!** What a concept!

This is a "how-to" book for individuals considering a career as a financial planner, and if you are one of those individuals, then you'd better know something right from the get-go:

People entering the financial planning profession today will have to define it.

There's help. Bob has been sort of canonized as the financial planner's visionary. He possesses this (some would term *peculiar*) knack of sensing where things are heading. I've been watching his uncanny prophecies come to fruition for nearly two decades now. It's been long enough, in any case, to get my full attention. If you are just entering this profession, you had better sit up and take notice too!

Once at the end of a speech to financial advisors, Bob told a story about an obviously successful retired person on the golf course with his buddies. You know the one…just like in the TV commercials for the major brokerages. In the commercials, someone looks at the satisfied retiree and asks, "Who's your broker?"

In Bob's futuristic version, people will ask, "Who's your financial planner?"

FPA President Bob Barry, CFP® summed it up in his speech at Success Forum[8] 2002 in New Orleans:

"I can not tell you how certain I am that the only way that we can make any true progress in defining a profession that will endure, is to define who we are. And I can tell you that if I ruled the world, by some date in the not so distant future, if you were holding yourself out to the public as providing financial planning, you'd be a CERTIFIED FINANCIAL PLANNER™ practitioner. I'd also hope that you wouldn't think of calling yourself a financial planner unless you were a CFP® practitioner. And, it's my wish that across this country, financial services firms that offer financial planning would know that they have to

---

[6] http://www.investorwords.com/
[7] http://www.bobveres.com
[8] The Financial Planning Association's Annual National Convention.

hire CFP® professionals to provide it, so that consumers would be clear, once and for all, that if they want financial planning they should go to a CFP® practitioner."

Names and ideas and models and scenarios have been tossed around in discussion groups with current practitioners all over the country, but they boil down to one thing: going forward, true financial planning professionals must take a holistic approach to helping their clients plan for the future. A background in psychology, an empathetic personality, and plenty of diverse life experience are just as important in this profession as is academic coursework in the financial planning process.

The Nazrudin Project has been instrumental in perpetuating this new landscape on the financial planning horizon, and in making it available to consumers. Innovative work is being done by some of the finest financial planners in the nation toward developing an infrastructure that will educate the public to the availability of this new breed of financial planner. You had better prepare for it if you expect to be a part of this exciting, dynamic, pioneering profession that is just now surfacing.

Members of the Nazrudin Project in the greater Los Angeles area participate in a bi-monthly get-together. We met while I was struggling to come up with a definition of the financial planner of the future for this publication. The ensuing discussion was both energizing and fascinating, but a specific, satisfactory definition continues to elude us.

Eric Bruck, CFP®, with the independent firm of Allied Financial & Consulting Services, Inc. in Westwood, California, reminded me of a Nazrudin chat awhile ago that used the metaphor of a jigsaw puzzle to illustrate a holistic approach to the financial planning process. The question posed was, "What's the most important *piece* to start with when putting the puzzle together?" Some thought it was the corner piece, or finding the edge pieces. Others thought sorting the pieces by color was the key. The logical piece to start with, of course, is the picture on the box top.

Without looking at the completed picture, it's much more difficult to assemble the many tiny pieces in the box. The financial planner of the future must first have the skill set to guide the client's focus to the picture on the box. This has nothing to do with which mutual funds to own or what type of insurance to purchase. It has to do with first defining a vision for living life to its fullest. Without the picture that identifies those present and future dreams, there is no viable place to begin a plan. How much money a client has, or the percentage a client is making on his portfolio, has no relevance without the picture on the box. The planner must put the paintbrush in the client's hand, and lend guidance and encouragement as the picture develops.

Taking this one step further, Eric suggests that "traditional" financial planners have put the cart before the horse. If the solutions are in the cart, then the cart belongs **behind** the horse. After all, how are solutions possible until you know where the horse is headed?

He continues to challenge the planner to discern the client's expectations in at least four distinct areas before even beginning to think what might be appropriate items to fit in the cart. Eric proposes the following as necessary ingredients of a fulfilled life:

- Health/Energy
- Sense of Security with the World
- Good Quality of Relationships
- Contribution to the Community

And let's not forget a possible fifth ingredient: simply, fun! There is no substitute for having the capacity now and then to just enjoy the moment.

Once the client has come to terms with these components, then, and only then, does Eric feel it is time to begin filling the cart, but only at a pace with which the client is comfortable.

While researching web sites and links for this book, I came across an article written by a CPA I had never met. Astounded by how perfectly the article summed up what I had been trying to explain from conception in this chapter, I picked up the phone and called Frank Sisco[9], CPA, PFS, a Personal Financial Specialist[10] and financial planner in Harrison, New York.

"Frank," I asked, "may I include your article in the appendix for Chapter 1 of my book for people considering financial planning as a career?"

His generous response led to an animated coast-to-coast conversation that lasted nearly an hour. In his article on "Sensitive Financial Services"[11], Frank has beautifully articulated what I see as the financial planning profession of the future. Certainly there will be clients who need the direction and guidance of financial planners for short-term or temporary projects. But I truly believe the financial planning professional of the future will deal with unique clients on a long-term basis, just like the ones Frank illustrates in his article. It takes a special person to tune in to the true needs and dreams of clients.

Take time now to read Frank's article in Appendix A. If you can't envision yourself doing what he describes for a sizeable portion of your clientele, then I suggest you reconsider financial planning as a career. The definition of *Financial Planning* may not yet be written in stone, but Frank's scenario is not far off the mark.

How Much Money Do Financial Planners make?

I don't know.

I'll admit right up front that I have a jaded eye when it comes to surveys, so it won't come as a surprise when I tell you I blame the Financial Planning Association's Annual Financial

---

[9] Learn more about Frank Sisco from his website http://www.thirdthousand.com or give him a call in Harrison, New York at 914.381.3737

[10] The Personal Financial Specialist (PFS) is the financial planning specialty accreditation held exclusively by certified public accountants (CPAs) who are members of the American Institute of CPAs (AICPA). A CPA must demonstrate experience and expertise in a wide range of personal financial matters before being awarded the PFS. http://www.cpapfs.org/

[11] See Appendix A

Performance & Compensation Study of Financial Planning Practitioners[12] for the common misconception that financial planners make a lot of money.

Let me begin by telling you that my good friend and colleague, Harv Ames, CFP®, a financial planner in Peterborough, New Hampshire, took me under his wing one afternoon and spent hours explaining exactly why the study is valid and accurate. Harv has a degree in statistical analysis and made an excellent presentation that I understood thoroughly. I just didn't buy it.

Here's why: According to the CFP Board's Annual Report[13], there were 36,307 CERTIFIED FINANCIAL PLANNER™ certificants in the country in 2000. I searched through the Study and found only that the questionnaire had been sent to "a diverse group of…participants ranging from small sole practitioners to large ensemble firms…with revenues over $10,000,000."

Since there are a whole lot more financial planners who are not CFP® Certificants that are members of the FPA, who commissioned the Study, I can only assume that the universe of "diverse…participants" from which to choose was much greater than 36,307. I received the questionnaire. I don't have it any more, but believe me, it was really long. I spent a couple of hours getting through the first few pages, and then the questions got too tough for me. After consulting with Ronnie, my paraplanner who also does our company's books, we answered a few more questions. Then some esoteric accounting terms that I couldn't even define came up and I threw the rest away.

The Study results include the 703 participants who responded to the survey. Seven hundred and three! I don't know about statistical analysis, but that doesn't sound like very many out of at least 36,307 identifiable financial planning practitioners. My contention is that those filling out the forms were mainly high producers selling commissionable products at large brokerages who are doing very little actual *financial planning* – and Harv.

Harv told me he completed the questionnaire and sent it in. Why wouldn't he? He grooves on this stuff! Once I began writing this book, I also began inquiring as to who sent back the questionnaire. My research was anything but scientific, but of the several hundred people I asked, perhaps 15% had received the survey. Absolutely no one that I asked – with the exception of Harv – had taken the time and effort to fill it out and return it.

My hypothesis is that the Study is enormously skewed toward the large brokerages, where staff can fill in the questionnaire utilizing published statistics from corporate tax returns and 1099s that the "participants" received showing commissions earned. Some of this shows up in the statistics, which report that the average sole-practitioner makes less than the planner does in an "ensemble" practice.

Well, duh! Even I have heard of economies of scale. What was new to me is the term "survivorship bias." Nowhere in the Study could I find anything about practitioners who

---

[12] http://www.fpanet.org/products/2001fpasurvey.cfm
[13] The CFP Board's complete 2001 Annual Report is on their website: http://www.cfp-board.org/press_anlrpt.html

8

had left the industry, yet I am aware that many who enter the profession cannot make it for a variety of reasons – generally due to misconceptions about income. They don't make enough money to support themselves – having entered the industry because they read the Study which showed the "average" income was lucrative, and discovering just the opposite! I'll bet none of those "under $5,000" planners participated in the Study. They were out looking for a job![14]

If you want to know how much money you can make as a financial planner, then find a financial planner in your area whose practice you admire, take the planner to lunch, and ask! Don't stop there. Ask them what they did to get where they are. Ask them about the cost in time, dollars, and family. Ask them if it was worth it. And then take a different financial planner who is doing what you want to be doing and invite them to lunch. Ask the same questions.

Not long ago, there was a posting on Financial Planning Interactive[15] by a college graduate expressing concern over whether or not it is a good time to be entering the profession. As Carl Abissi completed his internship and looked for work, he recognized that the industry has moved toward what he calls a "relationship approach." I think Carl is right.

"Many firms I have interviewed with," he shared, "have decided a recent college graduate may have no place in their program due to the fact that the grads don't have a demonstrated track record of success and accomplishments. They are looking strictly for experienced people with established relationships, past professional business experience, and with a CPA, CFP® or JD attached to their name.

"I have interviewed with firms of all types," Carl continued, "from traditional Broker/Dealers and insurance companies to small independent financial planning and high-end wealth management firms. In many cases I feel they are turning their efforts away from college graduates, toward seasoned professionals."

Carl is looking for answers to questions that have no answers. These are the same questions that will confront you. No one has the answers. No clear steps are there to guarantee you reach the magic doorway through which a career as a financial planner awaits you.

Make no mistake.

This is a book for people who think they want to become financial planners. It's not for those who want to be stockbrokers. It won't tell you how to invest your retirement funds. This book has nothing to do with selling investments or insurance. And it won't hand a new career to you on a silver platter.

---

[14] Other places to find information on a career in financial planning is the Bureau of Labor Statistics http://stats.bls.gov/ and from AdvisorBenchmarking.com, a most realistic picture is on http://www.advisorbenchmarking.com . Also take the survey at http://www.fabestpractices.com/.
[15] http://www.financial-planning.com/wwwboard5/

What this book will do is tell you what's out there, show you where to find the fundamental resources to prepare yourself, and give you a supporting hand. If that's not enough, then perhaps you're looking at the wrong profession.

Conclusion

When my daughter, Beth, was doing graduate studies toward her Physician Assistant[16] Certificate, she worked at Children's Hospital in Los Angeles. Once in awhile I'd visit her for lunch and she'd take me on a tour of the wing where she worked. It saddened me to see so many sick children, but watching their faces light up when they saw Beth was such a delight. She would pat someone on the back, give a hug to another, tickle a rib or two and get down on one knee to listen to a soft whisper, as the children clamored around for attention.

Next would come introductions to her Mommy amid much giggling as Beth asked a bandaged-headed boy what the Sultan had done with Billy, and applauded Susie's success – three whole steps, even with the heavy brace.

Weeks later, Beth would come home and I'd ask, "How is little Tommy?" She would tell me that he had died a few days ago, and then describe, with such pride, how a new child had overcome a difficult obstacle.

Beth has a gift. She can bring joy and laughter to these terminally ill children and somehow survive the everyday tragedies to remain upbeat and loving for the next ones.

"I'm so glad we have people like you in the world, Beth," I told her once. "I could never do what you do!"

"Mom," she replied. "You've been doing what I do ever since I can remember. It's just that I do it with medicine, and you do it with money."

Before embarking on any new career, take time to do some soul-searching. If you're going to be good at what you do, you'll have to know a lot more than you will find on the pages of a textbook. Yes, you need to learn the fundamentals, to pass the tests, to understand how the system works. But it's what bubbles up from down deep inside that will make the difference. Without passion for your chosen profession, you will miss out on the joy of it. Think long and hard before deciding whether you honestly have that consuming desire to be a financial planner.

If you do, then go on to the next page and begin your journey.

---

[16] http://www.aapa.org

Chapter Two

Back to School

"The FPA reaffirms that all who hold themselves out as financial planners should be CFP® certificants and rededicates itself to promoting the CFP® certification marks as the cornerstone of the financial planning profession."

Pretty clear edict. The Financial Planning Association, the result of a merger between the industry association, International Association for Financial Planning (IAFP) and the professional association, Institute of Certified Financial Planners (ICFP), passed this resolution in July 2000. Translation? If you really want to be a financial planner, you'll need your CFP® certification[17].

Things have changed considerably since, at the age of 44, I enrolled in the College for Financial Planning's course and simultaneously entered the University of Southern California extension Financial Planning Program. My UCLA kids cringe every time they see the USC diploma on my wall, but I think it looks cool.

I'm one of those students who needs to ask questions of a real, live instructor, and enjoys the intercourse from a classroom experience. There were 35 who showed up to begin the CFP-I class at the Hilton Hotel in Pasadena in 1983. Fifteen of us completed the course two years later. To this day, many of those are among my close colleagues.

Thinking back, the way we did it made a lot of sense. During the risk management course, we all went through an outside insurance program and sat for the Life & Disability and Variable Contract license exam. While we studied for the tax part of the CFP certification program, we enrolled in the H&R Block tax course in our neighborhood and became registered tax preparers. We took a five-day crash course together and passed the Series 7 securities exam while studying Investments in the CFP certification program.

At that time there was no certification exam and my years as a Realtor® qualified me for the work experience requirement once I passed the sixth course. Mid-way through the CFP certification program, I became a Registered Representative for a Broker/Dealer, and began my career as a financial planner.

Today the same four "E" requirements exist for those wanting to obtain the CERTIFIED FINANCIAL PLANNER™ certification. They are:

1. Education
> You will need to be knowledgeable in the following six areas of financial planning:
> > Insurance planning
> > Investment planning

---

[17] http://www.fpanet.org/cfpmark/index.cfm

Tax planning
Retirement planning
Employee benefits
Estate planning
2. **Examination**
    You will need to pass the CFP® Certification Examination
3. **Experience**
    You will need three years of relevant experience in personal financial planning (five if you have no college degree.)[18]
4. **Ethics**
    You will need to sign statements adhering to the CFP Board:
        Code of Ethics and Professional Responsibility
        Financial Planning Practice Standards
        Disciplinary Rules and Procedures

Selecting a School and Course of Study[19]

Choices abound! As of May 2001, there were over 200 CFP Board-Registered programs at 136 colleges and universities in the United States. Whatever you do, don't just jump into the first program you find. This is an important step in your career, and you want to give yourself the best possible education. Unfortunately, many classes are simply set up to help you pass the certification exam, not to teach you financial planning skills.

If you are going to earn your CFP® certification, here's how to get started:

1. Download or send for the Guide to CFP® Certification[20]

2. What is your purpose for acquiring the certification?

This may seem like an odd question, but it requires a little soul-searching. Some people "collect" letters to put after their name. Others figure it's probably something they should do, but they want to get it over with the cheapest, quickest way available.

For those serious about a career in financial planning it can be absolutely the best possible way to train. Place emphases on schools that reach out beyond the six required areas and offer classes in financial planning practicum and on developing and managing a practice.

Frequently there are posts on the discussion boards from people entering the industry who want to know whether they will get the best financial planning training from American Express or Merrill Lynch, or perhaps with an independent firm. You may learn outstanding marketing, sales or service techniques with any one of the hundreds of Broker/Dealers and financial planning companies across the country, but you will not learn how to prepare a

---

[18] View the CFP Board's Definition of Work Experience at http://www.cfp-board.org/cert_gibs4.html
[19] FPA Career Center http://www.fpanet.org/career/education.cfm
[20] http://www.cfp-board.org/cert_edpro.html

comprehensive financial plan for a client. The best way to learn that is by going through the educational process with a CFP Board-Registered program.

Unfortunately, the schools, faculty, teaching methods and presentation vary greatly. I was fascinated as I listened to students discuss their experiences during a "Bridge the Gap" session at Success Forum 2000 in Boston. Many were disillusioned and even angry at the quality of classes or support they had received from the institution they chose, while some praised their instructors to the hilt and felt the program they selected had prepared them well for entry into the profession. Clearly, it pays to shop around. It's a classic case of *buyer beware*! The CFP Board has posted a list of questions in the Guide[21] you should ask before plunking down tuition fees.

Like any other profession, there are some outstanding opportunities out there. I feel Jerry Mason, Ph.D, CFP®, CLU, ChFC during his tenure at Texas Tech University[22] set the benchmark. But logistics of earning a BA while attending on-campus classes in Lubbock, Texas may not be practical for many mid-life career changers.

3. How do you learn?

Some have the discipline to set a self-study schedule and stick to it on their own. Others need intense classroom interaction in a structured environment. I needed as much help as I could get, and signed up for both a self-study course and classroom instruction. At the time, my tuition at USC included a one-day crash course prior to each live test. Literally hundreds of students would gather on the USC campus to go over case studies, calculations, and generally get our act together. But back in the '80s, most of us didn't even own a computer! Today, the basic choices remain self-study and live on-campus classes with some online reinforcement.

The College for Financial Planning[23] in Denver started it all back in 1969, and the new (February 2001) kid on the block to offer the CFP® certification course is Kaplan College[24]. Coincidentally, a couple of the best-known instructors from the College for Financial Planning are now affiliated with the Kaplan program.

Kansas State University[25] began a hybrid program in September 2001.

Texas Tech and Kansas State are also a part of GPIDEA[26], the Great Plains Interactive Distance Education Alliance, a consortium of Human Sciences Colleges at ten universities. Students may pursue a degree offered by a single institution or multiple institutions. Each university brings a unique strength to the multi-institution academic programs. In a multi-institution program, a student is admitted at one institution and enrolls in courses at multiple institutions.

---

[21] http://www.cfp-board.org/cert_edpro.html
[22] http://www.hs.ttu.edu/medce/ffp/default.htm
[23] http://www.fp.edu
[24] http://www.kaplan.com → Certificate in Financial Planning.
[25] http://www.k-state.edu/ipfp/
[26] http://www.gpidea.org/

4. What's your time frame?

Unless you've been collecting financial experience in a personal financial planning setting approved by the CFP Board, you won't be able to place the CFP® certification marks after your name for at least three years (five without a college degree). I recommend you get started as soon as possible, but there's a lot to be said for working as a financial planner before starting the certification program. For instance, if financial planning professionals surround you, you have a ready-made advice and cheerleading group to help you through the tough parts.

If you have a well-paying day job, think about taking the classes during your off time. Most courses are designed for working professionals and anticipate a two-year completion date. Look at your calendar and your transition plan and see how the course works in. Socking away something from a job with steady income while studying could be a huge help during the first few lean years in practice.

If you're rarin' to go, others have proven it's possible to zip through the program and sit for the certification exam in record time. Take Michael Kapustin[27], CFP®, RFC, ChFC with Society Hill Financial Planning in Voorhees, New Jersey:

"It is possible to take the necessary courses and take (and pass) the test within 6 months. I know this because I did it several years ago.

"It takes a lot of discipline, a lot of time and an understanding family (in my case, a wife). In my opinion, it also takes a familiarity with most of the subject matter as the building blocks for the vast amount of learning that you will need to do. You don't need to be an expert. You won't be one after the test either! If you are not learning it, don't rush it. Some of the material is difficult, most is not. It is just a lot of information on a lot of different topics. This is a great time to learn. Make sure you learn the material for you and not just the test!

"To move along as quickly as you want, self-study may be the only option. I took the self-study courses from the American College. I was satisfied with the material and feel it did its part in helping to prepare me for the test. Take a prep course before the comprehensive exam. Dearborn's was outstanding for me." Six months??? Wow.

Tim Murray, CFP®[28] passed the Certification Exam in November, 2001, exactly one year after enrolling in Florida State University's distance learning program. He also took and passed the Series 7, 66, and Virginia Life and Health exam in the same year. "Just to give a heads-up on what it costs to take the certification exam," offered Tim, "I spent $600 for the exam, $550 for study materials, and $50 for a hotel room between testing sessions. It was a $1200 event that I did not want to repeat!"

---

[27] Mike Kapustin can be reached at SocHillCFP@aol.com
[28] Tim Murray can be reached at TMurray@CapitalPlanningDirect.com

5. What will it cost you?

Of course there is more to consider than just the cost of the course. Some packages come with materials included and some with free re-takes of review classes if you don't pass the certification exam the first time. Do your own financial planning. Compare costs. Will you have additional travel or shipping expenses? What about support? Break down the fee and add on the extras.

Don't forget the cost of taking "crash" courses just before the CFP® Certification Exam, and travel and lodging for the test site. The last thing you want to be is under pressure from freeway traffic on your way to the certification exam. Plan to indulge in some quiet time to clear your mind and be well rested and alert for the test. Besides, if you're late you lose. I mean, you are not allowed into the test, must wait until the next exam date to retake it, and shell out another exam fee!

Depending on the course of study you select, anticipate a rock-bottom budget of $3500 to get through the qualifying course work, reviews and the exam itself. If you need to re-take the exam or underlying courses, or enter into a degree program to prepare for certification, the costs could rapidly multiply.

6. How will you pay for the courses and CFP® Certification?

This question requires even more forward thinking about what you eventually plan to do as a financial planner. Many fine Broker/Dealers will pay, or reimburse you, for the cost of your CFP® certification. Some of them offer mentors or in-house classes of their own. If you are planning on affiliating with a Broker/Dealer, this is certainly a question you will want to ask them. Discounts are available from some schools for FPA members[29]. Many institutions offer a pay-as-you-go plan, and some require non-refundable tuition up front.

If you require special financing, see if it is available from the school you select. Don't forget to see if you qualify for the Lifetime Learning Credit[30] when you're filing your income tax return. Remember that a penalty free withdrawal from your IRA[31] may be a source of funds to pay higher education expenses.

7. Research schools

A complete list of CFP Board-Registered programs can be found in the Guide to CFP® Certification[32]. Once you've determined the sort of program best suited to your needs, make a short list of potential schools to contact. Phone or send for catalogs, or download appropriate material from the institutions' websites. Prepare a notebook or spreadsheet with

---

[29] If you are enrolled in a CFP Board-Registered Program, you can join the FPA at student rates.

[30] http://www.ed.gov/inits/hope/ Apparently the College for Financial Planning does not qualify. If this is a concern, check if your school is qualified to administer financial aid.

[31] http://www.irs.gov/forms_pubs/pubs/p5900110.htm

[32] http://www.cfp-board.org/cert_edpro.html

questions and a place to enter responses from each school, including the date and person you spoke with, and then begin comparing programs. Include the following in your questions:

    A. Verify information in the catalog is the most current.
    B. What, exactly, is included in the cost? Tuition, Books, Support, Etc.?
    C. Ask about fees and payment options.
    D. What is the anticipated weekly study time needed?
    E. What faculty support is available; when and how is it delivered?
    F. What is the pass rate for students who take the certification exam?
    G. How long before you should be ready to sit for the certification exam?
    H. Is there a crash course before the certification exam? Included?
    I. May you contact former students for references?
    J. Are career placement or intern programs available?

Tim Bennett, a recent graduate of NYU, suggests looking for schools in which CERTIFIED FINANCIAL PLANNER™ professionals teach most of the courses. "One of the problems that I had at NYU was that 70% of the professors were not CFP® practitioners, had never taken the CFP® Certification Exam, and had never done a financial plan. This was a shock to me because the NYU brochure specifically states that the faculty members have *a practitioner's view of financial planning.*"

Tim Murray, CFP® selected the Florida State University program for the following reasons:

    A. FSU has a good name (in general)
    B. Didn't have to pay for the whole program at once.
    C. Each of the courses had a very comprehensive "take home" midterm and final. Since I'd have to take the CFP exam for any of this to be worthwhile, why go through the stress of 6 cramming sessions for each course. I saved my energy for studying for the Series 7, 66, insurance, and CFP exams.
    D. The scheduling of their classes suited me well.

8. Compare schools and programs and make a decision

Do some serious homework here. Wherever possible, follow up on the information you have. Ask questions on the discussion boards or at industry meetings. Talk to people who have recently attended the schools you're interested in. If anything is in doubt, telephone the school again and get updated information.

"I would place the biggest emphasis on talking to former students," recommends Tim Bennett. "While the school can give you most of the information you need as far as the facts go, they will obviously tell you that they have an excellent program.

"Don't expect their brochure to tell you the truth," he continues. "To illustrate my point, in NYU's brochure they say that the three main things that the students are taught are to:

    A. Assess a client's needs and goals
    B. Structure an effective financial plan
    C. Evaluate actual plan performance

We did only a little of the first and absolutely none of the other two."

16

9. Enroll

10. Set yourself a study schedule and stick to it!

It won't be easy, but it most definitely will be worth it in the long run. Once you're in the system, you'll start meeting more people, knowing the "in" group, and who to ask for help when you need it.

Not only will the support from your chosen institution be there, but you'll be surprised to find in most cases the authors of your text books, and the financial planners whose works are cited, are available and willing to talk with you.

J. Jeffrey Lambert, CFP® Director, Personal Financial Planning Certificate Program University of California, Davis Extension suggests "putting together a study group for support, or at least connecting with others who are studying. College contacts, FPA, potential employers or on-line discussion boards could be used to organize. It pays to be a good networker!"

Preparing for the CFP® Certification Examination[33]

The Financial Planning Association[34] offers assessment tests through Kier Educational Resources and Dalton Publications. The tests are available to FPA members to help evaluate readiness to sit for the certification exam. They offer members review materials at a reduced price.

There are questions available for download from the CFP Board website[35]. A list of certification exam review course providers who have met certain criteria is also on the Board's website[36].

"Get a free ($15 for shipping and handling) book that Dalton Publications[37] has put together with questions from three previous CFP® exams that the CFP Board has released over the past seven or eight years," advises Tim Bennett. "It has explanations for each answer. The CFP Board does not provide explanations for the released questions that you can download from their web site.

"After finishing the CFP® certification program, I bought all of the Dalton books to review. They are excellent and worth every penny. I passed the CFP® exam the first time I took it. Go directly to http://www.daltonpublications.com." Numerous posts on the FPi discussion boards back up Tim's enthusiasm over the Dalton material. "Plan on spending at least 150 to 300 hours reviewing for the exam," says Tim. "If you've taken classes over a normal two year period, you'll need to review closer to 300 hours, since the material studied early on won't be as fresh in your mind."

---

[33] http://www.fpanet.org/career/cd_tools.cfm
[34] http://www.fpanet.org
[35] http://www.cfp-board.org/cert_smplexm.html
[36] http://www.cfp-board.org/cert_rvw.html
[37] http://www.daltonpublications.com

Another review course that has received consistently high marks is an on-site, 32-40 hour class in Florida taught by Kenneth Zahn, CFP®. According to his website, Ken has been teaching the CFP® Certification Exam review course since 1995. Complete information regarding cost and scheduling can be found at http://www.gate.net/~zahn/index.htm. A huge plus to help you gage the quality of his material are the "Scenarios" he includes on the web page. Ken provides a complete prestudy book. The prestudy is application and case based rather than academic. His condensed classroom book is designed to focus the student on the key areas of the exam. The two books have about 2000 questions and numerous cases.

Take preparation for the CFP® certification examination very seriously. This is one test you do not want to take a second time! The pass rate for the July 2002 exam was 51%, low relative to the 57% historical pass rate since the exam's 1991 introduction.[38] Recently, the CFP Board has been reporting the pass rate since 1995, when the transition to the two-day certification exam was complete, and including repeat test takers in the statistics.[39]

Caution! The CFP Board is very protective of their data bank of questions, and the ones released are often obsolete. The best use of these questions is to get a feel for style and composition. Do not accept the answers provided as accurate! As Jeff Lambert puts it, "This is not a load & dump exam! It is designed to test your ability to apply the material in practice."

In responding to a post on the FPi[40] discussion boards asking for the best ways to get ready for the two-day, ten hour certification exam, Nigel B. Taylor, CFP® suggested the following:

1. Obtain a couple of the previous examinations and review the questions carefully. Formulate your own answer and then make a comparative review of acceptable answers that are often provided. Remember, not every "correct" answer reflects real life. Many acceptable answers on the comprehensive examination are the answers the CFP Board in Denver and the examiners want to see.

2. In deciding upon the best method of study, classroom education or self-study, you need to be honest with yourself. Some factors for consideration are:
 A. Finding sufficient time in your busy schedule to set aside without distractions
 B. Finding sufficient energy to study and absorb the materials in more than your short-term memory
 C. Having access to a professional support structure (mentor, etc.) to assist you if the course demands exceed your ability to comprehend particular concepts. If you cannot set aside time to really study without having to send your spouse to the movies, if you have children at home who demand attention, or if you are not currently in the business and have no mentor or support structure to assist you, I would recommend you take a classroom course.

---

[38] http://www.cfp-board.org/press_archvdprapr.html#5-30-01
[39] http://www.cfp-board.org/press_archvdprjuly02.html#passrate
[40] http://www.financial-planning.com/shoptalk.html

3. Take a review class before the comprehensive exam – knowing the topic isn't always enough. Furthermore, you will be equally tested on the "first" thing you ever learned, as well as the "last and most recent" thing you learned so it's good to train for the examination, just as many candidates train for the CPA exam and the bar. As the passing ratios[41] show, many are unprepared for the sheer volume of knowledge they will need to impart over the two days.

When you're actually sitting for the two day comprehensive exam, consider this advice from Jon Lacy, CFP® with Lane Dickson & Lacy, LLC and a member of the UC Davis sponsored CFP® Certification Exam Review Course team.

"The CFP® Certification Exam is almost as much about Time Management as knowing the subject matter," suggests Jon. "You'll want to decide on a testing system that works for you." Here's a list of Jon's recommendations:

1. Answer all the questions you absolutely know immediately.
2. Circle the answer (in the test book) for questions you're a little unsure (marked for review)
3. Draw a box around the question number when you have no clue (marked for review)
4. Read the mini-case questions first before reading the case (helps you know what to look for)
5. The first pass through, never spend more than 2-3 minutes trying to figure out the question. Mark it for review and move on.
6. If you don't know (on 2nd review of the question) Guess and Go. Don't leave any question unanswered.
7. Watch for answers elsewhere. Sometimes a question will be answered in another question much later.
8. Don't let any question get you upset. Kicking yourself because you can't remember a fact or can't calculate a listed answer will only interfere with your ability to focus on the next question. Keep your composure.

Working With a Mentor

Before embarking upon a whole new career, I strongly urge you to line up a mentor to see you through the process. As you enroll in classes, interview with potential employers, study for exams and shop for software, there will be times when you'll feel like quitting. There will be better times when you need someone to celebrate with – someone who understands exactly what you're going through. A shoulder to cry on, a reminder of your goal, and a heartfelt "way to go!" can bring triumph out of discouragement.

You may even need a "team" of mentors, or mentors for different facets of the journey. A spouse may be an ideal mentor, or someone who turned you on to financial planning in the first place. Maybe it's a business associate who knows you well, or a trusted friend.

---

[41] 57% of all test takers had passed the certification exam as of 6/30/01.

During my career, I cannot begin to count the number of times I have called upon someone, for whom I held respect and admiration, to ask for advice. Yet I don't remember a single incident where I was rejected. Sometimes the contact has been invaluable.

A number of years ago, I was at a crossroads in my career. Totally stuck. A friend suggested I talk to other financial planners who had practices that looked attractive to me, and see how they got where they were. There were some excellent planners within a reasonable distance from my office. I had heard some of them speak at national conferences and had actually been introduced to a couple of them at local industry functions. But I was certain they wouldn't remember me.

Deciding which of the half dozen planners to call was a problem. There were things about all the practices that appealed to me. I wrote out a short script, promising to stick it out until someone agreed to talk with me, and then dialed the first number. I was surprised to be put through immediately. Identifying myself as a financial planner, I explained that I had heard/met them at the such and such meeting, and hoped they might help me.

"Sure! Let's have lunch one day next week." Not certain I heard correctly, I repeated myself, and was met with, "Why don't you make up a list of what you want to know, and we'll meet at noon." We set the date, and encouraged, I called the next planner on my list.

He, too, suggested a meeting, and asked if I was calling anyone else. I told him about my list, and that I was meeting the first planner for lunch. His response? He asked to join us for lunch. I stopped making calls and started my list of questions.

That luncheon turned my practice around. Not only were the two planners eager to tell me about their practices and help me employ some of their strategies, but they were interested in what I was doing in my office. Within six months, we were joined by the others on my list and set up a practice management study group that meets quarterly to this day.

During the initial months, I honestly felt I was the recipient of the greatest benefit. Before long, it became clear that these "mentors" of mine were deriving just as much good as I was from the collective brainstorming. Had I not made that phone call, asking for help, I've no doubt my practice would still be languishing out there somewhere.

The same holds true while you're working your way through the CFP® certification program. Contacts and friendships you solidify now, will serve you well as your financial planning career progresses.

Finding a Mentor

My naiveté during those early years continues to amuse me. Now that I'm in my sixties, I don't have time to waste. When I need mentoring, I go grab a mentor! I take it very seriously. A mentor should be specific to the subject requiring help. To paraphrase an old adage: if you want to know how to build a watch, you'll do better with a mentor who's a watchmaker than with a mentor who only knows how to tell time. That's why I've developed a list of what I'm looking for in a mentor, and don't just indiscriminately go on and on about my problem to any ear willing to listen. A mentoring relationship is not a one-way proposition.

The mentor must be:	**The mentored must be:**
Willing to teach	Willing to learn
Knowledgeable in the subject	Needing guidance in the subject
Able to articulate	Able to understand
A resource	A receptacle
Willing to spend time	Willing to take time
Caring	Appreciative
Approachable	Courageous
A problem solver	Able to apply solutions
Trustworthy	Deserving of trust
Passionate	Committed

When I'm seeking a mentor, I adhere to the following checklist:

- ❑ Define, specifically, the topic requiring a mentor
  - o Purpose
  - o Time frame
  - o Desired result
  - o Initial questions
  - o Outline or flowchart of anticipated project/goal

- ❑ Determine where/how mentors on this topic will most likely be found
  - o Industry
  - o Geographic area
  - o Preferred method for initial contact
    - ❑ Mail
    - ❑ Phone
    - ❑ E-mail
  - o Contact information

- ❑ Research potential mentors
  - o Current contacts
  - o Resources of current contacts
  - o Current organizational contacts
  - o Speakers
  - o Writers
  - o Internet
  - o Phone book

- ❑ Develop short list of mentors who appear to be compatible
  - o Name
  - o Contact information
  - o Reference source
  - o Results of contact

- ❑ Contact information and results
  - ○ Contact potential mentor
  - ○ Notes of initial contact conversation
  - ○ Entry into database (for current or future topics)
  - ○ Decision: affirm or reject agreement for current project

- ❑ Organize place and time to enter into agreement

When the Financial Planning Interactive discussion boards first appeared, I went there in need of support as my solo practice evolved. It was wonderful how forthcoming other planners were with ideas and recommendations. Sometimes I would dare to correspond directly with a poster to thank them for an answer and/or request additional information. Eventually, as I gained experience and expertise in my field, the roles began to reverse. Today, I moderate the "Getting Started/Career Development" discussion boards, and find myself being the mentor more and more.

One day I realized many of the same questions were being posted again and again by people new to the boards. I knew a great deal about getting started in financial planning, and it became obvious to me that I should collect the answers into a book. But I'm a financial planner, not an author. What did I know about bringing a book to life? Nothing. Time to grab a mentor!

After whipping out my checklists, it was a short path to Bob Veres. In the financial planning profession, he is considered by many to be a visionary. He writes for many related publications and seems to have his finger on cutting edge trends. He obviously knows how to write, gets published all over the place, is respected in the business, and appears to know everyone!

Oh, sure. Like I could just pick up the phone and give him a call. He probably doesn't have anything better to do than talk to me. LOL[42]!

So I chickened out and e-mailed him. That way he could respond in his own time – if he wanted to respond at all. There was no way for him to know that he had already been my mentor for years. I was flabbergasted when he responded in hours. Not only did he respond, but actually encouraged me; told me my book was long overdue, and asked for a copy of my premise. Before long, names of possible publishers showed up in my e-mail.

He volunteered (I didn't even have to ask!) to edit the first chapter I wrote, and returned it to me with invaluable notations. He suggested I talk with this guy and that gal, and include a chapter on thus and so. When I was bogged down and discouraged because I didn't have a committed publisher after a few months, he gave me a swift kick and told me to keep writing. Soon after, I discovered the world of ePublishing, and it was obvious that my book must be an eBook! Changes are rampant in the financial planning profession, and if I were to publish the traditional way, my book would be outdated before it ever hit the street!

---

[42] Internet shorthand for "Laugh Out Loud."

Suddenly I had a publisher, a format, a date, and access to Amazon! And contact with my mentor was more vital than ever! The hardest part is not abusing the relationship. Out of fear, I want to turn to Bob at every juncture. But I've been pretty careful to only bother him with what's really important. There is nothing in this for him except my appreciation. Yet he makes me feel accountable in some way, and that gets me through the next page…the next chapter. When there is a real problem, I know he will be there to guide me.

It's not easy to contact someone you hold in high esteem and just come right out and ask them to help you work through a problem.

A frequent poster on the Financial Planning Interactive discussion boards is Kay Conheady, a fourteen-year veteran of the Information Technology industry, who has decided to be a financial planner in her next life. She's holding on to her four day a week day job to pay the bills while she works through the CFP® certification material from the College for Financial Planning. The neat thing about Kay is the way she jumps onto the web site[43] and posts whatever is on her mind at the time. She's not frivolous. Her questions are thought provoking and well articulated.

It's the answers Kay receives that never fail to amaze me. She gets information and resource material from respondents with different areas of expertise. When she opens the door to her practice a year or two from now, she will be working with a terrific network of financial planning expertise. Kay will already know who to call upon when she needs help, be it in insurance, marketing, or finding the best college funding plan. She reminded me, tongue-in-cheek, that she's also learning whom **not** to call.

"One of the other very important things I'm learning by posting and following the FPi Getting Started forum (and others) is what the *hot buttons* and controversies are out there and how to present myself when I broach touchy subjects," explained Kay. "For me, it is much easier, psychologically speaking, to bare my inexperienced soul on-line rather than face-to-face!"

The Residency Program

Alfred E. Hockwalt, Director of Career Development for the Financial Planning Association invited me to the UCLA Lake Arrowhead Conference Center in October 2000 to observe first hand the much-touted FPA Residency Program[44].

What an eye-opener! I walked into the main lodge to see what appeared to be a darned good stage production involving a couple in their fifties arguing over some retirement issues while their financial planner tried getting to the heart of the matter. The audience consisted of eighteen rapt attendees and half a dozen industry folk, most of whom I recognized. Occasionally giggles or applause would burst from the group, and note taking on laptops and yellow pads was fast and furious.

---

[43] http://www.financial-planning.com/shoptalk.html
[44] http://www.fpanet.org/conf/residency/index.cfm?return=cc

The "actors" turned out to be Linda Barlow, CFP® and Dave Bergmann, CFP®, EA, CLU, ChFC, part of the extraordinary faculty transformed into case study characters. When the brief presentation ended, I followed Linda and a third of the audience out across the snow to a cozy cabin where the group nibbled on snacks and hashed over the impact of new information gleaned from the skit.

During lunch with Al, I was impressed with the enthusiasm, and the diversity in age, experience and occupational background in the room. Nearly everyone had recently passed the certification exam, and was in various stages of setting up a practice or looking for a position in the profession.

Tim Bennett, who passed the CFP® certification exam fourteen months after enrolling in the CFP® certification program at NYU in October 1999, was one of the residents at the session I attended. His company, Crystal Clear Financial Planning in Roselle, New Jersey is just beginning. It will be November 2005, before Tim has met the experience requirement enabling him to use the CFP® marks. Here is what Tim had to say about his week in California:

The FPA Residency Program

By Tim Bennett

I have always thought that the CFP® certification program taught at most colleges lacked a final class that covered two very important topics: how to do comprehensive financial plans and how to earn a living as a financial planner. So, imagine my surprise when I received a brochure about the FPA Residency Program that promised to teach that and more. It sounded too good to be true so I contacted several former residents (as the participants are called) to find out what they had to say. Every single one had glowing praise for the program. Veronica Hart insisted, "It was the best money I've ever spent on my career." Jeff Cedarholm added, "By learning tried and true methods from experienced mentors, my trial and error time has been cut down by years." And Deena Katz, one of the most respected financial planners in the country, told me that she has paid for all of her financial planners to attend. In fact, she was so pleased with what they learned there that she would probably send any new planners that she hires to the Residency Program as well.

After receiving so many wonderful recommendations, the only question I still had was which of the three Residency Programs to attend. My options were Bryn Mawr, PA in the spring, Denver, CO in the summer and Lake Arrowhead, CA in the fall. Laura Tarbox, the chair of Lake Arrowhead's program, persuaded me to attend the program in California by insisting that the beautiful location in the San Bernardino Mountains was well worth the trip. Of course, it didn't hurt that Tarbox had been recently named by Worth magazine as one of the 300 best financial advisors in the country and I wanted to find out how she became so successful.

It was with great anticipation that I arrived at the FPA Residency Program in Lake Arrowhead, CA. Tarbox was right. It certainly was a lovely location. We stayed at the UCLA

Conference Center, a place so popular that it is booked up a year in advance. I'd heard that the Denver program had rather plain accommodations so I was surprised by how nice our rooms and the meeting areas were. I was also looking forward to taking a dip in Lake Arrowhead. Unfortunately, because of the Residency Program's long hours, I never did make it to the lake.

The Residency Program is a very intensive weeklong boot camp that teaches new planners how to take the technical knowledge they learned in the classroom and use it in real life situations. The main emphasis is on three case studies, based on a couple at three different stages of their life. The couple is played by two of the mentors who try to make it very challenging and interesting at the same time. Since the case studies we used at Lake Arrowhead included, among other things, a Russian ballet dancer stepfather, an alcoholic son, and a toilet seat manufacturing company, we didn't know whether to laugh or cry. We ended up doing a little of both. We received less and less assistance from the mentors as the week progressed. We did the third case study almost entirely on our own. The progress we made in one week was amazing. On the first case study, we made the mistake of focusing too much on number crunching. By the third case study, we concentrated less on the financial planning minutiae and more on the clients' feelings, goals, and objectives. "The purpose of the FPA Residency Program is to teach you how to think and feel like a CFP® practitioner," explained Ben Coombs, one of the mentors.

In between case studies, the mentors taught general sessions on gathering client data, explaining difficult financial topics in a way that clients can understand, and managing client expectations. In the evening, we broke up into smaller groups for rap sessions. Each group chose which topic they would like to discuss in greater detail. Some of the topics were fee only vs. commission, starting your own financial planning business, the pros and cons of various financial planning software, and marketing. The final evening included one on one sessions where each resident got to pick the brains of three mentors of their choice. Much to the amusement of the mentors, I had brought a long list of questions with me to the Residency Program specifically for the one on one sessions. After they stopped laughing, however, the mentors gladly answered my questions.

The Residency Program taught me many important things. Here are just a few. I learned to listen carefully to clients, not only to what they said, but also to what they really meant. I also learned that clients want you to use words they can understand. I was eager to impress clients with my knowledge of Q-TIPs, standard deviation, and deferred contingent sales loads. Since I was confusing clients more than helping them, I figured out how to translate financial jargon into plain English. By the end of the week, I had also gained a great deal of confidence. I figured that if I could survive this boot camp, then most real clients would seem easy in comparison.

The program was a success due to the hard work and dedication of the mentors. Each one was an experienced CFP® certificant. Laura Tarbox, the chair of the Lake Arrowhead Residency Program, is so successful that she can afford to regularly turn away prospective clients with $500,000 to invest. Helping her lead the program was Ben Coombs, one of the original CFP professional's from the class of 1973. Coombs was instrumental in starting the FPA Residency Program (then known as the CFP Residency Program) in 1985 when he was president of the Institute of Certified Financial Planners. After a 10-year hiatus due to lack of funds, the program was revived in 1998 with Coombs' help and sponsorship by TIAA-CREF. The other mentors were two successful sole practitioners, Linda Barlow and David Bergmann, and Jeff Lambert, a national board member of the FPA. Since the mentors all had different backgrounds and specialties, they were able to give us a wide variety of viewpoints.

The cost of the Residency Program is $2,500, $2,250 for FPA members and $2,150 for early registrants. The cost includes tuition, room and board. While I initially thought it was expensive, I quickly realized that 60 hours of instruction from financial planners who usually charge well over $100 per hour was a bargain.

The program counts as three months of financial planning experience towards the CFP® certification. One creative resident thought that he could attend all three Residency Programs and receive nine months experience. Unfortunately, it doesn't work like that. Three months experience is the most you can get. In order to attend, you must complete the CFP® certification program required to sit for the CFP® certification exam. If you have a designation such as a CPA or ChFC that exempts you from taking the CFP® certification program, you are required to pass the CFP® certification exam. My fellow residents were a very diverse group. I thought that most of them would be in their twenties but their ages ranged from 25 to 55. They included attorneys, accountants, a teacher and even a doctor who wanted to work in the ER at night and do financial planning during the day. (He didn't mention when he planned to sleep.) There were also several experienced investment advisors and insurance agents interested in making the transition to comprehensive financial planning. No matter what their background, however, they all had one thing in common: they were very enthusiastic about becoming financial planners.

The benefits of the Residency Program didn't stop when it was over. Since then I have gone over my notes from the program several times, each time learning something new. I have also kept in touch with a few of the other residents so that we can bounce ideas off each other.

It's too early to tell how successful the residents of the recent programs will be but Charles Foster, a resident at the first program in 1985, has been named by Worth magazine as one of the best financial advisors in the country every year since 1996. In fact, he thinks so highly of the Residency Program that he has been a mentor at the Denver program for the last three years.

Since the Residency Program originated in Denver, it is the best known of the three locations and sometimes sells out several months in advance. Because the other two programs started more recently they often have openings available at the last minute. However, the accommodations and food in Lake Arrowhead and Bryn Mawr are superior to Denver so it's just a matter of time before the word gets around and they sell out too. The material taught is identical in all three locations.

The FPA Residency Program surpassed all my expectations. I learned more about "real world" financial planning in one week at the Residency Program than I did in two years studying for the CFP® certification exam. At the beginning of the program, Ben Coombs promised, "The mentors are going to give you some street smarts." They certainly did. If you're serious about becoming a successful financial planner, I strongly recommend that you find the time and money to get there.

A few weeks after my visit to Lake Arrowhead, Linda Barlow shared some of the evaluation comments with me. On a scale of 1 – 5, the only number I saw was 5. Considering my brief encounter with the group, I'd have to concur. If you want to get a jump-start on your career, get thee to a Residency Program!

"Our goal is to expand the number and the geographic locations of the Residency Program," Al told me.

For more information on the FPA Residency Program, e-mail Amanda Kutkas at amanda.kutkas@fpanet.org or Al Hockwalt at al.hockwalt@fpanet.org, or visit the website at http://www.fpanet.org/conf/residency. Check back often, since the website is constantly updated.

Looking for an entry level position as a financial planner[45]

Speaking of jump-starting your career, here's where the serious problem lies, and it has little to do with the need for new blood in the financial planning profession. Independent financial planners simply don't feel they can afford to hire help, and do not realize the incredible benefit an intern can bring.

My own experience, sad to say, is typical, from what my colleagues have told me.

Mine is a small, comprehensive, fee-only financial planning practice. For years my clients have come solely from referrals, and I've done no marketing. I have a paraplanner who does data-entry, keeps the books and runs my in home office, and a clerk who comes in once a week to file and get out mailings. I manage just under $25 million in assets for my financial planning clients, see most of them every quarter, and am comfortable with net income. I was not seeking growth.

A few years ago, I entered into a buy-sell agreement with the out of state economist who designs the investment portfolios for my clients. I am currently looking to transfer my business to him beginning in about 3-5 years, at which time I will work part time for him, seeing my clients and doing public relations work for what will become his business. He wants to buy a "growing" practice -- which means it's time to change some of its current characteristics. I was becoming complacent, and needed someone young and aggressive to bring in a new perspective -- someone to replace me, as comprehensive planner, and to eventually manage the office in the absence of the out of state owner.

With the help of a business coach, I envisioned this person. I did not spell it out, due to sticky employment issues, but what I had in mind was pretty specific: female, 30-40 years

---

[45] FPA Career Center http://www.fpanet.org/career/

old, CFP® certification, living in close proximity and willing to work out of my home office. I did no formal advertising, but talked to students at conferences (Texas Tech, Virginia, etc.) local networking groups, clients, instructors of CFP® certification programs in the vicinity and professors at local colleges and universities (there are half a dozen excellent campuses in my area.)

Over a two-year period, I interviewed over 20 individuals fitting the description I'd projected. While I met many very nice people, nothing clicked. Either I couldn't see the person working within the market I know is here, or I couldn't see myself working in the cramped quarters of my home with the person. I made one offer, to a woman who taught economics courses at a local university and had the CFP® certification. She refused the salary I offered. While she had taken the CFP® certification program several years prior, she had never practiced as a financial planner, had minimal computer skills, and no practical experience in a business setting. But I admit, I wasn't aggressively pursuing an employee, and could have been more diligent. I put the hiring process on the back burner.

One day I got a call from a student who asked for an appointment to discuss a job. I was preoccupied at the time, set the appointment date, and thought nothing more of it until a young man showed up at the door. I ushered him into my conference room and asked, "Why are you here?" It still amuses me that his response was, "I'm graduating in a couple of months and haven't found a job yet so my counselor told me to come and talk to you." (One of the professors I had talked with had passed my information on to a colleague.)

The next question I asked him was whether he knew what a financial planner was. His refreshingly candid response, "No." His BA was in business with a minor in finance. I told him to go find out what a financial planner was, and if it interested him, to give me a call the following week. Interview over. He even forgot to leave a resume.

Eight o'clock Monday morning the phone rang. He asked for another appointment, and came in with practically a term paper written on financial planning, his resume, a list of what he particularly liked about the profession, and a slew of questions about my specific practice. I hired him on the spot, pending salary negotiations, and invited him to lunch with my attorney to draw up an employment agreement. He both graduated from college and celebrated his 21st birthday subsequent to my hiring him. He has already begun courses toward the CFP® certification.

There is nothing about him that fit the profile I was seeking (nor was he looking for a career in financial services,) but we convinced each other. He lived in another county, there was the gender issue, age, and on and on. But it seems to be working, and here's why:

1. Maturity. Though he was only 21 at the time of hire, he possessed a serious, straightforward attitude never acquired by many. I can picture this young man earning the trust and confidence of my clients, and their children.

2. Realistic Outlook. He understood how to separate the "business" of planning (after all, he was a business major!) from the profession itself. He told me he anticipated it would take about 5 years before he would experience the income and client levels he expected to achieve. He managed to get his degree in 3 1/2 years. We're allowing two years for the CFP® certification program.

3. Initiative. He made a presentation to me, rather than waiting to see what I had to offer. It may sound backward, but doggone, it's hard to resist being courted! My company has a tremendous amount to offer, but I didn't have to say a thing. He took it upon himself to research my company and me, find out where we stood in the industry, know it was an profession he wanted to be in, consider his fit in my office, and go after it. Most often these days, students make the mistake of reading the glossy company recruitment brochure and wait for the company to make them an offer.

4. Work Ethic. First appointment, he showed up in suit & tie, shook hands firmly, answered questions honestly and directly. I was in slacks and a casual blouse, but he never saw that as a cue to dress down. Next appointment the suit and tie were still there. He asked about dress before coming to work the first day, has never been even a minute late to work, and when he's here, the work gets done.

5. Foresight. I know he was disappointed with my salary offer. Yet he looked past the initial period at future rewards, and took the time he needed to evaluate and compare options, before accepting the position. More important, he discussed his concerns with me so we could start out on the same page with a goal of working through each chapter together.

6. Eagerness. In the same way he researched the profession, he plows into everything asked of him with interest and enthusiasm. This is not to say he blunders ahead hit and miss. He presents drafts, makes recommendations, accepts criticism willingly, and keeps at a task through completion.

Could I have spelled all that out in a job description to a potential employee? My guess is, I'm just like a myriad of other independent financial planners who'd give their right arm for an employee like the one who fell into my lap, but they don't know what they're looking for any more than I did!

Employers, particularly independent financial planners, are afraid if they hire someone who doesn't work out, it'll open up a can of worms they haven't time to cope with, rendering them worse off. So they spend 80 hour weeks doing it all themselves, just like I did. Gosh! Just think where I could be now, if I'd had the right job description to start with!

An enormous plus I never considered is that my office is extremely computer literate and technology oriented, yet a huge amount of our time and money was spent bringing in a computer guy every time there was a glitch. We certainly couldn't afford a full time computer expert like larger companies and, luckily for me, computer skills are second nature to my new employee, just as they are to most college students who have graduated over the past few years.

My employee was able to show me how he could generate an increase in his income simply by saving me valuable time and money by not having to bring in outside help every time the computer locked up. Now that he's familiar with the proprietary programs we use, he can fix things faster than the computer guy, because he knows our unique needs! He keeps our web site current, and even talks tech geek when a glitch in our download needs reformatting – or whatever.[46]

Bridge the Gap[47]

Without question, one of the best places to encounter resources if you're looking for work as a financial planner is the "Bridge the Gap" Program during FPA's Annual Success Forum.

Scott M. Kahan, CFP® is part of the Strategic Team for Career Development for the FPA, and chair of the Bridge the Gap Program. He also heads up his own fee-only financial planning firm, Financial Asset Management Corporation, with offices in New York and Florida. He taught at New York University until 1997, is currently on the Kaplan College Advisory Board, and, in his spare time, teaches at Baruch College in their financial planning program.

"Everyone wants to be fee-only, working for an independent firm and making big bucks," Scott told me. "It's like everyone wanting a safe, liquid, high yielding investment. People want one thing, but reality is something else.

"The best thing to do is to start out with a good firm, learn the basics, but keep on the lookout for the company you want to end up with. When it's time to make a move, you don't want to burn any bridges!" Scott thinks the Bridge the Gap Program can help new planners sort through employment opportunities.

Unlike the Residency Program, which focuses on plan preparation and building client relationships, Bridge the Gap is all about marketing and building a business. The two go hand-in-hand and are geared for those just starting or with less than two years in the industry.

Bridge the Gap started as a special session during the last ICFP conference in Dallas, became a track at the first FPA convention, and has now become a "meeting within a meeting", with separate sponsors and a reduced conference fee. There is no better way to gain exposure to the financial planning profession than through participation in a Bridge the Gap Program. It's a terrific opportunity to learn which companies will best meet your needs as a beginning planner, and to compare them side by side. Meeting others just starting out and learning how they are getting their careers off the ground is a big plus.

In the future, Scott hopes to see Bridge the Gap become a model for local and regional FPA conferences, as well as having a role within local chapters. There is an urgent need to Bridge the Gap not only for new planners to get into the business, but also for older planners to transition out of the profession! Somehow the two have got to get together.[48]

---

[46] My first intern was with us for two years and has since moved on.
[47] http://www.fpanet.org/career/new_planners.cfm
[48] Tapes from previous Bridge the Gap sessions can be seen by checking the FPA link at http://www.playbacknow.com

Internships[49]

Obvious in every other profession but financial planning, working as an intern with an established firm is the best way to discover what it is you want and don't want to do with your career. Until a few years ago, financial planning was so new there were few masters under whom to study. That landscape has changed dramatically with the advent of degree programs in financial planning from highly regarded colleges and universities, public recognition of the CERTIFIED FINANCIAL PLANNER™ designation, and baby boomers seeking help with retirement options.

If I had my 'druthers, Jerry Mason, PhD., ChFC, CFP® would be King of financial planners, and his cardinal law would be that all firms must sponsor interns.

In the January/February 2000 issue of Financial Advisory Practice, Dr. Mason authored an article on internships that should be mandatory reading for every financial planning firm and student.[50] At Texas Tech University, where he co-founded the Center for Financial Responsibility, a minimum of 200 hours of participation in an internship program is required of all Family Financial Planning majors.

Texas Tech has an aggressive internship program, leading to a high percentage of placements at graduation. It's no wonder, when you see what these students have accomplished. Résumés for those seeking internships and entry-level positions can be found on their website.[51] The Family Financial Planning Program at Kansas State University[52] and the Family Financial Management Program at Virginia Tech[53] also help students enrolled in their programs obtain employment through online posting of résumés.

In Dr. Mason's opinion, an internship is a logical step between acquiring basic education and applying it in a fulfilling career. Unrealistic expectations on both sides are the main reason the new hire/company relationship doesn't work out in an estimated fifty percent of cases. He compares the internship to a courtship that, with honest communication, may lead to a commitment.

The biggest hurdle, Dr. Mason believes, is the interviewing process. Independent firms often don't know what they're looking for, and that can turn a prospective intern off. Turnover is high, with many young people staying only six to nine months.

Dr. Mason blames the employers, who, he claims, "do stupid things. They don't ask students to produce course work such as term papers, financial plans, brochures and workbooks. Another thing they don't do is check references," he continues. "Talk to professors and teachers. Find out if the student comes to class on time. Is the student's attitude positive? Grades aren't usually that important."

---

[49] FPA Career Center http://www.fpanet.org/career/internships.cfm
[50] Dr. Mason has offered to send a copy to anyone taking the time to get in touch with him.
[51] http://infre.hs.ttu.edu/resumes.htm
[52] http://www.ksu.edu/ffp/
[53] http://www.chre.vt.edu/ahrm/FFM/index.htm

Perhaps independent firms will learn one day soon. But in the meantime, the onus seems to be on the intern or person seeking a position. The jobs are there, but until more hiring firms get up to speed, pay attention to Dr. Mason's unconventional, but vital advice:

"Never look for a job. Look for a company with which you may want to be affiliated, and interview them. Be prepared. Be professional. Take business cards, plans you've done, resumes, and tell the company what you can do for them. Look at the best four or five offers you receive and compare firms.

"Once you accept the position understand that the education continues. Get all the education and training you can. Read every day." Pearls of wisdom from Dr. Mason. Heed them.

Money hasn't yet been mentioned here, and there's good reason for that. It's a taboo subject. Ridiculous, isn't it, that everyone pussyfoots around the compensation issue when the subject is financial planning? Believe me, it only gets worse later on, when the talk turns to commissions vs. fees.

But here we're talking about interns. My advice to you is to not let the money issue slide. Obviously you're not going to make a lot of money during an internship, but your employer certainly expects you to be providing a benefit to the company, and you should expect more than a few credit hours in compensation.

Ask for no less than minimum wage, or negotiate a fee based upon an assigned project. If you are unable to provide value equal to at least your cost, then perhaps it is too early to seek an internship. Ask around.

Where I am in Southern California, it is common practice to pay little or nothing for an intern. I think that's just plain wrong. If you are planning on interning with my firm just to sit back and watch how we do things, taking up my time to explain things to you, then I shouldn't be paying you anything. But if that's what you expect, you won't be offered an internship here. Should you come to me with an outline of how you could improve my website, or a proposal for a new marketing plan, or a design for increasing back office efficiency, then I would expect to pay you accordingly.

Some companies are noted for their superior internship programs. American Express Financial Advisors[54] and Northwestern Mutual[55] come to mind. Compensation packages for internships are already in place for these behemoth organizations. If you're talking with an independent firm, particularly one that is just awakening to the fact an intern could be of value, you may need to help them structure an appropriate salary.

The FPA has been diligently working on an internship program that should appear on the career center site[56] by now. Excerpts from a paper I wrote proposing a national internship

---

[54] (800) 328-8650
[55] http://www.nmfn.com/tn/careers--page_fr_intro
[56] http://www.fpanet.org/career/index.cfm

32

paper were published in the September 2002 issue of Financial Planning™ under the title "Blueprints for a Profession".[57] Efforts are ongoing to help new planners gain practical experience in the industry.

J. Jeffrey Lambert, CFP® Director, Personal Financial Planning Certificate Program University of California, Davis Extension, shared with me that the most difficult question he gets from students is one that does not have a neat and tidy answer. Students want to know where they can get a job, what they will do in that position, and how much they will make.

He tells students to:

1. Find out who you are and develop a personal vision and philosophy.
2. Read, listen and learn what others are doing.
3. Network and find a position that permits you to be on a career path that will allow you to fulfill your dreams and reach the heights of your potential.
4. Be patient as you continue to grow and develop the right opportunity for you.

Nevertheless, he is uncomfortable with his answers. Career path development has just recently become a priority for the professional associations. At this point, the financial planning career paths that are well developed are sales oriented.

Jeff is not alone in his concern. In the last couple of years, FPA has put significant work into developing resources to serve new entrants into the profession. He exclaims, "I am excited for those entering the profession now. With FPA's help both on a national and local level, it is possible to get much support for the development of your career. It may take initiative, creativity, soul searching and networking, but the resources are there."

One planner I know who us trying to create an intern/mentor program is Eileen Freiburger, CFP®, founder of On Your Side, Inc. Financial Planning Group[58] in El Segundo, California. Eileen's practice is based on a fee only, hourly as needed model.

Before opening her own RIA, Eileen had been a manager in brokerage companies, broker-dealers and banks. Early on, she realized as a sole practioner, she was missing the training, mentoring and coaching elements she enjoyed as a manager.

So, Eileen created a model that enables individuals enrolled in Board approved CFP® programs to begin assisting her on a project basis with her current cases. She exposes these individuals to her working model and gives them the opportunity to assist with data entry, web based software, projects and general paraplanning work. While the pay is minimal, Eileen's business plan includes giving the candidate the opportunity to "jump start" his or her own practice and learning curve. In addition, she has actively been seeking CFP®'s to join her. As you may eventually find in an hourly model, it's difficult to market, give seminars, network, meet with clients and actually do planning work! Eileen's invited others to come under her umbrella and have a sliding percentage of the cases she handles. For the

---

[57] http://www.financial-planning.com/pubs/fp/20020901025.html If you'd like a copy of the entire paper, including suggested workload and compensation, it's at http://www.nancysbooks.com.
[58] http://www.plannersonyourside.com/

interns, she wants to give them a taste of what her model offers. She hopes to eventually see more people open their own independent hourly offices, or if a candidate doesn't want to have the financial obligations or market their own company, she has invited some to join her firm She has high hopes of several branches of On Your Side, Inc. eventually being in Southern California.

NAPFA

Future planners who really want to pursue a career devoid of product sales should acquaint themselves with the National Association of Personal Financial Advisors[59]. I asked Warren Mackensen, CFP®[60] if there were any opportunities for entry-level planners within NAPFA.

"NAPFA has had a mentoring program in existence for some time for new planners who join the organization. A beginning planner is teamed up with a more seasoned planner. NAPFA also conducts a "Basic Training" two-day track at each of its four regional conferences in the fall, which would serve beginning planners well. Beyond that, there are local Study Groups that meet throughout the United States. The Study Groups, many of which meet monthly, are a great resource for beginning planners.

"We were all new planners at one time," jokes Warren. "At each conference, NAPFA ensures that there are sessions for all levels of ability and interest. We strongly foster education at all levels and never forget about the beginning planners.

"There is a special student rate for people enrolled in a CFP® certification program, and NAPFA offers a few scholarships at each conference to help defray students' expenses.

"Many NAPFA members hire interns. Of course this is highly variable depending upon many factors," explained Warren, "But members have the capability of posting résumés on the NAPFA web site."

SUMMARY

1. Enroll in a CFP Board certified program to learn financial planning principles.

2. Get a mentor.

3. Prepare for the CFP® certification exam and earn the certification.

4. Attend a Residency Program.

5. Discover options and opportunities at a Bridge the Gap Program.

---

[59] http://www.napfa.org
[60] Warren Mackensen created the ProTracker System Practice Management Software (http://www.protracker.com) for his fee-only practice.

6. Apply for an internship.

7. Begin your new career as a financial planner.

Sounds simple enough. However, the system has serious logistical problems. There is no obvious path leading from Point A to Point B. To me, it all seems backward. The profession is losing an enormous number of highly qualified potential financial planners who are gobbled up in a sales-driven culture foreign to their original intent. Consumers, who need the help of serious financial planning professionals in ever-increasing numbers, are the ultimate victims of this travesty.

Other vocations have predetermined career paths and until the financial planning profession has such, it will never achieve the distinction it deserves.

The CFP Board is working to "benefit the public by fostering professional standards in personal financial planning."[61] Dr. Mason was instrumental in creating the Center for Financial Responsibility at Texas Tech. The Financial Planning Association has made great inroads with the Residency and Bridge the Gap Programs and is developing a National Internship Program. College and Universities across the country and companies like American Express Financial Advisors have responded by providing competitions, scholarships and funding for promising students.

But like the "herding cats" analogy, there is no coordination. Professionals, companies, students and consumers alike stand to benefit from a cohesive effort to bring this industry together.

As the financial planning profession matures, the steps to take will become more obvious. Until then, ask questions, check references, find a mentor, put money in the bank and jump on in!

---

[61] http://www.cfp-board.org/cons_abtbrd.html

School Contact Notes

Chapter Three

Who's the Boss?

Whether in a solo shop, fee-only practice, or selling commissioned products for a major Broker/Dealer, financial planners are in business. As you go through the process of deciding where to begin your financial planning career, do not lose sight of the fact that **you** are the boss and, ultimately, **you** are responsible for the success of your business.

The E-Myth Revisited[62] is my favorite business book. In it, author Michael Gerber talks about every business owner having three "people" inside: the Entrepreneur, the Technician, and the Manager. The Entrepreneur is the visionary who sees Utopia in all its wonder. The Technician is the worker, focusing on production. The Manager is constantly organizing, keeping things in order. Each of these inner "people" wants to be the boss.

All three bosses feel they are working for the benefit of the company, yet conflict arises because there isn't one "boss" in charge. No two are willing to relinquish control to the third. While the Entrepreneur is looking toward the future, the Technician is busy doing what needs to be done today, and the Manager just wants everyone to stay in the system where everything is accounted for.

As you approach the time to make a decision regarding those with whom you will be working in your new career, you have a myriad of things to consider. I suggest you start by being selfish. Think about who you are and what you want. You're the boss! In what setting will you thrive?

Leslie Strebel, CEC, is a Certified E-Myth Consultant and fee-based financial planner. She is part owner of Ultimate Results[63], the E-Myth part of the Strebel Planning Group in Ithica, New York. "Most business owners strive for an efficiently run business that is growing in value while providing excellent service to clients in a pleasant environment with happy employees," she told me. "And plenty of time for the owner to enjoy a balanced life outside of work, of course!

"Yet most small business owners I talk with are only benefiting from very few of these visions," she continued. "They experience long hours, worry about profits, and have little time for kids. One day they find they are doing everything, and feel trapped, wondering where the vision has gone!"

I asked Leslie what could be done about this dilemma, and the answer, of course, was to not let it happen in the first place. Someone just entering a new profession is in the perfect position for prevention.

---

[62] The E-Myth Revisited: Why Most Small Businesses Don't Work and What to Do About It by Michael E. Gerber, Harperbusiness, 1995.
[63] http://www.strebelcpa.com/ultimate/index.html. Leslie can be reached at les@lightlink.com

"Determine your Primary Aim," she explained, "before doing anything else. Don't think about other people, or even about your business. Don't confuse your Primary Aim with goals for income, fame, or other tangible things. Just think about you. Think about your core values, beliefs and desires – what you truly want out of life.

"It's an intense process, and difficult for many of us because we're used to caring about others and doing things for them before ourselves. Once you know the attributes of your Primary Aim, formulate it into a short phrase," she said. "Helping you discover what's really important to you is one of the ways E-Myth coaches guide you toward building a successful business. The Primary Aim is just the first step of many in building a business that works, and serves as the foundation upon which everything else is done."

The most focused summary I have heard concerning what to look for as you consider how to begin your career as a financial planner came from Jonathan Guyton, CFP[®64] in an address to attendees at a Bridge the Gap reception in Boston during the first annual Success Forum, October 2000. He was gracious enough to allow me to reprint it here.

Words of Advice to the Next Generation of Financial Planners

By Jonathan Guyton, CFP®
FPA Career Development Chair

I.   The landscape for careers in financial planning has changed dramatically in the past ten years. As you survey it for your career opportunities:

  ➢ Never forget why you chose to be a financial planner.
  ➢ Associate yourself with a firm that looks like one you would want to refer your mother to.

II. Financial planners used to have customers who sought information and products. Now, clients seek knowledge and wisdom to help them make a lifetime of sound, fulfilling decisions – an advisory relationship where the financial planning process coupled with technical knowledge and people skills provides the tools to help people improve their quality of life.

III. For those looking to become practitioners, there seem to be two main points of entry to the profession at this time: Revenue Generator and Client Caretaker.

IV. If you seek to become a Revenue Generator:
  ➢ Look for a firm that demonstrates a commitment to the CFP® mark.
  ➢ What are their requirements for new advisors to earn the CFP® mark?
  ➢ What are their expectations of their existing representatives to earn the CFP® mark? What percentages have the CFP® mark now? What percentages are enrolled in the CFP® program?

---

[64] Read more in depth coverage from Jonathan Guyton, CFP® in the April 2001 issue of Journal of Financial Planning: http://www.journalfp.net/fpajournal/jfp0401-art15.cfm

➢ Do they reimburse CFP® for program and exam fees? If so, after how much production?

➢ How do they demonstrate their commitment to the financial planning process?
     * Number of client relationships per advisor
     * PR message that promotes financial planning to current and future clients
     * Software and data collection tools that facilitate comprehensive planning
     * Percentage of advisors that are FPA members

V.   If you seek to become a Client Caretaker:

➢ You will likely be joining a firm that began with one or two founding principals and has grown to the point where the principals can no longer handle all the clients. Find out what their vision is for the next 3-5 years. How important will your role be?

➢ What is their philosophy about how value is delivered to clients? Do they utilize the 'star system' (where value is provided through a sole advisor) or a team approach (where value provided by several professionals 'institutionalizes' the client relationship)? How many clients does each 'lead advisor' serve?

➢ How will they demonstrate their willingness to involve you in client meetings? When will this occur? What will your role be when it does? How will they ultimately provide an opportunity to establish relationships with clients that you will one day serve as 'lead advisor'?

➢ What are the current owners' hopes/plans to sell the business some day? How do they believe that having you join the firm will increase its value?

➢ Is adequate staff already in place for client service and administrative tasks?

➢ What are the opportunities/expectations for you to be involved in future marketing efforts?

When I first decided to write this book, it was with the notion that after reading "So You Want to Be a Financial Planner" anyone who wanted to would end up either working for an independent financial planning firm or starting one of their own. After countless hours of research, listening to story after story, attending conferences and reading myself cross-eyed, I have concluded that I was wrong. Maybe not totally wrong, but probably premature.

There does not exist today an obvious and clearly defined route from any other career to that of a financial planner.[65] Huge strides are being made as the Financial Planning Association develops the Residency and Bridge the Gap Programs, NAPFA reaches out with mentoring opportunities and the schools and universities offering the CFP® curriculum encourage planning firms to accept interns. Nevertheless, there is no clear-cut path.

---

[65] An exception might be the accountant who earns a designation in financial planning and adds product sales to the practice.

The primary reasons a financial planner new to the profession might want to begin with a Broker/Dealer or insurance company are name recognition, marketing support and immediate draw. The primary factor that determines future success, however, is the financial planner's fit in the specific office of the selected Broker/Dealer or agency. If you are not comfortable in your environs and enjoy being with those around you day after day, the stress will clobber you before you have a chance to find out if you could otherwise make it.

If you'd like some help, consider Akros, Inc.[66], and investment consulting firm. They will work with you to help formulate a business plan, set up operations, or introduce you to a Broker/Dealer commensurate with your profile. Debbie Castellani and her partner, Bill Conrad, have an eclectic background which includes management, analysis, marketing, sales and client relationship management.

Frank Gleberman, CLU, CFP® has enjoyed a distinguished career as a financial planner. He is a principle with The Century Benefits Group, Registered Representative of Jefferson Pilot Securities Corporation, and a Registered Investment Advisor with Economic Designs Corporation in Marina Del Rey, California.

Finding the Right Fit
By
Frank Gleberman, CLU, CFP®

There are a lot of two-way streets today, just as there have always been. Those two-way streets (spell 'em o-p-e-n a-n-d h-o-n-e-s-t r-e-l-a-t-i-o-n-s-h-i-p-s) are between practitioner and company, practitioner and client, practitioner and fellow practitioners, company and practitioner's client, etc.

There is no disagreement on the part of yours truly that:
1 - What we envision in the beginning is sometimes not the real world down the road.
2 - What some insurance or brokerage companies are today may not be what they will become in a few years.
3 - WE change and sometimes find another venue will fit our needs better.
4 - Some practitioners are far better off answering only to themselves and not an insurance company or brokerage.
5 - It is difficult (but not impossible) to obtain training personalized to ourselves rather than personalized to some insurance or brokerage company training executive.
6 - Even in the best of worlds, we do not always make the best lifelong choices . . . in marriage, in selecting friends, in selecting investment or in choosing the best company with which to develop our future practices.

But I certainly WILL reiterate that you should take the time to interview a sufficient number of companies to obtain a very broad view of the profession. Different sizes, different philosophies and other differences . . . just be sure to not limit your interviews to only one company in each category.

---

[66] http://www.Akrosinv.com/

If possible, be sure to look for established financial planners who are looking for an intern or junior partner. I believe you will feel much better about yourself if YOU feel your choice is the RIGHT one. Lord knows, establishing a practice has enough challenges that you don't want to base your early years on a false premise.

Be open and honest with the companies with which you interview. My take is that there are practitioners with most of them who mirror your objectives and with whom you can identify. If you can't find any of those folks in a particular company, then I believe I'd scratch THAT company off my dance card. No matter how good their training, it evidently hasn't been the RIGHT training. If that company won't let you interview practitioners, RUN, don't walk for the exit door from that interview. They're evidently hiding something.

When you DO find practitioners with whom you strongly identify, that also tells you something. And don't forget to ask them, as has been brought up on this string, "IF there was no penalty or loss in your compensation (commissions, etc.), would you leave this company?" And, "Why?" Those are honest questions that deserve honest answers. Right?

Above all, be true and honest with others. In that way, you're true and honest with yourself. Both ways, you are building a discipline that will also help you be true and honest with your clients.

BROKER/DEALERS[67]

Here's where I should put the A-list of super-special Broker/Dealers in the industry so you will know exactly whose door to knock on to get the *best deal* if you want to be a financial planner. *Best deal* being:

> *Outstanding payout*
> *Incredible technology*
> *Amazing training*
> *Fantastic brand name*
> *Remarkable etceteras*

Uh huh. Have you ever read the recruiting packages from these firms? Shoot, every last one of them has the most wonderful environment you could ever ask for, including all the bells and whistles, and your life with them will be perfect once you get through the interview maze and your name is on the dotted line.

---

[67] Most major financial planning publications put together an annual list of Broker/Dealers. Two places to start looking for a Broker/Dealer are the FPA http://www.fpanet.org/pub/resource (supplemental guide to the Journal of Financial Planning published in March) and FPi http://www.financial-planning.com/Surveys/broker/bdindex00.html (supplemental directory published in June)

Well, I had two major problems coming up with any list at all. First, the only people who would talk to me were the recruiters, reiterating the company line. They refused to allow me to quote their actual names, in case anything reeked of "not quite as advertised in the brochure." Second, talking to reps from various Broker/Dealers was fun, but I couldn't get their comments past their compliance people, in case readers misconstrued whatever it was they were really trying to say, or show, or not tell.

It doesn't matter what anyone said – or didn't. I've had enough experience, talked to enough people, read enough rhetoric on the discussion boards and possess enough gut reaction to name some names in spite of it all.

Be aware, every company has a faction that is out to defame them. Every Broker/Dealer of any size has a website set up by disgruntled clients or ex-producers to vent their anger and share their misery. Read it for what it's worth, do your research, and evaluate accordingly.

American Express Financial Advisors[68]

Yep. The big guns. Three things about them put them on my short list:

1. They throw money at the Financial Planning Association
2. They wholeheartedly support intern programs
3. They encourage education toward designations like CFP® and ChFC

The fact is, an inordinate amount of beginning financial planners start out with AEFA. What surprised me is the number that stay and build a career with them. I've not done a scientific study by any means, but my guess is the number is somewhere between 10% and 20%, and AEFA is diligently coming up with ways to increase that. In 2000, they rolled out their "Platforms" program.[69]

"Now we provide a career choice," says Mark Walker, Associate Vice President with AEFA, who claims the company uses the acronym WDYWFY" when talking to recruits. WDYWFY means 'What do you want for yourself?' It's the same question we ask clients!

"We encourage advisors to create plans for themselves as well as their clients," Mark explained. "When acquiring new advisors, we ask, 'What do you want out of your career?' We offer them a career with a floor, but no ceiling -- a solid platform upon which to build an independent practice backed by a great brand and a compliment of services including transition advice for planners wanting to expand their practices or to retire."

"In another year or so, I'll switch to Platform Two," Alex Bishop, a planner in Charlotte, North Carolina, told me. "I'll pay a monthly fee for the franchise agreement and proprietary

---

[68] http://www10.americanexpress.com/sif/cda/page/0,1641,1461,00.asp If this link doesn't work, try entering it manually.
[69] A 11/11/02 article by Jeff Benjamin in Investment News (http://www.investmentnews.com/) argues that the system may be stalled, and interviews some disgruntled franchisees.

software, but have my own practice, called something like 'Bishop & Associates, a division of American Express Financial Advisors'."

Alex tried to start his own firm once before, but found the biggest obstacle was lack of name recognition. "I'm confident I can go off on my own now," he said. "I've received fine education here, and I'm building a good fee-based business working as an employee on draw plus commissions."

Jeff Murphy, CUE Financial Group, started his planning career with AMEX after a six-year stint in the military, and still keeps up on things there, though he's worked elsewhere for eight years. "I worked there for about 22 months," he recalled, "which included the lengthy and extensive training program."

"I'd live at home if you can for the first year or two for a couple of reasons," he advises. "One, you may need to keep your expenses down, and two, even if you get off to a great start and make a ton of money, you won't have time to do anything except go home and sleep anyway for the first 18 months! They haven't changed THAT much.

"The first six months, I worked six days per week, at least 55-60 hours per week. For the first seven weeks, I was concentrating on studying for the Series' 7 & 63 and the insurance license, and memorizing the initial meeting presentation – 12 pages, typed, single-spaced, word for word! Saturday was phone calls from 9am 'til noon, Monday evening was phone calls from 6:30 'til 8:30, and Friday evening we called from 5:30 'til 7:30. Four days per week, there were 'classes' for half of each day on sales techniques or product information. The rest of the time was more phone calling or (hopefully) meeting with prospects.

"I forget the exact timeline, but the first six months or so, I got a ridiculously low salary, like $800 a month. Then I was on commission after that, but they gave a 'draw' of maybe $2,000 per month for 12 months. The worst part was that out of my paycheck (after the first six months), they deducted a ton of expenses: rent for the office, charge for the receptionist and administrative help, phone and long distance, postage on mailings, my computer lease if I didn't buy it (had to be through them), printer, EVERYTHING! On top of all of that, I had to spend about $1,200 out of my own pocket on day one before starting any training. That was for the Series' 7 & 63 and insurance license study materials, taking the exams, licensing costs, etc. Sounds bad, doesn't it?

"On the flip side, it was great training. Shortly after I left AMEX, I read an article somewhere that was about '*The Top 10 Companies to Work For...and Then Leave*', meaning to take your new skills and go elsewhere. AEFA was on the list.

"I still keep in touch with a guy I started with back in 1993 and he's still there and quite happy. Like everything, it is what you make it. Same with the leads. They are what you make them. You will certainly develop a thick skin calling those leads, but you can make some good money, too. If I was 22ish, single with no commitments and could live at home, I'd still do it again."

Raymond James Financial Services, Inc.[70]

Claude and I vacationed in Ashland, Oregon last year, and I couldn't help myself from stopping by the local Raymond James office on Main Street. When I walked out an hour later, I was ready to apply for a franchise.

These guys really have it together. Robby Harfst and Jeffrey Monosoff, CFP® are the sort of financial planners I'd feel comfortable sending my sister to. They told me of a recent client who wanted to know if she could afford to accept her company's early retirement offer. "It was a close call", Rob explained, "But we sorted through the complicated paperwork, ran Monte Carlo, and discussed the situation in light of her expectations."

When I asked if they did a complete plan for her, Rob laughed and said, "The cookie-cutter plans of the past are over. Our job is to listen and solve the problem currently facing the client."

They're able to do their job well because of the flexibility Raymond James offers. "Most offices are small, with only one to four reps, and are often family nucleuses with a husband and wife or father and son, plus a few registered assistants," Jeff told me. "Raymond James offers service for many different entities. There is a fee-only division, a group that works with institutions, such as banks, and then there is a boutique group of planners like we are. We do what fits best with the client's particular situation, and use the most appropriate compensation method for the job."

"Every Raymond James office is unique," added Rob, who has owned his office since 1988. "There is no commonality. One reason for that is the complete absence of edicts from the home office on how to conduct business. There is no pressure to sell product or charge a certain way.

Raymond James is definitely worth a look, if your goal is to ultimately open an independent office under a Broker/Dealer's umbrella.

Waddell & Reed [71]

In 1983, I started with this firm. They were a bunch of "good ol' boys", but somehow I seem to have a soft spot for them. They're on my list for one reason: They are financial planners.

Really. It's difficult to find a Broker/Dealer who puts financial planning first, but I think Waddell & Reed does. The problem is that they have proprietary products. The W&R Funds are okay, but I really hate the idea of being tied to a prescribed line of products. Maybe it comes from the days when I was with Waddell & Reed, and the United Funds were undergoing a routine audit by the SEC. Clients are suspect of that little "these funds are undergoing an audit by the NASD" sticker they put on the prospectus.

---

[70] http://www.rjfs.com/
[71] http://www.waddellreed.com

Waddell & Reed has a FAST Program (Financial Advisor Skills Training Program) to help you get off to a good start. A combination of classroom instruction and one-on-one coaching prepares you to "obtain appointments from people in your personal target market by using professional presentations that explain your services," according to the brochure.

"I was too chicken to start as an independent," says Gayle Johnson, a financial planner in Grand Rapids, Michigan. "Changing careers after nearly sixteen years in the non-profit sector, was a big step. I took six months off to research firms in my area, study for licensing, and interview potential Broker/Dealers."

Finally settling on Waddell & Reed because of their emphasis on financial planning and client relationships, Gayle applauds the great training and support she received. "They practice what they preach," she admits. "I had a good experience with them."

Gayle spent a lot of time thinking about what she was leaving behind when she decided, after two and a half years, to seek out an independent firm. I asked her how difficult it was to leave Waddell & Reed.

"They had no non-compete clause in the agreement I signed," she explained, "but all of the mutual fund products I sold were proprietary and couldn't be moved. At the time, all of the insurance products with Waddell & Reed were proprietary as well[72]. Waddell & Reed is an excellent company to represent and my reasons for leaving were not at all due to any lack of satisfaction with my Broker/Dealer. I was motivated by my total dissatisfaction with the "politics" at my local office.

"I'm much happier at **FNIC**[73]," she told me. "I was able to transfer many accounts at NAV. Now I'm compensated by a combination of fee-based planning, commissions on mutual funds and insurance, and am growing my number of wrap accounts. I wanted to be independent from the beginning."

Royal Alliance[74] (A SunAmerica Company)

The goal of this company is "To be the industry's premier Broker/Dealer for independent financial professionals." I like the independent part. In discussions I've had with reps, it sounds like they mean it. Royal Alliance makes my list because of three things:

1. They have brand recognition (SunAmerica)
2. They don't push proprietary products
3. They foster independence

---

[72] Some Broker/Dealers manage their own (proprietary) family of mutual funds and reps are often encouraged to sell those funds to their clients first. When a rep changes Broker/Dealers, money invested in proprietary products would need to be sold if the client were to move accounts to the rep's new firm. This may incur undesirable income tax impact for the client, leaving the client with no choice but to remain with the original Broker/Dealer.

[73] Financial Network Investment Corporation: http://www.fnic.com

[74] Recruiting contact at Royal Alliance is Gary Bender, Vice President and Director of National Recruitment. 800.821.5100.

Gary Charlebois owns Pension Portfolios in La Verne, California, a traditional commission-based business selling investment products through Royal Alliance Associates, Inc. I talked with John Colston, an independent contractor with Pension Portfolios, who told me, "Royal Alliance is committed to maintaining a platform for independents. There are a few proprietary products through the parent company, but absolutely no push to sell, or do anything, except follow compliance guidelines.

"Compliance is really the main issue," John insisted. "The New York corporate office conducts compliance audits, the Managing Executive[75] reports to a Regional Manager in their territory who in turn reports to the corporate office.

"Reporting requirements have tightened up, all applications and trades are submitted online utilizing Vision 2020, Royal Alliance's proprietary Internet-based system. Royal oversees the use of "A", "B" and "C" share mutual funds and other products such as variable annuities. Compliance is a major topic of discussion at our annual meetings more than in the past."

When I asked John if Pension Portfolios had considered switching Broker/Dealers, he replied, "No. Royal Alliance offers every type of program anyone could want. Each office can design their own way of doing business as long as they are compliant. We are happy with our commission/fee structure. We have no motivation to change. The same issues probably exist at other independent Broker/Dealers."

Brian Fenn[76], CFP®, CLU, ChFC, who left Royal Alliance to form his own fee-only practice in Charlotte, North Carolina, might disagree. "I was a different breed," he claims. "I was working with Royal Alliance, but compliance became a problem. They wanted me to state on my ADV that I had a 'conflict of interest' because I had a relationship with them. I certainly didn't consider my relationship with them a conflict of interest! But when a 'fee-only' client questioned the compulsory 'securities through Royal Alliance' I had to place on my business card, I began to wonder, why do I need a Broker/Dealer? They weren't set up to handle a practice like mine."

When I asked Brian if he could think of a better way to start out than with a Broker/Dealer, he agreed that, "Until the industry does a better job of working new advisors through the system, beginning with a Broker/Dealer makes sense. "Keep the vision of where you really want to be while getting the skills," he advises. "Work and network and you'll get there eventually.

"There's a huge need for hourly practices," Brian feels. "I'm thinking of starting a separate division in my corporation just to provide hourly services." This brings us to the next type of working arrangement you might consider:

---

[75] "Managing Executive is Royal Alliance jargon for the Registered Principal who has On-Site Jurisdiction (OSJ). Gary Charlebois is the OSJ. He is required to hold a Series 24 Registered Principal's license.

[76] Brian Fenn owns Carolina Capital Consulting, Inc., a fee-only RIA specializing in doctors and dentists. http://www.3ccc.com

Others

It would be an impossible task to find information on all the available Broker/Dealers in the country and list the pros and cons of working with them. That's a job for you to do, in any case. Only you will know why you entered this profession, where you feel comfortable working, and what you love doing.

Solicitation from Primerica, WFG/WMA and agents with other multi-level marketing companies are often the first contact individuals have with "financial planning". I'll go out on a limb here and comment that agents with these companies generally keep to themselves and refrain from participation in the FPA or the rest of the financial planning community in general. Controversy surrounds their business practices. Perhaps the best summation of the situation I've seen was on a March 2002 post on the Financial Planning board at FPi: http://www.financial-planning.com/wwwboard8/messages/3736.html. This isn't an original post, but it presents a rational view of a divisive issue.

To help you compare Broker/Dealers, Financial Planning Interactive[77] offers comprehensive analysis on over 62 firms. Rank and sort firms by payouts, revenues and services, or select up to four firms for in-depth comparisons.

Just to get you started with inquiries, check out C.J.M. Planning Corp.[78] (caters to accounting profession), Commonwealth Financial Network[79] (active recruiting campaign) and H.D. Vest Advisory Services[80] (a tax professional's slam dunk)

TURNKEY OPERATIONS

The Garrett Planning Network, Inc.[81]

"When I read about Sheryl Garrett's training program in Investment Advisor Magazine[82], I signed up right away and got in on her second training session. It's exactly how I wanted to practice," said Veronica Hart, CFP®, a planner in College Station, Texas. "My business plan flowed straight from Sheryl's model."

As part of their plan to integrate more financial planning into their culture, Merrill Lynch created the position of 'Planning Associate' for Veronica. "I went to Merrill with the intent of doing financial planning, and that's what I did," she claims. "They are really trying, and they do encourage reps to get their CFP®, but they have a very big boat to turn around," she said. When Veronica became pregnant with her second child and the doctor told her she had to reduce the stress she was under, she took the opportunity to leave.

---

[77] http://www.financial-planning.com/cgi-bin/broker2.pl
[78] http://www.cjmplanning.com
[79] http://www.commonwealth.com/
[80] http://www.hdvest.com
[81] http://www.garrettplanningnetwork.com/ Also check http://www.NUCO.com for a copy of Sheryl's book, "Garrett's Guide to Financial Planning: How to Capture the Middle Market and increase your Profits!"
[82] http://www.investmentadvisor.com/

"Merrill has plenty of resources to devote to training, compliance, etc. If I ever made an error, Merrill Lynch made it right. Period. But I wanted to do financial planning, and I could see the Merrill managers weren't excited about it." She left after more than five years.

"This was a difficult financial change for me, but I was prepared, because I'd been thinking about it for years. I wanted to focus more on relationships and less on transactions and production," she said. "The difference is like night and day. There is no comparison! My time is flexible. Sheryl has provided me with all the tools she uses, which has saved me hundreds of hours. The model works really well for most Americans. It's how they're used to paying for services. They understand, accept and appreciate an hourly rate."

Dan O'Leary, CFP® has been a commissioned financial planner to the middle class for over 15 years. He credits Sheryl's Network with turning his business around. "When I started," he says, "my marketing plan was 'anyone with any money who could fog a mirror' was a potential client. Today that approach is a recipe for disaster!

He feels that the market for fee-only or fee-based services to middle income clients is enormous. Dan urges you to "Find out for yourself. Open the yellow pages and call every listing under 'Financial Planning'. Pose a question, such as, 'I just became eligible for my company 401(k) and would like help selecting investment options. What do you charge for this service?' I'll bet less than ten percent will be willing to help, and they don't advertise that service.

"Sheryl offers a 'soup to nuts' business system," Dan continues. "You don't have to reinvent the wheel. You can come home after the training and be on-track."

The Garrett Planning Network, Inc.
By
Angie Herbers

The Garrett Planning Network, Inc., founded by CFP® Sheryl Garrett in July 2000, is a group of like-minded financial planning professionals who are dedicated to offering Fee-Only Hourly services to people from all walks of life and income levels. Our services are geared toward Middle Americans, do-it-yourselfers, and consumers desiring periodic advice. Membership in The Garrett Planning Network offers financial planning professionals a complete turnkey business model, coupled with ongoing training and support designed to help them reach and serve a huge, untapped market. Members of the network receive a comprehensive set of practice management and marketing tools – proven strategies to manage a Fee-Only Hourly business.

I work alongside Sheryl Garrett to help financial planning professionals decide if Fee-Only Hourly financial planning is the right fit for them. We work directly with established practitioners who wish to either incorporate Fee-Only Hourly planning into their existing Fee-Only practices or transition their existing commission- or fee-based practices to successful Fee-Only Hourly practices. We also help new planners who wish to establish their own Fee-Only Hourly practices. The Garrett Planning Network's unique 3-pronged system of turnkey materials, comprehensive training and ongoing support helps members not only streamline their start-up process but maximize their success over time.

The Comprehensive Training Program offered is a three-day event, conducted at our headquarters in Shawnee, KS. It is designed to help members get a successful start. Directed by Sheryl Garrett personally, this program walks members step-by-step through the workflow process. It clearly demonstrates our systems and efficiencies, and provides valuable coaching and information on "best practices" for a Fee-Only Hourly planner. We learn how to use the recommended software programs. We discuss practice management issues such as marketing, compliance and how to efficiently track and bill our time. We observe mock client meetings and role-play how best to introduce ourselves in business settings. We learn how to secure client engagements, and discuss ways to present our financial plans and/or analysis to clients so that the client wants to refer friends and return for additional services. Our marketing consultant spends an entire afternoon with the group to answer questions on creating effective collateral materials, web sites, marketing plans and more. We discuss how to work with the media and develop press partnerships.

The Garrett Planning Network's "Pathways to Success Retreat" is our annual meeting, aimed at bringing the entire membership together. We offer a variety of educational tracks addressing popular financial planning and practice management topics. This Members-Only retreat is included, tuition free, as a benefit of membership in The Garrett Planning Network, Inc. The retreat offers members the opportunity to grow their practices and gain valuable insights from keynote speakers and retreat sponsors. Most importantly, perhaps, the retreat gives members the opportunity to share ideas and resources in both formal and informal settings. We discuss what works in all areas of promoting and managing their practices. We are a motivated and generous group, filled with highly accomplished professionals who enjoy sharing their insights with other like-minded practitioners.

Cambridge Financial Advisors, LLC[83]

Margaret Opsata, a freelance finance writer interviewed Bert Whitehead, MBA, JD, founder of Cambridge Financial Advisors, LLC for Financial Advisor Magazine in 2000.[84] Cambridge advisors are compensated by a retainer, which includes tax preparation and amending previous returns. I was intrigued by the operation and was recently able to meet Bert and spend a few days with him and several of his advisors.

One of the Cambridge advisors is Robert J. Schumann, MBA, CFP®, who compared the system with Sheryl's network:

"Last week I had a prospect who got my name and the name of a local member of the Garrett Planning Network (GPN) from the NAPFA website. The prospect followed NAPFA's advice and interviewed us both. The family was a typical middle-income household with gross income of around $65,000. Husband and wife were young school teachers (he fulltime, she part-time) with a small child. Their household income was about

[83] http://www.cambridgeadvisors.com/
[84] http://www.cambridgeadvisors.com/main/Adv_News/Articles/Bert_Crusade.html

$65,000.   The Cambridge fee was around $5000. The GPN fee was $1500.   After studying both offers, the family chose the Cambridge system.   Why did they decide to spend $5000 instead of $1500?   I believe they decided based on 'value' rather than 'price'.

"The Cambridge system is comprehensive, holistic and focuses on taxes. I took three hours to study the family's tax returns from 1998-2000. The Cambridge retainer included amending previous tax returns for numerous errors. The total projected refund, including interest, on the three amended returns was over $3000. $5000 - 3000 = $2000 net fee.

"Now let's compare what else the family got for their $5000, in addition to more than $3000 in tax refunds. The Cambridge retainer included tax preparation, amended returns, tax planning, portfolio review, asset allocation, cash flow analysis, budget, record keeping, insurance review, goal setting, estate planning, investment strategy, investment implementation and year end tax planning. Included in the price were simple wills, powers of attorney for health care and living wills. The GPN retainer offered a limited 8 hours of advice in 3-4 appointments.   The Cambridge retainer was open ended with unlimited appointments, telephone calls and follow-up questions.

"A limited retainer is not comprehensive, holistic financial planning.   It's modular financial planning similar to that offered by insurance agents and brokers.   In my opinion, Sheryl Garrett's greatest contribution is that she has made modular financial planning available to the masses on a fee-only, hourly basis. She has eliminated the conflict of interest created by a compensation system based on product sales/commissions.

"While fee-only, hourly financial planning is a great and much needed service, I believe my middle America school teachers suggest that in the end the market will choose the Cambridge system or variations of it because it has five inherent advantages:

    1) Includes tax preparation
    2) Includes wills and advanced medical directives
    3) It's comprehensive and holistic
    4) It's an open retainer
    5) Flat fee retainer using value based pricing versus an hourly fee

"Taxes are the 'elephant in the kitchen' for most of Middle America. There is great value in getting the elephant out of the kitchen.   The more complex the code becomes the more that becomes true. We amend about 60% of all returns that come to us. For the 40% who don't need amended returns, we offer a limited retainer that is very similar to the standard GPN retainer.

"That's not to say the Cambridge system is perfect. The biggest threat to the Cambridge system is the proposal for a flat tax. The biggest weakness that I see in the Cambridge system is the time spent studying the old tax returns of the 40% who don't need amending. The second biggest weakness is the time and experience it takes to become proficient at reviewing tax returns.

"One could also argue that one system is not better than the other because each meets the needs of different segments of Middle America.   If we differentiate the market into price vs.

value preferences and modular vs. comprehensive service needs, it would appear that both systems fit needs. I personally believe that the demand for fee-only financial planning is so great that advisors using either system will prosper. Meanwhile, by focusing on taxes, Cambridge has made comprehensive, fee-only financial planning affordable to most Middle Americans."

The Alliance of Cambridge Advisors
By
Ed Fulbright, CPA, PFS

The Mission of the Alliance of Cambridge Advisors is to create, grow and support a thriving professional community of like-minded fee-only financial advisors who share and leverage their knowledge, resources, and experience and who are recognized as being at the forefront of holistic financial planning for the benefit of their clients. We have all received training on the Cambridge System and are free to alter it to suit our individual practices.

The system focuses on the Tax Planning & Preparation, Estate Planning, Simple Will Preparation, Record Keeping/Cash Flow, Portfolio Analysis/Investment Strategy & Implementation, Retirement Planning, Insurance, Goal Setting/Life Planning, Marketing, Preliminary Appointment/Presentation Appointment, Limited Retainers, Administrative Issues and Supplemental Materials (ADV preparation, choosing a custodian, complementary programs like NAPFA's Basic Training and FOSTER, etc). It is not a planning by the pound system. It is a recommendation and implementation system at your client's speed. It is a very personal financial planning system.

Our clients are people who cannot afford to make mistakes. These clients include people who have up to 5 to 10 million in assets. Most planning systems focus on the rate of return of your portfolio. It is not an AUM (assets under management) fee system but a retainer fee based upon the client's net worth, income and complexity.

The Cambridge System focuses on helping clients relate to the 10 most important factors to becoming and staying financially independent by knowing "How Much Is Enough":

1) How much money do you make? 2) How much do you save? 3) How much debt do you have? 4) Are you properly housed? 5) Is your house properly leveraged? 6) How stable is your primary relationship? 7) How much risk are you taking outside your portfolio? 8) How is your health? 9) How much tax do you pay? 10) Finally, what is the return on your investments?

During the first year, you are provided a coach/mentor to help you get around the barriers you discover.

I joined Cambridge Advisors five years ago for the following reasons:

It is a proven and validated system.

It includes areas of concern that you can control. You can influence rate of return thru asset allocation but you cannot control it in the short run. You can control how much they save and pay in taxes.

It saved me from paying the high price for unproven education, which could be higher than the first year fee. Mistakes or a lack of business has its cost, too.

Network of advisors with different areas of expertise to assist you with problems or questions.

It allows me to work with people of all income and net worth levels.

I stay a Cambridge Advisor for the following reasons:

The great sharing of knowledge of other advisors including software.

The referrals from other Cambridge Advisors more than paid for my initial fee and renewals. It continues to save me money by helping me to avoid mistakes and find innovations that improve my business performance.

For more information about the Cambridge System, I would recommend that you visit www.cambridgeadvisor.com and/or purchase Bert Whitehead's Book "Facing Financial Dysfunction" from www.bertwhitehead.com. Bert is the founder of the Cambridge System. You are welcomed to email me at edf@moneyful.com with your questions.

If this type of system appeals to you, do your homework. Other similar arrangements are out there, most notably Sherry Hazan-Cohen, of Dream Achieve®,[85] in Plano, Texas. Her focus is on values-based planning, and she offers a package that includes hourly financial planning and personal achievement coaching.

Assante Management Inc.

When I decided to add asset management services to my fee-only practice in 1995, I contacted Reinhardt Werba Bowen Advisory Services. Assante Asset Management Inc.[86] has purchased RWB, but the philosophy has remained the same and it is still a perfect match for some of my clients. They do 100% pf the reporting, saving me a ton of time.

"As a turnkey asset manager provider (TAMP) as they call themselves, Assante provides back office services that I could not have provided at the beginning of my career," claims Craig Martin, CFP®, ChFC, MSFS, with Family Wealth Consulting Group in San Jose, California. "They do hiring, management, training, payroll and firing. I have no personal or economic need to do that employee stuff myself. I have looked at what it would cost me to hire, train, manage and replace such a staff, and it's probably 35 to 60 basis points per year."
Assante is almost a pure play in Modern Portfolio Theory, using institutional asset class funds provided by Dimensional Fund Advisors (DFA)[87], while allowing the advisor flexibility to create unique portfolios. "They provide web-based reporting that is both time

---

[85] http://www.dreamachieve.com If you contact Sherry, be sure and mention Robin Vaccai-Yess, who highly recommends her!

[86] http://www.assante.com/us/

[87] http://www.dfafunds.com/

and dollar weighted, and monitor costs by tax lot number, giving me year-round tax planning ability," Craig said.

SEI[88]

If you will have clients with $100,000 or more in assets to invest and are interested in a fee-based turnkey program producing back-office support, consider SEI.

DOING IT YOURSELF: FEE-ONLY ASSET MANAGEMENT

Sheryl Garret wasn't around when I left FNIC to start out on my own with a vision of charging flat fees for projects or by the hour. RWB (Assante) wasn't around either. Aside from the fact that I nearly starved to death (but it was a different time and consumers weren't yet ready for fee-only planners like they are today) there was another problem.

I began by offering financial planning for a flat project fee or consulting at an hourly rate, but did not manage assets. Most people, no matter what the financial issues involved, need to invest. As part of the planning process, I would give general recommendations for their portfolios and send them off to find a broker. If pressed, I would recommend three or four I knew from my days in the registered rep world.

What I found was that I quickly got out of the loop where my client's investments were concerned. In spite of my brilliant work, the reps making the specific investment choices for my clients were playing havoc with my financial plans! Sometimes it would be a year before the client would return for a review, and the rep may have simply rebalanced the portfolio and not taken capital gains into consideration, throwing the tax planning off. Maybe the rep called the client to recommend a change and the client assumed since I had given them the name of the rep I knew about the change. Most of these were little things, but things that had the potential for significant impact on long-range planning. I soon realized I needed to have more control over the day-to-day dealings in the portfolio.

It was years before things actually ended up as I originally visualized. Today I hire an economist who designs the portfolios for our clients, and we work with an outside money manager for individual stocks. We are the bottom line. We gather the information, do the financial planning and tell the economist what the objectives are. He designs the portfolio, and explains to me why it is good for our client. We make the presentation. Once the client and our team agree on the portfolio, the account is opened with Schwab and our staff makes the trades. Every day the prices and holdings download into our portfolio management system, so when a client calls or comes in, we have up-to-date information about their investments, including current capital gain information.

We charge an annual retainer, which includes financial planning, portfolio design, managed assets up to a specific dollar amount, and allows the client unlimited phone calls and meetings. It's an ongoing process, and so far hasn't been abused where our time is concerned. When something comes up, the client calls, instead of worrying that it'll cost too

---

[88] http://www.seic.com/iag

much. We refer insurance business, but remain involved in the process, which is included as part of the retainer. We still offer an hourly rate for consulting, and have a "simplified financial plan" which costs the client $500.

The way we work gives the client a choice of payment options appropriate for their needs. We outsource what we don't enjoy doing, and refer when additional expertise is required. Since most of our clients are on retainer, our income is fairly predictable.

Institutional Services

One of the biggest obstacles facing those wishing to include asset management services in their financial planning practice is finding an institution without a requirement for $25 million or more under management. Schwab, Waterhouse. and Fidelity have all upped their minimum for new advisors. That does not mean you can't go to them with a good business plan and get them to relax their policy on a case-by-case basis. Be persistent if you want to work with them, but be aware that there are other options.

EAInvest[89]

We recently began opening accounts with EAInvest as an alternative to Schwab. They are a relatively new independent financial advisor's platform offering custodial, clearing, technology and training services. Due to a surprise merger with BenefitStreet Inc.[90], the firm will give fee-only advisers the ability to manage 401(k) assets. Service is highly personalized and responsive, and the company has no plans to serve retail clients. They clear through Pershing, but all contact is with a personal representative assigned to each advisor. Transactions can be downloaded into Centerpiece and Advent. Technical support is superior. New advisors and established veterans moving business to a fee-only environment will find EAInvest a good firm with which to do business.

TRADEPMR[TM][91]

There is no minimum account size for clearing through this relatively new discount broker. The company was started by a group of advisors unhappy with service they were getting from the big firms. They insist they will have no more than 25 new accounts per advisor, compared with 150 accounts per advisor at Schwab and Waterhouse.

They have over 7000 funds available with no transaction fee. Stock trades are $14.95 per trade for unlimited shares, less than half Schwab's fee. I talked with Michael Baldwin at the firm and was surprised to learn they download to both Centerpiece and Advent. I was impressed with the friendly reception I received from my phone call and the frank answers to my questions.

---

[89] http://www.eainvest.com/
[90] https://401k.benefitstreet.com/
[91] http://www.tradepmr.com **Send for the demo.**

INSURANCE COMPANIES

Northwestern Mutual[92]

Jess M. Swick, CLU, ChFC, AEP[93], has been with the Northwestern Mutual Life Insurance Company for over thirty years, beginning his career while still in college., and has found the occupation to be intensely satisfying.

"Northwestern provides significant resources for its Representatives," Jess told me over breakfast. "They provide incredible tools, software programs, and of course products to help people with important planning issues. When I am with a client, I do not think about income. I think about providing a quality service," he said. "If I help my clients get what they want then I will be appropriately paid." Back to that in a moment.

Jess does personal and business planning and does a darned good job. He's proud to represent the Northwestern Mutual Financial Network, and was eager to show me the company's ten page detailed data gathering form, which he goes through with every client. "With the fact finder, you gather vital information about the client that directly relates to their financial plans, goals and dreams. Insurance companies have become full service agencies to compete in today's environment," he explained. From the looks of the consumer material he displayed, they are doing a top-notch job of it. The company has invested a significant amount into software, training and other resources for their agents.

Jess loves working with people and if he's not able to help a new contact he believes it's either because the timing or the chemistry not right. His philosophy is that if he meets with enough people, he will solve a lot of problems, which means he will provide a lot of products.

This brings us back to compensation. Jess tells his clients he gets paid in four ways:

1. The satisfaction of knowing he has helped.
2. He receives referrals, indicating they are pleased with his services.
3. Commissions from the sale of products
4. Referring his clients to other professionals who help them with other services and needs.

Jess is one of those quiet "pillar of the community" types who are always ready with a helping hand. He has coached AYSO for 20 years, serves as President of the Board for OPARC, a non-profit organization dedicated to "enabling people with disabilities to reach their full potential", is on the board of the Claremont Community Foundation, is active in Kiwanis, is Moderator of his Church, is on the board of directors for the Financial

---

[92] http://ww2.northwesternmutual.com/tn/global--nmfn_home_pg
[93] The AEP (Accredited Estate Planner) designation is awarded by the National Association of Estate Planners & Councils to professionals who meet stringent experience and education qualifications including two graduate level courses administered by The American College. Learn more about it at http://www.naepc.org

Representatives Association (7500 members) of the Northwestern Mutual Financial Network, and a 25 year member of the Million Dollar Round Table.[94]

I asked Jess about new people entering the financial services industry, and what sort of person might consider applying to Northwestern Mutual.

"Entrepreneurs make the best candidates. Those who are self-starters, who want to work for themselves and control their own destiny." he responded. "Northwestern has an exceptional training process both locally and in Milwaukee. Our new applicants are carefully recruited and about only ten out of 100 are offered a contract," Jess continued, "however turnover is very low. New representative have to really hustle. The beauty is, you only need to work half days – any twelve hours. But it is worth it. Especially with Northwestern Mutual!"

John Hancock

Charles G. McKenna, currently with WFG in New York, spent twelve years with John Hancock – the last six in management.

"I was part of a small office that had less than 30 planners. Everyone was strongly encouraged to pursue industry designations. In fact, Hancock would reimburse you most of your expenses for the classes if you passed.

"Our regional VP was big on education and training and he did not like managers splitting cases with reps. My manager never split a case with me and I never split a case with any of my staff unless the lead was totally generated by me. For example, if I had a client from my book of business give me a referral; I would ALWAYS bring a new candidate with me on the appointment. I would do all of the work and show the rep every step of the way what I was doing. I would then give the rep 25% of the case. I would never take a percentage of the reps business that was generated by their leads. Neither would any other manager that I had worked with while I was with the company.

"As a Sales Manager, my compensation was based on overrides of my reps. On first year reps I would earn 49% of their base commissions. If that new rep did not last a year then I was "charged back" a percentage of his stipend salary or training allowance. After the first year, my compensation went to 28% override. After the third year, it was 15% and after the fourth, it went to 7% where it stayed.

"My GA would only allow me to bring on one new rep per quarter in each of the years I worked in management. He wanted me to make sure I spent enough time with the rep to teach them. Selling skills was a weekly class. Selling was not the answer but rather an emphasis on clearly presenting options to the prospect and helping them select which was most appropriate for them. We could choose from two systems: Financial Profiles or Expert by Sterling Wentworth. Both were great programs for comprehensive planning.

---

[94] http://www.mdrt.org/ Million Dollar Round Table is an association of primarily insurance-based financial services sales professionals.

"We encouraged, and required, cold calling for the first quarter of a new rep's career. After that, we insisted that they look to alternative marketing methods.

"Out of the 26 people that I recruited, only three are still with Hancock. Another 20 are still in the industry. In my last three years of management not one of my first year reps earned less than $75,000 FYC. The last two years all of my first year reps made over $100,000 in commissions and bonus. Those are very atypical numbers and were part of the reason that I climbed to be among the top ten managers in the company.

"Perhaps ours was a unique office but I know that the offices near me had similar results. Perhaps it was our region. He even encouraged us to give away our books to our reps.

"Hancock wasn't and isn't perfect, however, it was a great place to start and to learn. Make sure you have a very professional setting in the potential office and that the manager is respected. Ask to see the productions sheets for annual production clubs and you will get an idea of what is going on there."

To help you understand the very different experiences well-qualified and interested people can have with the same company, I refer you again to the discussion boards at Financial Planning Interactive. Here, you can read what Tom had to say about his experience with the same company. Differing views will be found within any company. Their diametric opinions are at http://www.financial-planning.com/wwwboard5/messages/4306.html

What to ask insurance companies

Rev. Frank J. Szewczyk, MBA, M.Div., a former financial planner with a major insurance company who currently has a "personal coaching practice helping people create a life worth living", suggests anyone considering an insurance company ask the potential manager these questions:

1) What is your personal ratio between hires and those who are still in the business? Companies have nationwide ratios but you want to know what YOUR manager's retention rate is for one, three, and five years.

2) What type of training will I receive, computer based, video, etc?

3) How long will the manager work with me? (Caution: most managers work with a new agent for a short period and move on to the next recruit.)

4) Will they assign you to a mentor? (This can be critical to your long-term success)

5) Will they teach you how to prospect and use lead lists, seminars, and other methods besides friends and family?

6) Are they financial planners or financial sales organizations? A needs analysis is different from a full-blown financial plan. Try to determine if the goal of the representative is to sell a financial plan/needs analysis to sell more products or is the goal to give the client a plan for long-term success.

In terms of companies, most have some sort of training program but again it depends on the local manager. For what it is worth, if you are housed out of the main office for the local organization versus a branch you tend to have access to more training. Obtaining one's CFP is the best technical training someone can receive.

A Different Approach, from a Related Industry

"My Man in Dallas/Ft. Worth" and I met online through the FPi discussion boards, and became instant friends. Kevin owns a Property & Casualty Agency, representing Nationwide Insurance & Financial. He offers P&C, Life (traditional and variable products), Health and Commercial Insurance. In addition, he has brokerage agreements to secure those insurance products not offered by Nationwide (LTC, Medicare Supplement, etc.) for his clients.

Definitely… *The Road Less Traveled*[95]
By
Kevin Michael Lynch, MBA, CFP ®, CLU, ChFC, RFC, RHU, REBC, CSA
President, K. Lynch & Associates, Inc.
Dallas-Ft. Worth, TX
sav4later@aol.com or lynchk3@nationwide.com

My entrance into financial planning has not been like so many of my brethren. I did not come to financial planning from insurance or investments but rather I came to insurance and investments through studying to enter financial planning.

I achieved my college degrees through part time studies over a fifteen-year period, culminating with my MBA in May 1985. Shortly after graduating at age 34, I discovered the concept of "financial planning" and The College for Financial Planning, Denver, CO. I began my CFP studies in 1987 and finished them in September 1991.

Beginning in 1991, through an "internship" with The Equitable Life Insurance Society, known today as AXA, I completed my Series 6 & 63 and became licensed for Life & Health as well. At the end of my internship 120 days later, I was not convinced that the general manager of the Houston, TX Equitable office was the person to properly train me for a career change and I remained in my original career field, Auto Sales Finance. (AKA Ford Motor Credit, GMAC, etc.)

I did continue however, working with a few friends and colleges over the next few years, providing financial services and basic financial planning under a registered DBA "Per$onal Financial Planning." In 1998, I was presented with an opportunity to make a career change and build a property & casualty insurance agency. My original business plan called for me to build a book of business with 2500-3000 policies in force and then to devote myself to serving those clients as their financial planner. This would mean never having to make a

---

[95] From "The Road Less Traveled: A New Psychology of Love, Traditional Values and Spiritual Growth" by M. Scott Peck, MD.

cold call, as I would be calling on clients with whom I already had a relationship.

My carrier, Nationwide Insurance & Financial, had a great "Financed Community Agents" Program and I launched my agency in November 1998. Over the next 44 months, I built my agency to 2200 policies in force and completed additional studies in the field of insurance and financial services. These studies included completing the requirements for and earning the following industry designations:

Chartered Life Underwriter (CLU), Chartered Financial Consultant (ChFC), Registered Health Underwriter (RHU), Registered Employee Benefits Consultant (REBC) and most recently, Certified Senior Advisor (CSA.)

Would I recommend this entree into financial planning for you? Probably not, but it worked for me.

The down side of my plan to become a practicing CFP: while I do have a book of business that contains @1400 families, these clients know me first and foremost as their P&C Agent. Making the switch from providing a "commodity" type product to a service, such as financial planning, is not a natural progression for the majority of my current clients.

On the upside however, what my P&C book of business does provide is a solid base of income from which I can now build a second profit center, under the umbrella of my current incorporated business, K. Lynch & Associates, Inc. With the income stream from my P& C agency, I have the base necessary to begin the process of incorporating Values Based Financial Planning into my practice. My first prospects will be the 100-150 client families within my current book that have the means and the motives necessary to utilize my financial planning services.

From this initial group of clients I plan to build a stream of referrals and within the next five years have 100 clients providing a minimum annual fee based income of $3500 to $5000 each...while retaining ownership, but delegating day to day operating control of my P&C business.

Will this plan work for you? I don't know but it is the path I am now on and the path upon which I plan on reach my personal and professional goals. Whatever path you choose I wish you God Speed and Good Fortune.

WIREHOUSES[96]

When I "talk" with beginning practitioners on the industry bulletin boards, one of the most frequent questions is: should I start out with a member firm or wirehouse? These are the companies that are most actively recruiting people into the financial services industry, and a

---

[96] Check out an informed response to a question regarding Merrill Lynch on the FPi discussion boards: http://www.financial-planning.com/wwwboard5/messages/4377.html

big part of the initial discussion centers on their training programs. Isn't this a great way to get training in the business?

The answer, of course, is yes and no. Although several of the larger brokerage firms have stepped up their training in financial planning, the ex-brokers I've talked to generally think there was a lot more hype than substance to the training they received. Scott Dauenhauer[97], who worked with three different brokerage firms in his career before he launched his own independent firm, has recently written an essay about his experience. "The programs focus solely on sales and product training," he says. "I attended one such program and 95% of the training focused on cold-calling sales and learning proprietary product. Brokerage firms want 'salespeople', not highly skilled financial planners."

Many people getting into the business will find the sales (and especially the cold-calling) process repugnant and degrading. Your real training comes if and when you manage to acquire a client through this process, and you begin to gain some real-world experience in helping people organize their financial lives. If Scott and others can be believed (and I think they can) this is going to be largely a self-teaching experience.

You should also recognize that working for one of the larger firms will reduce the things you can recommend to a client or prospect. "A public company owes its first loyalty to the public shareholders," says Scott. "The people who own stock in a company must have their interests protected. A public brokerage firm's loyalty cannot be 100% to their customer."

In the real world, that means that you are expected to direct client assets in directions that are most beneficial to the company. In fact, your income will depend on it. "A broker is paid a percentage of the revenues that he/she brings to the firm--typically 25-40%," says Scott. It is not, however, that simple. Brokerage firms determine the payout percentage for each individual "product." They control product flow by paying higher amounts for product the firm wants to move (sell). Each firm works differently, but depending on the product a firm wants to emphasize, they will pay a broker a higher percentage of the revenue to induce him to sell what the company wants him to sell. For example, if the company wants a broker to sell a "wrap account," they may tell the broker that he will receive a higher percentage of the fees they generate from that particular wrap account. If the broker wants the higher revenue, he/she will migrate toward selling that product.

"A more blatant conflict," says Scott "is a practice that people thought was eliminated a long time ago. Some brokerage firms pay their brokers more for selling proprietary (company managed) mutual funds." To be fair, he says, most firms have eliminated this practice. However there is still at least one major brokerage firm that still pays brokers up to 25% more commissions to sell their company managed mutual funds over other competing funds. In addition, the more company-managed funds a broker sells the more perks he receives. Whether it is a trip, an expense account, or personal gifts, he may not receive these perks if he sells other companies funds.

---

[97] The entire essay can be found on Scott Dauenhauer's web site: http://www.meridianwealth.com

Finally, says Scott, the broker many times is under tremendous pressure from management to sell the latest mutual fund offering from that brokerage. "Many branch managers," he says, "have compensation tied to the amount of proprietary products the branch sells. The manager's interest is in getting the highest bonus possible so he, in turn, puts the pressure on the brokers to 'pound the phones,' and sell their 'latest offering'."

It goes unspoken that if a broker does not participate in selling the new offering, then things will not be easy for him/her. "I know of one broker who was told, 'I don't think this firm is the right place for you,' after the broker refused to sell the new fund offering," he says. "It turned out that he was the only one to not submit to the pressure. He eventually left that firm. I can't begin to tell you how many voice mails and e-mails I received from management to sell the 'new' offerings. I never succumbed if it was not in my client's best interest. Be aware that the pressure is on the broker to sell certain products or else he/she risks losing their job. The conflicts don't stop there, they go on, but I think you get the picture."

But wait a minute; why does the planner who works for a wirehouse get only 25% to 40% of the commissions he or she generates through the recommendation of investments? The answer takes you into a murky world that Scott calls "The Broker Food Chain"--which, he says, even the brokers don't usually fully understand.

Does all of this mean that you cannot work with a large public company and still do a good job for clients? Not necessarily; but it does mean that it can be harder. Be aware that the company expects to be reimbursed for its training efforts. If you become successful, and you decide to leave the firm, many companies will file legal claims that the clients you've been working with at the firm are the "property" of the firm. They will file a temporary restraining order (TRO) on you, barring you from talking to these clients after you've left.

It doesn't matter if you are looking at working for a large institutional brokerage, an independent Broker/Dealer, or a small independent planning firm. The point is, **read the employment agreement and ask questions!** Pay particular attention to what will happen to *your* clients if you leave the company.

In many cases - I would say most - these TROs (as they are commonly known in the business) are not upheld, and the courts recognize that clients and consumers have the right to select anybody they choose as an advisor. But the legal bills and temporary injunction against talking to clients when you leave can be a factor in your decision as to whether the wirehouse brokerage training is as great a deal as the recruiter might make it sound.

BANKS AND CREDIT UNIONS

Many banks and credit unions are affiliated with Broker/Dealers today and offer an increasing range of financial planning products and services. Payout tends to be on the low end, but the experience in a relatively safe environment can be valuable.

Robin Vaccai-Yess, CFP®, owner of Center for Financial Wellness, Inc.[98] suggests working in a bank environment or for a bank-owned Broker/Dealer has added difficulties. "There are very stringent regulations in place to ensure that the customer understands that the investment products being purchased through the Bank Rep are not FDIC-insured. Because of these additional disclosure requirements to customers/clients, many Registered Representatives find the additional paperwork a hassle. No one expects to walk into a big brokerage firm or wirehouse and find FDIC-insured products, although they are available today."

WHAT TO ASK BEFORE YOU SIGN

Questions you'll want to ask of **any** company you interview:
1. How do you train new reps/employees? Will I have a mentor?
1. How many people have been with the company over 2 years?
2. What's the average production in the office?
3. How many hours a week will I be expected to work?
4. Will emphasis be on financial planning or gathering assets?
5. What products and services will I provide to clients?
6. How much support staff will I have?
7. Will I have quotas to meet? Proprietary products to sell?
8. How is compensation earned? Salary? Draw? Commissions?
9. What expenses will I encounter?
10. Are there any Medical/Dental/Life Insurance benefits? What's the cost?
11. Is a pension plan available?
12. What about tuition reimbursement for CFP®, ChFC, etc.?
13. What happens if I want to leave? What REALLY happens?

Jon Lacy, CFP®, is a frequent and well-informed poster on the FPi discussion boards[99]. He reminded me to point out that whomever you go to work for, there will be trade offs. "There is no free lunch," he intones. "If a firm is going to help pay for your licensing, pay for your office/phone/etc, and pay you a starting salary - there is going to be a cost. You will be expected to 'produce' - make money and do it fast. There will be pressure for you to sell products. Ultimately," he says, "you decide how you will work with clients (fees vs. commission, selling vs. planning, etc.)"

In addition to his activities with the full service (both fees and commissions) financial planning firm, Lane, Dickson & Lacy, LLC, in Diamond Springs, California, Jon teaches Investment Planning as part of the CFP Board registered curriculum at UC Davis. He teaches with the UC Davis sponsored CFP® Certification Exam Review Course team, serves on the Board of Directors for a non-profit organization and is on the local School Board.

His advice to newcomers entering the profession: "Once you're licensed, affiliated (B/D or RIA) and designated (CFP or other) GET ACTIVE (in your community.) There is a tremendous need for professionals to serve. Working in a Corporate Customer Service

---

[98] http://financiallywell.com
[99] http://www.financial-planning.com/shoptalk.html

Environment for over six years prior to entering Financial Planning, I learned a very simple truth: People don't care how much you know until they know how much you care."

Non-Compete Clauses[100]

Just after publishing in September 2001, I received an e-mail from a reader who was disappointed that I hadn't devoted much space to non-compete clauses. I agree it's important, and would like to re-print, anonymously, his experience:

"I really had not heard of non-compete clauses until I read AEFA's several hundred page franchise agreement and came to that section. It certainly isn't talked about and to me is a critical aspect of a job decision. I guess they didn't want me to know about it... I've been sponsored by AEFA for all my exams and was about to sign their agreement. The non-compete clause was like hitting a brick wall for me.

"Their non-compete clause states that there can be no financial contact (signing up a new account, selling insurance, or any financial advice) for a period of one year after termination. After six years, the non-compete expires. AEFA has a P1 track in which you are an employee and a P2 track in which you come in as an independent contractor. I fully understand having the clause for P1 advisors, where all expenses are paid. Because of the rigid schedule AEFA has for new planners (60 hours per week including EVERY Saturday morning; I have three young children and an aging mother), I was going in as a P2 to plan my own business (and time) and was paying for EVERYTHING, including the right to use "the name". It just didn't make sense that I should be paying for all that and they keep my clients if I leave. It's simply out of balance in my mind.

"After consulting with some other FP friends of mine, they unanimously stated that they would not sign that deal. I didn't."

FEES vs. COMMISSIONS

Eventually you'll need to deal with the issue of compensation, so you might just as well start forming some opinions now. Warning: Some real rabble-rousers out there are waiting to jump into the fee fray at the drop of a hat. My advice? Don't take the bait. Look at the argument from as many angles as possible, figure out what you will be most comfortable with, and then get to work helping clients with their financial planning.

I'm a fee-only financial planner and registered investment advisor. I receive no commissions whatsoever for anything. Once upon a time, I held all the necessary securities and insurances licenses, but they have all lapsed or become inactive. For me, it was a decision that evolved from the simple fact that I wanted to do financial planning and didn't want to sell anything except myself. I have to admit, the idea of getting up every morning knowing

---

[100] In August of 2001, Waddell & Reed lost an arbitration case against a former broker who claimed they made defamatory remarks to his clients in order to retain them for the firm. http://www.careerjournal.com/myc/legal/20010813-simon.html

that I had to find another client in order to implement a transaction didn't set well with my personal mindset.

John Lewis, CFP®[101] feels much the same way, but understands how difficult it is to go it alone.

"Most new reps can't afford to take the fee-based route from the beginning due to the lower, initial pay-outs. So, many go the transactions route and collect commissions off the sale of Class A or Class B mutual funds, for example. If you have to make your quota, the manager isn't interested in how well you are doing meeting your Year 1 projections in a 5 Year plan. How are you doing today, this week, this month, this quarter?

"Assume you're a star and you have accumulated $10 mil in mutual funds assets. In the second year, your trails are $25,000 based on the $10 mil the previous year (and no growth). If you keep a third of your GDC, you're staring at about $8K-9K. Guess what? You have to shake the trees again to find more prospects, in order to get back to where you were. You're stuck in your own version of 'Groundhog Day'.

"I'm a fee-based independent rep. I left the insurance world after two years to make a go of it on my own. It stinks sometimes, but I'm gonna survive. I'd recommend forgoing the commissions route on investments, build a stream of income, charge a fee for the creation of a financial plan, sell some insurance products because your clients will need them, and develop a well-rounded financial planning practice. After all, we tell our clients to diversify; shouldn't we, too?"

Some of the neatest people I know are commissioned salespeople in the financial services industry. Many of them are highly regarded CERTIFIED FINANCIAL PLANNER™ practitioners with respected Broker/Dealers, giving their clients wonderful, unbiased advice, and no doubt making three or four times my annual income. I've been there. I'm more comfortable charging a fee for taking a holistic view of my client's needs, which includes non-financial concerns, and sending them off to an expert in those areas that need more attention than I'm qualified to provide.

If you're coming from a successful background in sales and the thrill of the close is near and dear to your heart, then that is exactly what you should be doing! You have an incredible talent that shouldn't be wasted! It simply boils down to integrity. I'm referring to that gut feeling that tells you what it is you are doing is honestly the best possible solution that you believe is available to your client at this moment in time. You won't be able to do that unless you have the education and experience as a financial planner, and you have enough accurate information from your client to know the product you're selling is appropriate to the situation.

Compensation is relevant. Just don't let it interfere with how you can best serve your client.

---

[101] http://www.johnglewis.com/

IT DOESN'T ALWAYS WORK

My enthusiasm and just plain love for this profession has made it difficult to keep personal bias out of this publication as much as possible. If you are to accurately evaluate your own potential in this industry, it is only fair you have exposure to both sides. So it is with deep gratitude that I include the following courageous and unedited memoirs from a colleague:

My Journey Through a Financial Planning Career

by Edward Mora

It's not always easy to look back at a crucial career choice and admit that it wasn't successful. My experience in the financial planning industry spanned from 1993 to 2000 and was marked with deep lows and exhilarating highs, many extraordinary relationships (some I would rather forget), and many lessons learned. After much soul searching, I ultimately left the industry I devoted 7 years of my life to. I wish to share my experiences in the hope that they will shed light on the reality of building a successful career as a financial planner.

Over the course of my financial planning career I attempted probably every angle possible for a financial planner – running my own practice, working on commissions for a large insurance company and a boutique financial planning firm, and being a salaried planner and manager for a boutique planning firm. Along the way I earned an MBA, became a Certified Financial Planner (CFP®) and Chartered Financial Consultant (ChFC), and obtained a Series 6, 7, 63, 65, and insurance license. In addition, I was the author of a bi-weekly financial advice column in a local paper and very active in the local chapter of the Financial Planning Association. I truly was committed to the profession and expanding my knowledge base.

When I joined the industry, working on commissions for a large brokerage or insurance company was the only option to get experience. There simply was not (and still isn't) a defined career path for those who would like to pursue financial planning on a salaried basis. Earning a living off commissions was extremely difficult and required a lot of faith to continue. I joined a large insurance company straight out of college and in my first year, I made a grand total of approximately $10,000; not enough to live on and consequently I went into debt. I remember thinking at the time that I had wasted a whole year in "sales" and it wouldn't look good on resume. Since I had put in the effort to get my Series 7 and insurance license, I figured I'd give it another six months.

Well, six months later I decided to become a salaried planner for a small firm in Century City. This was actually an enjoyable experience from the aspect that I could accrue the benefits of helping individuals plan for their future, but not have to worry about paying my rent. I worked there for a roughly a year and half, earning around forty thousand a year. I ultimately left the firm not for dislike of my job, but because my boss was very difficult to work for and the environment was just too hostile for my liking. This however led me to my brief stint as an independent planner.

At the time I was leaving this job, my mother informed me that her company was offering early retirement to thousands of its employees. I thought it was an opportunity I couldn't pass up, so I quickly registered with a small broker/dealer and was on my way. I put on a couple of seminars, acted like I had experience galore (though I was only 25! – there is another lesson here, 'perception' is everything) and closed a bunch of rollovers. I think I made around sixty thousand dollars from front and back-end loaded mutual funds in those two frenetic months. But it was at this point, where I think I realized that making the "big dollars" in financial planning wasn't going to happen for me.

Knowing that I made this money through an "easy" connection, I tried to get referrals to extend this winning streak. As with my early days, here is where I just wasn't very adept. In addition, I knew if I wanted to really make this a successful business I would have to reinvest much of those earnings. To a 25 year old with that much in the bank, the idea of being able to actually have a decent investment portfolio and being able to afford some small luxuries was simply too much to pass up. Bottom line, I chickened out and wasn't willing to take the risk of continuing on my initial success. However, my gut instinct and inability to bring in additional prospects let me deal easily with this fact. I took off for Argentina for three weeks to figure out what my next step was.

I decided that a salaried planning position was the route for me and joined another independent planning firm, helping them to establish their investment management department. During the next three and half years I really stepped up in the education department, achieving the ChFC designation, then challenging and passing the CFP® exam. I was on a roll, so I decided to get a business degree from Loyola Marymount University in Los Angeles and eventually graduated summa cum laude with an MBA in Financial Decision Systems in 2000. Throughout my time at this firm, I helped to acquire and manage $75 million in investments and build a thriving financial planning and executive compensation practice. Commensurately, I rose from a technical analyst to Vice President of Investments in that short time.

Admittedly, I was enjoying good success at the firm but the reality was, as is the case in most relatively small planning shops, the pay was simply not that inspiring. When I left, I was making about sixty thousand a year (that included my quarterly bonuses) even though I managed the most profitable part of the business. When planning my career with the president of the firm, I inquired about what it would take me to earn $100k, and the answer was basically: "You'd better become a producer to make that kind of money."

Well, one thing that getting my MBA during the peak of the Internet revolution taught me was that there was plenty of money to be made with good industry experience and a business degree. So I positioned myself as such and secured a job with a Big 5 firm as an e-business consultant focusing on the financial services industry. I am still helping clients, but not on the "front line"; rather, my clients are American Express, Zurich Financial, and Morgan Stanley. And the difference in pay? Well, my salary almost tripled, so I can't complain there.

In summary, financial planning was a very interesting though unprofitable career for me; however, it can be very profitable career for some. Here are some things I learned during my journey:

Ed's Parables:

- **If you're not very good at the prospecting/selling part of the business, you will never make a lot of money** (there is, of course, many definitions for "a lot" of money). Put another way, do you want to cold call every day to make fifty thousand a year?

- **If you choose to work for a large brokerage or insurance firm, expect pressure and quotas to sell proprietary products.** There is very little financial planning done at these firms -- mostly investment planning.

- **Getting a CFP®, ChFC, or other credentials will not guarantee you more clients.** However, the education you will receive is well worth the effort. In my opinion, the CFP® is by far the best and most respected designation.

- **The most knowledgeable planners I worked with were at independent firms and fee-based.**

- **Despite what the Jobs Almanac says, financial planners have a lot of stress and not a lot of free time!**

SUMMARY

Morris Armstrong, CFP®, CDP[102] was a "career changer" who became a financial planner after 23 years as a banker. "I managed portfolios of currencies, deposits and bonds. Millions of dollars were transacted on my word alone, a far cry from the broker-dealer environment," he told me. "It was exciting, stressful, fast-paced, stressful, afforded plenty of opportunity to travel, stressful and paid well," he joked. "In a retrospective moment, playing the *coulda-woulda-shoulda game* I can sure see things I would have done differently." Today, Morris is owner of Armstrong Financial Strategies[103], a fee-only Registered Investment Advisor in New Milford, CT.

Morris came up with ten things that he's learned over the years – some of them the hard way:

Lesson #1: Thoroughly research the industry and companies

Lesson #2: Read very carefully all of the paperwork; seek written clarification

Lesson #3: Don't plan on much assistance; you are on your own

Lesson #4: You do not have to accept every person as a client

---

[102] Certified Divorce Planners (CDPs) are financial specialists who have successfully completed an intensive training program from The Institute for Certified Divorce Planners (http://www.institutecdp.com/.) They are trained in the complex financial issues of divorce.
[103] http://www.armstrong-financial.com

Lesson #5: Never forget that you are selling your services and yourself

Lesson #6: Develop and follow a business and marketing plan

Lesson #7: Learn to wisely prioritize and allocate time to all facets of life

Lesson #8: Thank people who do something nice for you

Lesson #9: Take the time to learn the software; know how the information flows

Lesson #10: Become active in your community financial planning organizations

Looking over Morris' list, I would have to agree. Taking his lead, I recommend the following:

ACTION LIST

- Seek career counseling and/or read Gerber's book.

- Get a handle on your "Primary Aim."

- Write a vision or mission statement.

- Research companies with a philosophy embracing your vision.

- Interview everyone and learn everything you can about the company before making a decision.

Chapter Four

The Dreaded Regulatory Stuff

Anyone can call himself or herself a financial planner, right? Yep. But consumers are getting pretty savvy, and they no longer accept just "anyone" as their financial planner. As recently as the early nineties, it was rare that a potential client asked me about my credentials or background. Today, I'm surprised when a prospective client doesn't come in loaded with a list of questions that put me in the hot seat! Then they often whip out the answers from the last planner they visited and compare notes before hiring an advisor[104]. In fact, it's not unusual to have them come in with a computer printout about me, generated from the Financial Planning Association web site.

You aren't going to want clients who hold back information and run off at the drop of the market, any more than your client would want a planner who didn't keep informed and in compliance. To get started right, you'll need to make some serious decisions.

Plan for Yourself First

Begin by envisioning what you'll be doing in five years, and then backtrack to determine how you will get there.

- Learn what worked for others.

- Attend Financial Planning Association chapter meetings[105] and conferences[106].

- Read trade journals and visit financial planning web sites.

- Interview Broker/Dealers and independent practitioners, particularly those doing what you want to do.

- Participate in discussion groups[107] and ask questions.

- Take your time, keep an open mind and stay flexible.

With few exceptions, you need to register in some capacity with a governmental regulator in financial services in order to be paid as a financial planner[108]. Once you decide where you

---

[104] http://www.fpanet.org/plannersearch/index.cfm
[105] http://www.fpanet.org/chap/index.cfm
[106] http://www.fpanet.org/conf/
[107] http://www.financial-planning.com/shoptalk.html
[108] The states are all over the map as to who must register. In many states, the definition of "investment adviser" will also include, "a financial planner who provides investment advisory services." Seek competent advice pertinent to your state to be certain you follow proper

want to begin, the path to register is relatively easy to navigate. Your first decision is whether you will start your own independent practice, or work for someone else. It boils down to three possibilities.

Three Ways to Become Registered:

1. Registered Representative (RR)

When you work for a Broker/Dealer, your supervisor, manager, or employer will tell you what licenses, exams and registrations you need to sell the products and services they offer. The company might provide classes to help you pass the first time. They will instruct you on what forms, agreements and records to keep, and what payout, commissions or salary you'll receive.

You will be a Registered Representative under your Broker/Dealer's NASD registration. Should you ever change your Broker/Dealer, you will need to transfer your registration to your new Broker/Dealer.

2. Investment Advisor Representative (IAR)

If you join an independent firm, you will register as an Investment Advisor Representative (IAR) of the independent advisory firm. Again, your supervisor will tell you how and where to register.

I think the best way for someone new to the financial planning industry to begin, is by interning with a good independent firm. The problem is that independent firms haven't generally awakened to the fact that interns can benefit them every bit as much as they can help the intern! Once you find a firm you like that is willing to take you on as an intern, go for it! You may eventually end up a partner. You might be able to negotiate the expenses of getting licensed and registered as part of your employment agreement.

3. Registered Investment Advisor (RIA)

The scary way is to jump right in and do it by yourself! The main advantage to becoming a Registered Investment Advisor on your own is also the main disadvantage. Whether you do it right or wrong, you're the bottom line.

The rest of this chapter will assume the reader is considering an independent practice, and will be responsible for making all of the decisions.

---

procedure and obtain appropriate licensing and registration. This is especially true if you intend to sell or advise on insurance issues.

Things You'll Need to Know Before You Register:

1. Business Form

If you start out on your own, your first concern will be your business form. Will you be a sole proprietor, corporation, Limited Liability Company, partnership or something else? There are books written on the pros and cons of business forms and I urge you to do plenty of research and get information from your accountant and legal advisor before making a final decision.[109]

2. Fee Schedule

How you charge for your services is integral to your ADV filing and your agreements, so it must be determined early on. Always think "disclosure". Your ADV must always contain current and accurate information. Amending your ADV later to include a different payment method isn't a problem.

3. Custody and/or Discretion

You don't want either. Don't even think about it! Custody means you have your client's money or securities in your possession. Discretion means someone else may have custody, but you can get it if you want. Both are rampant with conflicts of interest and additional compliance procedures. The more control you have over your client's money, the more regulatory hoops you need to jump through. Just don't go there.

4. Client Contract or Agreement

Before transacting business, you and your client must understand exactly what is expected from each of you. Unfortunately most contracts, out of necessity, require esoteric and often cumbersome language to protect the interests of both parties.

For fifteen years, I tried to perfect an agreement that wouldn't make me feel like apologizing every time I handed it to a client. I gave up. I still apologize, and then make my client read through it thoroughly with me before they sign. In the end, I know we're both more comfortable knowing we understand the specific terms of the engagement.

Don't ever simply copy another planner's contract and use it as your own. Make certain it is a true representation of how you personally do business, not what you think looks good! Your ADV will mirror your contract, so the two had better agree.

Your contract will need at least the following elements:

---

[109] BFi has a basic comparison chart to help recall the differences in the most common entities. http://www.bizfilings.com/learning/comparison.htm

A. Parties:
> Your name or company and the name of your client. This may seem straightforward, but there are a number of considerations to be made. If your client is married, is the spouse a de facto client? Are life partners considered a single client? Identification of your client may affect other parts of your agreement.

B. Services:
> An explanation of what you will do for the client, and how your services will be delivered. I have different contracts depending upon the engagement. One agreement covers continuing financial planning and asset management provided under my retainer, and another deals with hourly consultations and short-term projects. I've seen effective contracts that list items to be checked off if they are to be part of the engagement. Unless you are an attorney or accountant, this may be a good place to document that you will not be providing legal or tax advice. If you don't analyze property and casualty insurance, so state.

C. Authorizations and Implementation Procedures:
> Things you can do, like trade in your client's account, deduct fees from your client's account, and the steps that must be followed to enact transactions.

D. Responsibilities:
> Things you expect from your client, such as copies of financial documents, income tax information, completion of questionnaires, attendance at consultations, cooperation from your client's other advisors, etc.

E. Confidentiality:
> Your privacy policy statement, and any exceptions, in writing. Should your client wish to allow you to share information directly with his or her other advisors, define the nature of the information and documentation necessary to do so for each specific instance.

F. Term:
> How long the contract will last, and how to cancel it, if your client changes his or her mind after the contract is signed. Spell out whether the contract is for a specific project with a set deadline, or will continue until written notification from one of the parties within a specified period.

G. Compensation:
> How you will get paid. This section needs to be very specific. Consider such issues as minimum account size and billing in advance or in arrears (Billing in arrears or as work progresses is best from a logistical standpoint. If you bill clients in advance, that amount should appear on your balance sheet as unearned income until earned.) State whether pro rata billing will be from the time the contract is signed, the money deposited or an agreed upon date. Define the date and/or period of asset valuation if necessary. Identify what

will be specifically excluded from the compensation arrangement, such as brokerage, legal or accounting fees charged by a third party.

H. Basis of Advice:
Where you get your information. Generally, your recommendations will be based on analysis, education, documents and other sources that are available to the public. You do NOT make recommendations based on insider information.

I. Conflict of Interest Disclosure:
Other interests you may have that could affect the service you provide, such as involvement in another business venture, affiliation with a particular securities or insurance firm, etc. Include a listing of the states with which you are registered.

J. Miscellaneous Provisions:
Arbitration or mediation clauses, notification of changes in ownership, how consent should be obtained in case of assignment, receipt of ADV by the client, effective date of the contract, etc.

K. Acknowledgement:
Signatures of the Parties, testifying that they have read and understand the contract and agree with the terms. Also include the date the contract was signed.

Once you have finished writing your contract or client agreement and believe it contains all the necessary information, I strongly urge you to have an attorney knowledgeable about securities contracts take a look at it. At the very least, troubleshoot with a mock client. Go over each section and play "What if… ." Be brutal.

Pretend it's five years from now and your "client" is unhappy with your service, investment performance, manner of compensation, etc. How will your contract help avoid lawsuits, yet be fair to both you and your client?

Set up a scenario where it's five years from now and your client, Mr. & Mrs. X, are ecstatic at the advice, performance and service you have rendered. But Mr. X calls to whisper in your ear that he is leaving Mrs. X, wants you to sell everything and send the proceeds to his Swiss bank account. What can/should you do, according to your contract?

Use your imagination. Pick up the business section of a major metropolitan newspaper on any given day and put yourself in the shoes of the financial planner being sued, arrested, accused or convicted. Also pick up a copy of Katherine Vessenes' book, *Protecting Your Practice* [110]. Then take another long, hard look at your contract. Don't miss the opportunity

---

[110] Protecting Your Practice by Katherine Vessenes. Bloomberg Professional Library. 1997. http://www.wealth.bloomberg.com/wealth/books/protect.html Ms. Vessenes also has a disk available as an add-on purchase, which contains sample documents and contracts.

to attend one of Katherine's presentations at a meeting or conference. She makes protecting your practice, and other legal and ethical considerations a whole lot of fun!

Some of the compliance services, such as the Consortium and National Regulatory Services, offer mock regulatory exams, which walk you through an audit and leave you prepared for the real thing.

Getting Registered:

If you receive compensation (commissions, fees, wages, prizes, etc.) for financial services, you must register with the Securities & Exchange Commission or the state in which you do business. The magic number is $25 million under management, with a little wiggle room between $25 million and $30 million. When you have authority to exercise any sort of control over client assets in excess of $30 million, you must be registered with the SEC.

If you're just starting out, you won't be managing $25 million, so check with your state at http://www.nasaa.org → find regulator. Find out what they require in order for you to do business.

Note: Most states have a de minimus exemption that allows you to work with a few clients (generally 5) in that state without registering, as long as you don't have an office in that state. If your first clients are friends and relatives in other states, this may be particularly important!

If you begin your own practice, you will become a Registered Investment Advisor (RIA) and have your own ADV.

I have no idea what ADV stands for. It's probably an acronym for "Advisor Registration", but in any case, in most states, you need to be registered. Your ADV is the document evidencing your registration.

The Series Exams and What to Expect:

Series 7: General Securities Representative

Every full service Broker/Dealer will require this exam. Passing it will qualify you to register with the NASD as a General Securities Representative (Registered Representative) and sell stocks, bonds and mutual funds. You will be allowed six hours to take the 250-question test. A passing score is 70%.

The Series 7 is a difficult test. You are advised to plan at least a six-week study period to familiarize yourself with the material. I highly recommend a live, hands-on, five-day cram course immediately prior to taking the exam. Believe me, you don't want to have to take this test a second time. Do what you have to do to get through it, and get on with your life!

Caution! Sometimes the company you work for (typically an insurance company or bank) may sponsor you for only the Series 6, and explain that's all you need since you will be selling only mutual funds and variable contracts under their jurisdiction, not individual securities. Don't buy that! If there is even the slightest possibility you may work one day with a full-service firm, you'll have to have the Series 7. Get it over with right from the start.

Series 63: Uniform Securities Agent State Law

In addition to the Series 7, you must pass this exam in order to sell securities in a given **state**. The Series 63 isn't exactly fun, but compared to the 7, it should be a piece of cake! There's a lot of common sense involved in the questions, but it's best taken right on the heels of the Series 7.

You'll need to learn a lot of legal terms, and consider ethical issues, so spring for a workbook or a course, and take the time to study and pass the first time through. You will have an hour to answer 50 questions, and need a score of 70% to pass.

Series 65: Registered Investment Adviser Law Examination

Whether you're working for an independent advisor or striking out on your own, if you will be holding yourself out as a financial planner, this is the one you'll probably need. It's required in most states in order to become a Registered Investment Advisor (RIA) or Investment Advisor Representative (IAR). The exam contains 140 questions to answer within a three-hour period, but only 130 are graded. The remaining 10 questions, which appear randomly, are pre-test questions. A passing score is correctly answering 68.5% of the 130 questions.

A registered person associated with a Broker/Dealer will also require this license to sell wrap-type products and be engage in fee-based asset management along with their commissioned products.

With permission from General Counsel at NASAA, here are some sample questions from the Series 65 and 66 exams, which were revised beginning in 2000 to include more financial planning issues. The questions also appear on the NASAA website.

SERIES 65 & 66: sample questions (the answer is bold)

1. Using multiple asset classes in an investment portfolio reduces which of the following?

    1. Liquidity risk
    2. Credit risk
    3. Interest rate risk
    4. **Market risk**

---

2. Under the Securities Act of 1933, which of the following is NOT a security?

   1. Futures contracts
   2. Corporate bonds
   3. Investment contracts
   4. Stock options

3. Under the Uniform Securities Act, "sales" include which of the following?

   I   Giving a security as a bonus for a securities purchase
   II Making a bona fide loan of stock
   III Entering into a contract to sell a security for value

   1. III only
   2. I and II only
   3. I and III only
   4. I, II, and III

4. Which of the following statements is true about required minimum distributions for traditional IRAs?

   1. They must begin when the individual retires.
   2. They must be completed over a five-year period.
   3. They are mandatory as of April 1 following the calendar year in which the owner reaches age 59 1/2.
   4. They are mandatory as of April 1 following the calendar year in which the owner reaches age 70 1/2.

5. A husband and wife are 55 and 57 years old, respectively. The husband plans to retire at 62 and the wife at 65 and both are healthy. What is the most appropriate estimate of the time horizon for their retirement portfolio?

   1. 5 years
   2. 7 years
   3. 8 years
   4. 20+ years

CERTIFIED FINANCIAL PLANNER™ practitioners, as well as Chartered Investment Counselors (CIC), Chartered Financial Consultants (ChFC), Personal Financial Specialists (PFS) and Chartered Financial Analysts (CFA) are exempt from taking the Series 65 in order to become RIA's or IAR's in most states.

Caution! Passing the CFP® certification exam does not automatically qualify you for the designation, however. You must also meet the three-year (or five-year without a college degree) experience requirement before actually using the CFP® certification marks.

If your Broker/Dealer doesn't have a study track available to you, or if you plan to test on your own, there are some good courses available. Check your local schools and universities, or begin an online search[111]. To learn more about the Series 63 and 65 tests, see http://www.nasaa.org →Main Menu →Exams.

Since 2000, I have served on the North American Securities Administrators Association (NASAA) Exam Advisory Council. The Council was charged with modifying the content of the Series 65 exam to include investment vehicles, economics, ethics and legal guidelines, within a financial planning environment. My participation includes writing and reviewing items for the Series 63 and 65 tests. When I accepted a position on the Council, I had no idea the incredible amount of concern that went into writing the questions. The test development organization is committed to preparing an examination that will test competence. A tremendous amount of time and expertise is devoted to weeding out "trick" or unclear questions. If you are serious about becoming a financial planner, then I'm convinced you should have the knowledge required to pass the exams.

As of March, 2002, several states and Puerto Rico did not require advisors to register. For the rest, proof of a passing score on the Series 65, **or** a passing score on both the Series 7 and Series 66[112] is prerequisite to registering. Check your state at http://nasaa.org →Find Regulator.

Preparing and Filing Form ADV:

Beginning in January of 2001, online transfer of Form ADV Part I became available through the Investment Advisor Registration Depository (IARD) for RIAs currently registered in many states. It is not possible to file Part II on-line yet, but eventually, all Registered Investment Advisors will file ADV Part I and Part II on-line and Part II will be available to the public. It costs $150 for a one-time set up fee and $100 annually, plus the renewal fee charged by the state(s) in which you register.

At present, initial filings must still be submitted on paper in many states, and require a notary. To learn more about the IARD system, see http://nasaa.org →Investment Advisor →IARD. Form ADV on the IARD system is the same for both the SEC and the states requiring Investment Advisors to register. You can see all 81 pages of instructions and the form at the SEC website http://www.sec.gov/divisions/investment/iard/iastuff.shtml. The

---

[111] http://www.aitraining.com
http://www.bobeder.com/
http://www.businesssavvy.com
http://www.dearborn.com
http://www.proformware.com
http://www.stcusa.com/
http://www.trainingconsultants.net/
http://www.nasaa.org → Exams → List of Study Material Vendors
[112] The Series 66 focuses on state law and is already built into the Series 65 exam. The Series 65 is a comprehensive (securities, law, financial planning) state exam. The Series 7 is a federal securities exam only, and doesn't deal with state law. The Series 66 is the unified state law portion. A person holding a Series 7 wanting to become an RIA would probably have an easier time passing the 65 than the Series 66.

"old" form can be downloaded from the same site. Take a look. Might as well see what you're up against!

Caution! I cannot emphasize enough the importance of getting currently accurate information from the home state in which you intend to set up your office and practice! The rules for each individual state are constantly changing. At some point, everything will be done on-line. But we're not there yet!

Fortunately, help is available. There are compliance people, attorneys, other advisors and state regulators who can help you process your ADV. When I first registered, I sent away for the form that arrived in a big package with incomprehensible instructions. I had to look up most of the words, but finally filled the thing out and sent it in, only to have the state send it back. The California Department of Corporations and I went back and forth so many times we practically had our own postal franchise before we were finished. To tell you the truth, I was never comfortable that I knew for certain just what I was admitting to by answering some of the questions the way I did.

A few years later, when I went into partnership with another advisor, we hired Nancy Lininger with The Consortium[113] to fill out the Partnership ADV. She grilled us for hours with tough questions about how we did things and set us straight on the best way to develop our business. The ADV was accepted as submitted the first time through.

When the partnership fizzled, I learned how to withdraw my ADV and took the chance of registering by myself again as a sole proprietor. This time, thanks to Nancy's meticulous explanations of each facet of the ADV, it was accepted immediately. I got smart and purchased a floppy disk (well – it was a long time ago and now I download it from the Internet) with my ADV from National Regulatory Service (NRS)[114].

Today my corporation uses EZ-2000™, NRS's registration forms software, which lets us easily update our ADV whenever we have to file an amendment. Now, instead of printing a bunch of copies (which we are required to give to clients prior to working with them) that may become outdated with a change, we print on demand. I'm not sure how the IARD system will coordinate with NRS, but on the last update from NRS, all our information had been automatically transferred to the new ADV forms. Another company with similar software is National Compliance Services, Inc. (NCS)[115]

Tips from Nancy Lininger of The Consortium:

I called to ask Nancy if she had any hot tips for new advisors filing their first ADV, and she jumped right in with what turned out to be three pages chuck full of information. Listen up! What follows can save you a whole lot of time, grief, money, and a bottle of Tylenol. Here's a boiled-down version of what she told me:

---

[113] http://www.liftburden.com
[114] http://www.nrs-inc.com →Investment Adviser
[115] http://www.proformware.com →Investment Adviser

1. If you "borrow" language you like from someone else's ADV, for crying out loud make sure it agrees with what you do! I have seen so many ADVs with inconsistencies. The wording might look good, but if it says, "bill in arrears" and you actually bill in advance, you're setting yourself up for real trouble when the auditor comes calling.

2. In theory, advisors should understand all the rules before filling out their ADV. In practice, the form looks simple, but an inadvertent answer could end up giving you custody when that's not what you intended at all.

3. Begin with your marketing plan. Know what services you provide, and the fee you will charge. It's easier to transfer what you're doing to your ADV than to try and fit what your ADV says into your practice.

*4. Know how you are compensated. You can call yourself "fee-only" if you have **no** Broker/Dealer affiliation. Some Broker/Dealers[116] allow you to retain a separate RIA. If, in addition to your RIA, you are a Registered Representative of a Broker/Dealer, you are fee-based, fee-offset, or commissioned, but **not** fee-only.*

5. Disclose ALL business activities where required. If you sell shoes one day a week, you are engaging in a "business activity" which must be disclosed.

6. Know whether you have discretion and/or custody. If you are a trustee for your client, have general power of attorney, or can deduct fees without complying with specific procedures, you may have custody and be subject to regulatory hoops you haven't acknowledged.

7. Have an agreement, in writing, disclosing all fees, conflicts of interest, scope of the engagement, and a clause that disallows you from assigning your client's account without written confirmation.

8. Once your ADV application has been submitted, WAIT until you get authorization before giving advice.

9. While awaiting authorization, set up files for proper record keeping under the SEC rules, prepare your Policy & Procedures Manual (a.k.a. written Supervisory Procedures) (even if you are only supervising yourself), Privacy of Consumer Information documents, and research errors & omissions insurance. (Coverage is not mandatory.)

10. Keep your ADV current! File amendments when required (at any time during the year material changes occur). At a minimum, file annually to reflect the number of clients, dollars under management and percentage of time devoted to financial planning and other activities, and make your annual ADV offer to clients.

---

[116] See Chapter 3, "Who's the Boss" for Broker/Dealers who allow outside Investment Advisor registration.

Tips from Katherine Vessenes[117], JD, CFP®, *Protecting Your Practice*

Katherine on Notes:

"Get good processes and procedures in place from day one, so you can say, 'I **always** did *xxx*'! File notes are the number one most important thing! Have a good filing system, with original, contemporaneous information."

> **Nancy Note:** I can't help inserting here something I learned during my days as a Realtor® that has pulled me out of the line of fire any number of times. I buy those duplicate phone message books at the office supply store, and place them by every phone. Each time a call is made or comes in, the name, date, and brief comment of the discussion is recorded. The original is placed in the client's file, and the carbonless copy remains in the book to be filed. There is a contemporaneous record available for audit of each call in case it's ever needed. Today we can just enter those notes directly into ProTracker.

"Ask every client: 'What are your specific goals? What expectations do you have of me as your advisor? What expectations do you have of your investment returns?' Make note of the responses. Give a copy of the notes to your client and ask them to initial if they are accurate. Do it right there while you're with the client! If the responses are out of line, make a note of it and have the client initial the note!

"When you see a lot of clients, pretty soon they begin to run together. Make notes about how you feel about clients, about their goals and expectations. Keep them in a central database so your entire staff can see them when the file is opened."

Katherine on Compliance Manual:

"**Read it!** Know what's in your compliance manual. It takes about forty hours to complete a compliance manual. There's help available, but be careful! I've seen some nationally known firms with horrible contracts! Don't just copy stuff. Be sure your compliance manual contains specific information about **your** operations."[118]

Check out the premier issue of Bloomberg's Wealth Manager in the archives at http://www.bloomberg.com →Wealth Manager (features and archives)→Your Practice. Katherine's article on "Worry-Free Compliance" recommends fifteen steps to ensure your compliance manual is compliant! You'll need to subscribe, but you'll be glad you did! Bloomberg's Wealth Manager features excellent articles by top industry professionals!

---

[117] Katherine Vessenes, JD, CFP® is president of Vestment Consulting in Shorewood, MN, which provides practice management, compliance and marketing consulting to the financial services industry, and author of *Protecting Your Practice,* Bloomberg Press. She can be reached via e-mail at katherine@vestment.net or by telephone at 953.401.1045.

[118] Beth Dickinson at riaserve@aol.com, a colleague of Vestments Consulting, can give you quotes as to the cost of preparing a compliance manual.

Katherine on E&O Insurance:

"I'm amazed at how few fee-only planners have it! It's like saying if you're wearing a seat belt you won't have a car accident! It's stupid to think you can't get sued if you don't get commissions!"

The SEC has a letter that addresses common compliance issues discovered during audit at http://www.sec.gov/divisions/ocie/advltr.htm. It's well worth reviewing.

The Consortium, NRS and NCS all offer compliance products, service, and software to make your life easier. First, talk to other advisors. Find out what they're using and how happy they are. If you don't have a Broker/Dealer with a compliance department at your disposal, you definitely need a source that will keep you updated. The Consortium publishes a friendly monthly newsletter for $25 per year. Ask for a free copy. NRS lets you download a PDF file with their newsletter. Check out the "free stuff" on the NCS site while you're at it.

Record-Keeping Requirements:

As an independent advisor, you're required to keep your Policies and Procedures Manual, Notice of Privacy Policies and Practices[119] (effective 7/1/2001). Client Contracts, Investment Policy Statements, Form ADV Part I and Part II and certain other records available for audit at all times.

In 2000, proposed amendments to Rule 204-2 under the Investment Advisers Act of 1940, would permit investment advisers to "*create and maintain any required records using any form of electronic or micrographic media, as long as the adviser:*
1. *Arranges and indexes the records to permit easy location, access and retrieval of any specific record.*
2. *Provides promptly (no more than one business day after the request) any of the following that an SEC examiner requests:*
   a. *A legible, true and complete copy of the record in the medium or format in which it is stored;*
   b. *A legible, true and complete printout of the record; and*
   c. *Means to access, search, view, sort and print the records.*

When maintaining records electronically, the adviser would also be required to establish and implement policies and procedures to reasonably safeguard the records from loss, alteration, or destruction, to limit access to the records to properly authorize personnel and the Commission, and to reasonably ensure that any reproduction of an original record is complete, true and legible when retrieved."

---

[119] The FPA has guidelines and sample forms available free to members, and regulatory services have sample Policies and Procedures Manuals, Notice of Privacy Policies and Practices, Client Contracts, Investment Policy Statements, etc. for purchase.

Currently, NASAA has adopted the SEC Recordkeeping Requirements for Investment Advisers under Rule 203(a)2[120], which, for most advisors, includes the following:

1. Journal
2. Ledger
3. Memorandum of each order
4. Check books, bank statements, canceled checks and cash reconciliation
5. All bills or statements, paid or unpaid
6. Trial balances, financial statements, and internal audit working papers
7. All written communications
8. List of all discretionary accounts
9. Copy of all powers of attorney and discretionary authority
10. Copy of each agreement
11. Advertising and reasons for recommendations of specific securities
12. Record of every security transaction (of RIA)
13. Record of every security transaction (non-RIA)
14. Form ADV Part II, and dates given or offered to clients
15. Agreements, disclosures and receipts of fees paid to solicitors
16. Performance calculations
17. Complaint file
18. Investment policy statements for each client
19. Written supervisory procedures
20. State and/or Federal filings (applications, amendments, renewals, correspondence, etc.)

Prepare a filing system and diligently maintain these records from day one. In our office, we have a filing cabinet with twenty files, each bearing the appropriate label. Our operations flow chart provides for copies of all appropriate documents to be placed in the proper compliance file at the time of execution. Inside files for required records that do not pertain to our business, we place a written statement that the record is not applicable to our company.

Errors & Omissions Insurance:

Do you need it? Probably. Back in the days of limited partnerships and heavily loaded mutual funds, few planners were insured, and there were fewer firms willing to insure them. In the 21st century, lawsuits over the LP debacle have subsided and consumers have a vast variety of investment options with a myriad of cost structures available. Now that financial planning and asset management have come into their own, coverage and costs have become reasonable, and E&O insurance is affordable, even for the sole independent practitioner. You don't expect your home to burn to the ground, but you probably have homeowner's insurance. Your health may be terrific, but you still maintain health insurance. I know you're a great driver, but you need automobile insurance.

---

[120] Complete text at: http://www.nasaa.org → NASAA Library → Investment Adviser Recordkeeping Requirements.

I'll never forget a seminar I attended a number of years ago. The speaker was a well-regarded planner who had prepared a financial plan for her long time client. A life insurance policy was recommended, but the policy was never purchased and the planner hadn't followed up on that particular issue. Years later the person for whom the policy was intended, died. The survivor sued the planner for not insisting that the insurance be purchased. In this case, the court ruled there was no negligence on the part of the planner. Yet the event took a year away from the planner's practice, cost over $50,000 in defense, and the emotional toll was devastating.

Your practice should be protected. The Financial Planning Association lists carriers who currently insure financial planners[121]. Depending upon the nature of your practice, personal background and credentials, there may be discounts available. Costs and coverage vary greatly, so shop around.

My Experience:

I talked with Tony Bougere, Sr. VP of Marketing, asked him to tell me about The Cambridge Alliance[122], and what I had to do if I wanted to apply for professional liability insurance with his firm.

"We specialize in service to our policyholders, and help them prepare their practices for protection," he told me. I was surprised to learn how proactive Cambridge is in encouraging their policyholders to contact them if they are concerned about a particular situation.

"We'll investigate to mitigate the circumstances if necessary, and recommend procedures to prevent an uncomfortable incident from getting blown out of proportion and becoming a claim." Tony went on to say it was not unusual for Cambridge managers Nancy or Bud Bigelow, to recommend changes to client contracts or suggest methods of reducing risk exposure.

The process was painless. I applied online to receive an application packet, which included a list of questions I should ask before applying for professional liability insurance, a specimen policy, brochure, the application, and a checklist of submission requirements. I sent the completed application with Parts I and II of my Form ADV, samples of my client contracts and LPOAs, plus a copy of my current Certificate of Insurance (so I could arrange for prior acts coverage) to a broker in my state.[123]

Cambridge specializes in small to medium size Registered Investment Advisor firms, and welcomes applications from newly emerging practices.

---

[121] http://www.fpanet.org/ → Resource Directory → Insurance: Errors & Omissions
[122] http://www.cambridgealliance.com
[123] Applications must be submitted through a licensed surplus lines insurance broker in the state where the insurance is to be placed.

SUMMARY:

While the compliance and regulatory side of things may seem like a big headache, you'll have an even bigger headache if you don't do it right the first time. Chances are good that one day you'll be audited, or even sued. It'll be really nice if all your books and records are pristine from the start and you don't have the frustrating task of undoing all the problems.

Action Plan:

1. Decide on your game plan:
    A. Broker/Dealer
    B. Employee/Independent Contractor
    C. Your Own Business
        a. Develop Business Form
            1. Obtain physical location, business license, fictitious name, etc. as applicable
        b. Check NASAA for proper registration and examinations in your state
            1. Prepare for and pass required exam(s)
        c. Determine Compensation Structure
        d. Prepare Client Contract or Agreement(s)
        e. Set Up Record-Keeping Files
        f. Research E&O Insurance
        g. Submit Form ADV

Chapter Five

Setting Up Shop

I lean back in my office chair, prop feet up on my desk, and sip iced tea. My eyes are closed, and a smile is on my face as I contemplate my dream of the perfect practice. I envision my office, my clients and colleagues, my daily routine, and the relaxed yet dynamic outlook of my future...

I open my eyes and look out the window, where I see green. There are lots of trees, and birds singing. A quiet, rural residential area with privacy. Easily accessible. I feel comfortable here in my chair, looking out the window, seeing what my clients will see, listening to the birds, relaxing. Yes. It's a nice environment in which to contemplate my clients' financial concerns and develop solutions. My dream places me on the walkway outside and I step through the front door.

An inviting entry area, with current lifestyle magazines, and today's edition of the Wall Street Journal. My receptionist is engaged in welcome chitchat as coffee is served. Venturing down the hallway and into:

My private office. I see wood. A warm, serious place with a simple, spacious desk. An ultra-thin big screen monitor, showing beautiful worldwide landscapes, waiting only for my touch to become instantly alive with anything I wish to explore. A file. A research piece. Audio and/or visual contact with a colleague or client across the country. Historic records all efficiently archived and securely backed up. On one wall is a bookcase filled with slim leather-bound client binders containing minimal necessary information, in preparation for the next appointment. Beside the binders are some of my favorite professional books. I wander into the next comfortable office and greet members of:

My competent team of advisory professionals, paraplanners and clerical personnel who are diligently contacting clients, preparing reports and arranging engagements. Weekly staff meetings keep everyone informed. We all have Internet access to everything we need. Those advisors choosing to work in remote locations join the meetings through video conferencing. Everyone sets their own hours and decides on their work sites.

Our completely integrated software provides for a single entry to seamlessly flow from initial prospect contact to client, and on into comprehensive financial planning, asset allocation, portfolio management and information dissemination back out to the client. Data is automatically downloaded and backed-up daily, and is constantly available to advisors and clients through the Internet.

Peeking into the conference room, I find a spacious, oval table surrounded by comfortable chairs, each with a console to accommodate audio/visual equipment and computer connections. In one corner is a cozy arrangement of loveseats and coffee table for more intimate meetings. A credenza with refreshments and supplies fills space on one wall, and another serves as a control area containing a large screen, computer activated presentation equipment, and reference library. This room is designed for quick rearrangement into a small theatre for educational sessions.

Across the hallway is the rest room with fresh flowers and sparkling tile, good lighting, colorful tissues and clean cloth towels refresh visitors as they come and go. I return to my private office and settle into my chair to contemplate:

A normal workweek. It's flexible. Four days a week, business takes priority. My day starts at the gym to work out four or five mornings each week, a couple of them with a personal trainer. I'm in the office by nine, checking e-mail and preparations for the day's events. My staff sees that my schedule is in front of me and agendas and reports are ready for client meetings. Sigh. I knock myself upside the head and

Come back to reality. I consider for a moment that actually, I'm not so far from my dream after all! The single-entry software is finally available, but I've learned to live without it. It's too expensive to replace all the other programs now, and too time consuming to convert all the data.

By year-end, documents will have been scanned and the ceiling-high-stacked storage boxes will have been shredded. We will be well on our way to an office with less paper, if not paperless.[124]

My wonderful staff does keep me on track, and schedules are flexible. Mike, my portfolio designer resides in another state, yet through advanced communications systems, we are constantly in contact.

For a long time, I felt I couldn't afford another assistant, yet when the opportunity came along, I took the chance and hired an intern.

I look out the window, where I actually do see lots of trees, and hear birds sing. Life is good, and I love what I do!

That's what my office is like. It certainly didn't start out that way, but things were different in 1983, when I was a Realtor by day and a student pouring over financial planning textbooks by night. I started out with a Broker/Dealer, and for a time I had an office in their branch. To stay closer to my client base, I added an office in an executive suite, and eventually moved out of the Broker/Dealer's office entirely. Soon after, I became an RIA, converted to a fee-only practice, and let my securities licenses lapse.

When a new complex was built nearby, occupants of our suite were solicited for space in the new building. An attorney, a CPA and I, all tenants of the executive suite who enjoyed the networking companionship we had established, signed an agreement to rent space in the new

---

[124]If the concept of a paperless office appeals to you, read "The Paperless Office" by Gary Stauffer in Appendix G.

complex. Our intention was to share the expense of hiring a secretary/receptionist and purchase office equipment, while keeping our practices separate.

I let my lease expire, put my desk, chairs, and filing cabinets in storage a month before our agreement was effective, and went on vacation. We were to move into the new offices in June. It was actually November before the new complex was approved for habitation, but by the end of July I needed a place to meet with clients and to work, so I moved my desk, temporarily, from storage into a bedroom vacated by one my kids. The CPA and attorney encountered similar problems and found office space elsewhere.

The move scared me. I felt it was unprofessional, and my clients would feel the same. I was afraid I would spend time playing with my dogs or doing the laundry instead of working. Oddly, just the opposite happened. I found myself working more than ever. Before, if I had a dinner meeting, I would leave the executive suite, attend the meeting and head home after to get a good night's sleep. Now, I would leave my home office for the meeting, return at eight, stop for a moment to check e-mail, get involved in an unfinished project and find myself falling into bed at midnight. I had no problem leaving the laundry alone, and with most clients, the dogs were assets!

Remarkably, another thing was happening. It was the attitude of my clients. Instead of dwelling on my appearing out of place or unprofessional, they seemed more relaxed, and tended to open up more. Once I became aware of that, I realized I had discovered the perfect place for my office. As the kids left for college and marriage, I commandeered the bedrooms for additional office space. I have never looked back! Today I have two separate offices, a conference room, storage room, reception area, and access to the rest room and kitchen. It has worked out beautifully! When I need space for a seminar or reception, there are schools, conference facilities and hotels available to cater any function. Meantime, the overhead is great.

What do you see out your window?

"I chose a home office for convenience and overhead," claims Joseph Ponzio, a financial planner from Elmwood Park, Illinois who chose to start out in a home office. "Do some people ultimately choose not to retain my services because of a home office? Sure. But those might not be my target clients anyway. Because of such low overhead, I can maintain a small number of clients and still make a great living. Ultimately, as I bring on other staff (I currently have one advisor with me) we may choose to set up an office." Before deciding on his home office, Joe asked himself the following questions:

> Can I concentrate on work at home?
> Can I walk away at the end of the day and have family time?
> What level of overhead to I want/can I afford?
> Will people view a home office as unprofessional (or smart)?
> How many? (enough to justify higher overhead?)
> Why? (are these the clients I want long-term if I want to work from home?)
> Will I invite clients to my home or visit them at theirs?
> How will they view either?

Will this cost me a significant amount of business?
What will I do when additional staff is needed?

Joe adds, "Don't forget to get a Post Office Box. I used to have mail come to the house, but I do not trust the Post Office to deliver the important stuff (nor my neighbors to not throw it out if it comes to them)!"

How Three Set Up Shop:

A thread on the FPi Getting Started/Career Development discussion board revealed the process used by three financial planners who recently struck out on their own. Their stories are re-told here with permission:

Mike McCarthy, CFP®

I have had my CFP® since 1995 and worked for a consulting firm from 1994 - 2000 managing part of the Broker/Dealer. I had my Series 7, 24, and 63. I did very well there, but could never shake the desire to go out on my own.

Fortunately, my wife is a teacher, so we have some income to pay the basic bills. I knew that I wanted to be independent and fee-only. Keeping my Series 7 was not important to me.

So, I set about forming an S Corporation and I started the process of registering as an RIA in Illinois. I could have really suffered through that process and tried to do it all on my own, but I decided to pay National Compliance Services[125] the $1500 to guide me through it. It was money well spent. I would have spent $300 - $500 on the ADV software anyway, so the extra money to have them do everything was worth it. They were great and I recommend them to anyone in a similar situation. You also get turnkey compliance manuals and customer agreements that you can adapt for your use. Since these are necessities for an RIA, these were an added important feature.

Finding a broker-dealer to go through as an independent advisor wasn't easy. Schwab wants you to have $10 million under management before they'll even talk to you. This is a brand new practice, so that's out of the question.

Fidelity was not an option for me because my former employer was Fidelity's #1 competitor in the 401(k) business. If I went with Fidelity, that would have infuriated a large segment of my potential clients.

TD Waterhouse told me that you need to have at least $10 million before you get all of their advisor features, and then tried to appear generous by saying that I could have clients open accounts and manually get power of attorney on all of them. But they wouldn't set up direct debit of advisory fees or any other advisor features. Then I saw one of their reps at a trade show and he said that they really are willing to work with anyone, regardless of amount of assets under management. So, I didn't know whom to believe there.

---

[125] http://www.proformware.com/

I probably would have pursued TD Waterhouse more, but then I saw that CSFBdirect[126] was opening an advisory service and was doing it aggressively. I had some contacts there from the work at my consulting firm, so I was able to work it out with them despite my being a new advisor with no clients to start with. I am now set up with them and I am very pleased. They're new to the advisor side of the business, but they have some former Schwab people heading it up and I've been impressed.

I did a lot of reading on what software to buy. I ended up going with Morningstar Principia Pro Plus for Mutual Funds and Stocks, the MoneyTree Suite, and Allocation Master from Frontier Analytics. Each of those packages does something different. Morningstar allows me to screen for investments and do reporting. MoneyTree performs some of the more sophisticated financial planning analysis and has Monte Carlo analysis. Allocation Master does the efficient frontier modeling.

Finally, for portfolio management software, I chose TechFi's web-based AdvisorMart. They have received great reviews and I want my clients to be able to look up their accounts on the Internet. They do all of the downloading for you too, which is a huge plus and time saver. Advent was too difficult to use for a small advisor, and I think Techfi's stuff is better than Centerpiece, even though they have the same target market.

Finally, I am renting office space for $600 a month. Now, all I need is some clients to help me pay for all of this!

David J. Moran, CLU, ChFC, CSA
The RTA Group

My background is insurance based. I grew up in the captive agency system working my way through the ranks as an agent, sales manager and home office trainer. In that time, I earned my CLU & ChFC, won all kinds of awards and felt pretty good...until. Until I decided that the best way for me to succeed in the future was to build my own business in the fee-based financial planning and investment management arena. In '98 when I left the insurance business there were very few options to explore that would give me the total independence I desired.

I didn't just jump into the fee-based business with no clients and no assets. I dove in face first! To wit, two small children (ages 4 & 5 at the time). My wife and I have always felt that the most important thing we could do for our relationship and for our kids is for mom to be home with them, full time.

So, no clients, no income, just a business plan - and away we go!

After interviewing the Broker/Dealers and insurance companies (posing as financial planning firms,) I set off to register in Massachusetts as an RIA. I had the requirements of series 7, and ChFC as well as work experience. I hired National Compliance Services[127] to handle the ADV writing and filing. I highly recommend them to anyone thinking of

---

[126] http://www.csfb.com/ 866.655.5655
[127] http://www.proformware.com/

89

registering as an RIA in their state - they have the contacts and experience to help you avoid the inevitable mistakes.

I spoke with Schwab, Waterhouse, Vanguard and Fidelity. I opted away from Fidelity because it was my concern that I would be fighting an uphill battle to create my own "brand" with their name so prominent on all marketing materials. Vanguard wanted $1 million in Vanguard funds to start (yeah, right) and Schwab didn't take me too seriously. TD Waterhouse on the other hand made me feel like I could actually pull this off! They returned my calls and although they wanted a substantial commitment after 12 months, I went with them. I am extremely delighted with their service, follow-up and technology. A shameless plug for TD Waterhouse Institutional Services at this point isn't out of line, is it?

I chose Centerpiece[128] as my portfolio management software for some of the same reasons I chose TDW. Their people made me feel like I could pull it off. I spoke with IA's who use the program (as well as others) and felt pulled between Advent and Centerpiece. The Centerpiece sales guy threw in some extras and sealed the deal.

As for planning software, I use LifeGoals LGX[129] program. It's okay, I think. My problem is that being a sole proprietor I make decisions and have to give them time to work without the advantage of bouncing ideas off other people in the office. (I do talk to myself a lot but find I don't like some of the answers!)

For funds and stocks, I use Principia[130] - and like Centerpiece, I'm sure that I am utilizing about 35%-40% of the capabilities at this point. When deciding between marketing my practice and learning the ins & outs of software I always choose marketing.[131]

The reality is that I have begged, borrowed and borrowed some more to make this happen. My office is a "dedicated suite" in my home, a/k/a the basement. When scheduling meetings I give the prospect the option of meeting at my place or theirs. It runs 70-30 at theirs. I go out of my way to make it easy for people to do business with me.

One more recommendation for anyone crazy enough to do it this way: Read, read, read. Read everything you can on owning and running your own business. A book that helped me tremendously is "The E-Myth" by Michael Gerber[132]. The first edition was written in the 80's with a revised version put out more recently. I can only comment on the older one because that is the one I read! What it taught me is the importance of systems. Having systems in place for all the activities of the business lets you run the systems that run the business. Once you grasp that philosophy, it takes all the mystery out of it!

---

[128] http://www.schwabperformancetechnologies.com/ Centerpiece is currently available only to new users who custody assets with Schwab. The only other major choice today is Advent.
[129] http://www.lifegoals.com/fps/
[130] http://www.morningstar.com/products/clmppro.html
[131] Learn more about Dave's marketing campaign in Chapter 6: Marketing 101.
[132] The revised version is The E-Myth Revisited by Michael E.Gerber, Harperbusiness, April 1995. http://www.amazon.com/exec/obidos/ASIN/0887307280/o/qid=992907327/sr=2-1/107-8086869-3133337

The real reason I've done it this way is so I can be there for my family. I get the kids on the bus in the morning and am there to get them off after school. I haven't missed a school play or a baseball game yet. They're only small once...

Scott Dauenhauer, CFP®
President, Meridian Wealth Management
http://www.meridianwealth.com/

I opened my office at the end of 2000. I went through NCS and they were a big help. They are currently helping me transfer my information to the IARD.

Schwab told me that they would let me in with no assets as long as I hit $3 million by the end of the first year. If I don't, then they will charge me about $600 a quarter. I don't know if they offer this to everybody, but they offered it to me. They have been very helpful and very responsive; I can always get somebody within a couple minutes, no hold time.

I bought Principia[133]. I also bought AASim[134] from financeware.com and am test-driving Naviplan[135]. I haven't really found a software program that does what it says. My primary software is Excel. I also purchased the Text Library System[136], which for the price is a great value. It helps you automate your practice and makes it so you are not re-inventing the wheel. It is a great tool for keeping in contact with your clients, prospects, and centers of influence.

I went another step, which added significant costs, but I believe will pay me back and then some in the end: I hired Millennium Advertising[137] to write and produce a personal brochure and postcard as well as stationary and logo that all matched. They did an incredible job. I use the postcards as my primary marketing piece (they are all 4 color.) This set me back about $12,000 including the printing (I printed a huge amount.) I also started my own website and used AdvisorSquare[138]. They do an o.k. job but they charge too much on a monthly basis. I spent a lot of time on the content (probably too much) and I am constantly updating the site with articles that I write and articles written in the press that I feel are appropriate.

I use Advent[139] for my portfolio accounting. This was a big decision since it cost me about $4,500, plus a yearly licensing fee. The software has a huge learning curve that I am still on. The reason I chose them is because I think my practice is more focused on the middle class and I didn't want to have to pay a minimum fee for each client. It wasn't cost effective for me to use AdvisorMart[140], though they were my first choice (very cool concept.)

---

[133] http://www.morningstar.com/products/clmppro.html
[134] http://aasim.com/
[135] http://www.naviplan.com
[136] http://www.financialsoftware.com
[137] http://www.milladv.com
[138] http://www.advisorsquare.com/advisorsquare/intro/
[139] http://www.advent.com/index.asp
[140] http://www.techfi.com/Products/AdvisorMart/advisormartoverview.htm

Instead of renting office space, I work out of my home. I was working out of our second bedroom, but my wife and I are having a baby and my office is being turned into a nursery. Now I am remodeling the garage to make room for my new office. When I meet with clients, I use an executive suite by the name of REGUS Business Centers. They rent me space by the hour to meet with clients and the place is primo. They model their business on Ritz-Carlton. They also answer my phones and give me a prestigious address. I pay $175 a month for that service, plus the hourly fees to rent the conference rooms. I haven't had any client complaints. They actually like the idea!

My wife is a Teacher, and her income is definitely helping as I start this venture. I am actually marketing my services to public school teachers. There are no fee-only planners in my area marketing to them; only annuity reps. Needless to say, there is a lot of room for growth. We have over 19,000 Teachers in Orange County. I am working my butt off and wearing more hats than I ever dreamed, but I love it.

What We're Using At NLJones, Inc.

First, I need to tell you I've learned the hard way not to be married to any software. It's much more important to stay flexible with constant changes in products and services. That said, here's the run down on what works for us at the moment.

We are a financial planning and asset management firm, clearing through Schwab Institutional[141].
General Office: MS Office 2000
Contact Management: ProTracker[142]
Financial Planning: FPLAN[143] Advisor Plus or MoneyGuidePro[144]
Portfolio Management: Centerpiece[145]
Asset Allocation: Frontier Analytics Allocation Master[146]
Analysis: Morningstar Principia Pro[147]
Client Education: Kettley's Backroom Technician[148]
Form ADV: EZ 2000 from National Regulatory Services[149]
Backup: Burn weekly CDs, and backup daily with @Backup.com.
Bookkeeping: QuickBooks Pro
Research: Internet (I have dozens of sites bookmarked)
Paperless Office Solutions: Gary Stauffer (gstauffer@sbcglobal.net) with ECS Imaging[150]

---

[141] http://www.schwabinstitutional.com
[142] http://www.protracker.com
[143] http://www.fplan.com
[144] http://www.moneyguidepro.com
[145] http://www.schwabperformancetechnologies.com/
[146] http://www.allocationmaster.com/
[147] http://www.morningstar.com/products/clmppro.html
[148] http://www.kettley.com/
[149] http://www.nrs-inc.com
[150] http://www.ecsimaging.com

MAKE A LIST AND CHECK IT AGAIN AND AGAIN

If you're starting out with a Broker/Dealer and plan to maintain space in your Broker/Dealer's office, or if you'll be joining an established practice, then your costs are pretty much pre-defined. You may be responsible for some sort of space rental agreement, might need your own computer, and may have to pay a fee to log onto proprietary software systems. But that expense should be minimal compared to the cost of opening your own office.

If you'll be on your own, I strongly urge you to do a little dreaming. Opening a home office was strictly a happy accident for me, but looking back, I sure wish I'd thought of it from the beginning. Give some thought to where you expect to be five years from now, and begin with that in mind. It never hurts to be ahead of the curve when negotiating space and technology needs.

In the Appendix E you'll find a suggested list of things you may need before you open the doors on your own private practice. Much of the cost will be dependent upon the location and cultural setting at the time and place those doors open. My office is in Southern California, but in San Bernardino County. Things cost a lot less here than they do just a few miles south or west, in Los Angeles or Orange Counties. Of course, my homespun style and fee schedule reflects expectations from middle-income clients that may be quite different from the multi-millionaire professionals in Century City.

SOFTWARE

One necessity we all have is software. I've often joked that my financial planning software is a yellow pad and pencil with a good eraser. But the fact is, I can't get much further than a ballpark guesstimate with my yellow pad. Those brief notes and rough estimates will eventually need to be input to specialized software that will spit out multi-color graphs and charts and precise calculations for my client.

My dream office included an integrated software program to include contact, asset, report, and education management. I'm convinced no such thing exists today in the financial planning world. We're told the profession is too new and too small to warrant such extravagance. I personally think that's a crock, but being a complete klutz with computer programming, let alone installation, I'm in no position to bargain. At Success Forum 2002, I saw some hope! Too late for me, but take a look at Interactive Advisory Software (IAS) by Optima Technologies.[151]

---

[151] http://www.optima-tech.com/optima/framesets/main/content_fset.jsp?main_content=about_optima_fset.htm

To illustrate what I mean, here's a recap of a recent exchange on the Quick Talk List, a terrific discussion board used by registered members of AdvisorWorks[152], a community of investment professionals. The operative word here is professionals. These people have all been in the business many years!

Question.

I could use help deciding which financial planning software to use. I really like *M-Plan* and the presentations, but they have no education module and the interface is not intuitive. *Lumen Systems* is decent, but lacks depth and the presentation is not the best. *Naviplan* is also rudimentary, lacks flexibility, and offers poor client presentation. I have used *Financial Profiles* and it doesn't offer enough flexibility and is also simplistic.

Response 1.

Go to the *Easy Money Suite*. We left *M-Plan* for the same reasons, plus it had no Long Term Care module and their promises to add modules over the last year and a half have never materialized.

Response 2.

I have used *Financial Profiles* in one form or another for about eight years. It certainly has its drawbacks. I have also reviewed other programs and haven't found a better fit. They **all** have drawbacks. The one positive thing I will say about *Financial Profiles* is, they seem to work at updating and improving the software. One of the main drawbacks I have heard in the past has been its "life insurance bias." I don't even print the recommendations section. I do them all in a word document. And, depending upon the client, we add *Financeware.com* and *StockOpter*. Also, for client education we use *Kettley Backroom Technician*.

Response 3.

I have used *Financial Profiles* for four years now and haven't seen anything come along that's better as an overall program. I do the same thing with regards to recommendations (customized Word document) but use their Recommends Title page. *Financeware.com* doesn't seem as comprehensive as *Financial Profiles*.

Did you look at *Naviplan Extended* or *Integrate* (excel based)?

Don't bother with *MoneyTree*.

Response 4.

I'm curious why you said, "Don't use *MoneyTree*." We changed to it two months ago from *M-Plan* because it is four times faster to use, its output is easier for the client to understand, and they seem to be very quick about anything we ask for. Have you looked at the recent version?

Response 5.

I disagree with the comment about dismissing MoneyTree. As a MoneyTree user, I have found it easy and simple to use. The Golden Years Retirement planner gives year-by-year real tax data (indexed as well) for a real time super accurate calculation of year-by-year income and expenses during retirement, which hold up to good audit tracking. You have an excellent choice of up to 63 report pages (tabular data and charts) and can customize the text report to suit your own writing style.

---

[152] http://www.advisorworks.com/

It's very reasonable in cost and the support is very good. Data can be shared easily with their full financial planning *EasyMoney* program without multiple entries. Both retirement planners (the very basic "down and dirty" *Silver* and the more comprehensive *Golden Years*) offer a full Monte Carlo simulation.

Don't dismiss *MoneyTree* until you have ordered the free fully functioning demo, tried it for yourself and compared the costs with the competition.

Response 6.

I'm currently using/evaluating both *MoneyTree Suite* and *Lumen Financial Planning Professional (FPP)*.

Generally, I think *MoneyTree* is easier to use and produces more professional reports in some areas. I especially like *MoneyTree's GoldenYears* software for people who are in or near retirement.

Alternatively, I think *Lumen's FPP* is a more comprehensive and more versatile analysis tool than either *MoneyTree's EasyMoney* and/or *GoldenYears* software. *Lumen's FPP* software allows you to view and modify intermediate results and you cannot view or access to the intermediate results in *MoneyTree*. *MoneyTree's* software does include Monte Carlo Analysis and they provide several stand-alone tools.

I don't believe there is or ever will be a "best" financial planning software package. Pick one that you feel comfortable with the plan on using other tools to fill in the gaps. In addition to the software features, you would consider the availability and quality of technical support.

FYI: I have two biases that affect my comments. I belong to the Garrett Planning Network, Inc. and they recommend *MoneyTree Software*. That is one reason why I acquired *MoneyTree Suite*. I'm also an independent financial planning software consultant and I provide those services to *Lumen*. That is one reason why I have and use *Lumen FPP*.

Yikes!

I did have conversations with some pretty heavy hitters in the industry, and here are the candid results of those encounters. Stay awake! New stuff is coming down the pike every single day. Don't miss out on the product you need because you weren't paying attention! And don't, for crying out loud, be stuck with an obsolete product because you think you can't afford to change! In today's financial planning environment, you simply can't wait for the perfect solution. You must be prepared to upgrade or even switch entirely to a new format! Purchase financial planning software with the intention of replacing whatever you have within a few years. And keep your fingers crossed that before long one of those techie geeks will finally make a name and fortune for him/herself with an integrated program. Please!

John Olsen, CLU, ChFC

John Olsen hosts the Software/Technology Boards[153] for Financial Planning Interactive, which is where I was introduced to his comprehensive knowledge. Today, when I am considering a new software program, John is one of the first people I contact for information. If it's out there, John's taken it for a test drive.

---

[153] http://www.financial-planning.com/wwwboard2

FINANCIAL PLANNING SOFTWARE

By John L. Olsen, CLU, ChFC

The first difficulty many practitioners (especially new practitioners) encounter with "financial planning software" is that the term itself is as precise as "financial planning" – which is to say, so vague as to be virtually useless. What does it *mean*? The frustration wrought by this confusion is evident from the question often voiced by planners:

"What IS financial planning software anyway, and how can it help me in my practice, and how can I decide which program or programs to buy?" Let's attack this question by breaking it down to its three components.

What is "financial planning software"?

That term covers a lot of ground, but generally refers to computer programs, which help the user perform one or more of the following general tasks:

Retirement Income Planning. Here, the focus is on *projected income levels.* Programs in this category may use "deterministic" modeling (assuming that a chosen rate of return on assets – individually, or as a group – will be earned, each year, with no variation, for the entire period.) Often, the user may input one [unvarying] rate for pre-retirement and a different [unvarying] rate for post retirement) or "stochastic" modeling, such as "Monte Carlo simulation" (where *variations* in the chosen rate are considered.)

Estate Planning. Here, the focus is generally upon "net wealth transfer to heirs". Some EP packages do little or no *cash flow* analysis. Some make *required income* a *constraint*, funding any shortfalls in income by liquidating assets. Nevertheless, the focus is *usually* upon one or two Future Values (e.g.: Net To Heirs at 1st death & 2nd death.)

Investment Planning / Portfolio Management. Here, the focus is on *the type of assets owned and how they perform.* This category includes "straight analysis" programs, such as Morningstar's "Principia" and Wiesenberger's "Investment View", "asset allocation/portfolio optimization" packages, such as Frontier Analytics' "Allocation Master" and Advisoryworld's "Power Optimizer". Recently, some software vendors have combined portfolio optimization/asset allocation with Monte Carlo Simulation.

Client/Task/Asset Database Management. This category may be more in the nature of "housekeeping" than "planning". It includes *Client/Contact* management programs such as "Act" and "GoldMine" and *Client/Contact/ASSET* packages such as EZ-Data's "Client Data System", "dbCams", and "Centerpiece". These packages are more focused on record keeping than on projections.

Tax Planning. Most packages which are devoted *strictly* to tax planning are intended for the Accounting market, but nearly all programs in the other categories we're looking at take Income Tax into consideration. Some also consider Estate and Gift Tax.

Cash Flow / Debt Management & Planning. *Debt management* is one area in which the software manufacturing sector has fallen down on the job badly. A few programs permit some limited analysis of "debt what ifs". *Cash flow*, on the other hand, is a large component of some FP software but a minor consideration in others.

"Capital Needs Analysis". "CNA" programs have been in use in the life insurance industry for decades. Typically, they seek to show a Net Present Value - the *total dollars needed today* to fund clients' goals for Survivor Income if Client/Spouse dies, Income if Client/Spouse becomes disabled, Retirement Income, and Education Funding.

"Comprehensive" Financial Planning packages. These programs attempt to do several – or even *all* – of the seven tasks listed above.

2. How can this software help me in my practice?

First and foremost, a software package is a *tool*, not a Magic Wand. What it *won't* do is enable you to perform planning and management tasks that you don't understand. For example, if you haven't any idea how to complete an Estate Tax Return, getting the 706 preparation program from Zane's or ProBATE Software is just asking for trouble.

Second, even if you feel comfortable in a given area of planning, you don't want to use a software package, which "does" such planning as a "Black Box", the output of which you can be assured is "right". *No* software package is certain to be free of "bugs" and "glitches" and *all* of them produce results based on *assumptions* - some of which may not be explained fully in the documentation (as if anyone ever reads documentation.) Facts which lead to a couple of Operational Rules:

1. If you don't know the assumptions that underlie the results you're examining, you can't possibly know if those results make sense.

2. If you aren't sure of where a number came from, you can count on being asked.

That said (and if we haven't scared you off the idea of using *any* software,) let's look at how using financial planning software, of one or more of the types described above, might be a *good* idea - how it can help you in your practice.

A *lot* of planning is mere arithmetic. Computers do arithmetic a lot faster and more accurately than humans do. Moreover, some of the math in financial planning is complicated enough that most of us simply *can't* do it "by hand".

"What if" is the very essence of financial planning, and "what if" scenarios are difficult, if not impossible, to do without computer help, especially if we're examining the impact of changes in *several* variables. The best FP software packages allow us to model the effect of a whole assortment of different assumptions and possible strategies.

Your Time Is Money. Not only can you, using appropriate financial planning software, do planning which you wouldn't even attempt without it, but you can do so relatively quickly. The value of your billable hour is enhanced.

Presentation Is Everything. A really good FP program can produce text and graphics, which look simply *terrific!* Some even allow you to customize the text and format. For "in person" planning (where you are actually doing "what if"s, right in front of the client,) some packages allow you to see the result of a changed assumption or value immediately, right on screen. The *impact* on the client is often enormous.

Your Practice Is A Business. As planners, we often spend a distressingly large portion of our time simply running our practices. Billing, correspondence, compliance (every planner's favorite task,) and the like take up otherwise-billable hours. To the extent that you can do these tasks *more quickly, accurately, and efficiently,* you "increase the hours in your day".

3. How can I decide which program or programs to buy?

While the process of selecting financial planning software is anything but easy (which is why planning firms and individuals hire the author to help them do that,) asking yourself a few key questions – and spending some serious time and effort in addressing those questions – can make it more bearable.

A. What do you want the thing to do? The decision process starts right here. Give a *lot* of thought to this question, because, if you don't have a pretty clear idea, you won't be able to make a good decision.

BE SPECIFIC! Include what you *want,* what you *need,* what you *don't want*, and what you *don't need.* Specify *why* you feel as you do.

WRITE IT DOWN!

B. Ask other practitioners how they would answer this question. Not only will you hear ideas you hadn't thought of, but when you put the responses you hear into the perspective of what you know about the nature of the respondent's practice, you'll get a better idea of the Nature of the Problem.

C. Reduce what you have to an itemized list of FACTORS. Make sure that there's as little overlap as possible. (Each factor should be both specific and unique.)

D. Make up a spreadsheet. The first column should list the programs you're considering, *beginning on the SECOND line.* Assign each FACTOR you have identified to a separate column (headed by the name of the FACTOR on the *first line.*)

WEIGHT the FACTORS. Apply a Weighting Factor (e.g.: 2.0 = VERY important to you; 1.0 = "neutral" [neither VERY important nor VERY unimportant;] 0.0 = VERY unimportant to you) to each FACTOR you've identified. Enter this WEIGHTING FACTOR *on the second line of the spreadsheet* (directly beneath the corresponding FACTOR heading.)

MAKE A PHOTOCOPY OF THE SPREADSHEET you just made (or, if you're doing this on a computer spreadsheet, **COPY THE RANGE** to an area to the right of the existing spreadsheet.)

Score each program for how well it handles the factor in question ("RAW SCORE") and enter the scores in the appropriate cells.

Multiply the RAW SCORES in each column by the WEIGHTING FACTOR for that column and enter the result in the corresponding cells of the second spreadsheet (or tell Excel to do it).

ADD UP THE WEIGHTED SCORES FOR EACH PROGRAM. The higher the number, the better the program *for your particular needs.*

This procedure won't *guarantee* that you'll end up with "the perfect software library", but you will have reduced the task to manageable proportions. At this point, you should have only a few packages to evaluate.

E. What constraints will you apply? This includes:

Hardware limitations. Will you use it on a Network? (Some packages won't run on one, or cost a lot more for a Network version.) Will you want to swap files between a desktop and a laptop? (Some packages make this easy; some don't.)

Who will use it? Consider the "learning curve". A *lot* of software is purchased and then shelved because it's simply too hard to learn for the folks who will have to use it.

Cost. Make sure you take into account the *ongoing maintenance fees.*

Compatibility with other software. Unfortunately, most financial planning software doesn't talk to other financial planning software. But some programs do and most will (eventually.) *If you expect to be able to use a program with one or more other programs, make sure you ask the software manufacturer for SPECIFICS on this point.* (Vague promises of "cross-application compatibility" won't cut it!)

F. How will you and your staff learn the program? Most planners decide on "do it yourself", which is rather curious, given that we're in the business of helping clients to *avoid the pitfalls* of this strategy. Consider these factors:

Are you a "pro" at learning/teaching software? If not, then an *amateur* will be running your training program.

How much would hiring a "pro" cost, in billable hours?

Do you really want the aggravation?

If you decide to "do it yourself", make sure that you know what sort of training the software manufacturer provides (other than manuals, which aren't "training" at all.)

If you decide not to try to *learn* the program or programs you purchase by yourself, you may want to consider whether you want to make the purchasing decision on that basis. A software consultant who is familiar with the strengths and weaknesses of *all* the programs out there (or many of them, at any rate) *and* who understands the financial planning business may save you, not only time and effort, but money as well. After all, isn't that what *you* do for your clients?

***

The author, John L. Olsen, CLU, ChFC, is Principal of Olsen Financial Group, located in St. Louis County, Missouri. John is a financial and estate planner with over 28 years' experience. In addition to providing insurance, financial, and estate planning advice to his own clients, John consults with other financial professionals on estate, financial, and insurance issues and cases. A growing part of John's practice is **financial planning software consulting***, which he provides to individuals and firms, usually on a "web-assisted" basis (in which John and the client are "virtually" sitting together in front of his computer.)*

John may be reached at:
Olsen Financial Group
131 Hollywood Lane
Kirkwood, MO 63122
314-909-8818
FAX: 314-909-7912
Email: jolsen02@earthlink.net
Web site: http://www.olsenfinancialgroup.com

Carol A. Grosvenor

One of the first computer gurus in the financial services industry, for fifteen years Carol put her two degrees in Computer Science to work designing systems, writing reviews, speaking at conferences and helping hundreds of financial planners acquire appropriate technology for their offices.

I caught up with Carol in May 2001, at the Southern California Financial Planning Conference where she moderated a Master's Track panel on Technology. She recently retired from her position as a computer consultant and become a Registered Representative with Financial Network Investment Corporation.

Now on the financial planner's side of the table, she's setting up her own system. I asked her what software she would recommend for someone just starting out.

"There are six areas to consider," Carol explained. Below, in the order of importance she gave them, I've listed ***Carol's Choice*** selections with comments:

1. **Contact Management:** This is the most important software you'll need. This is where you keep track of appointments, conversations, commitments and tasks. You need to know who you talked to, what you said, and what to do.
    a. ACT: Simple and inexpensive

b. GoldMine: Comprehensive. I love their family contact card. ***Carol's Choice***

c. ProTracker[154]: Tailored to financial planning. The best of the three for financial planners, but I'm concerned that there is only one man behind the company. What if something happens to him?

2. **Analysis:** To provide securities analysis and compare stocks, mutual funds and variable annuities, and rank them for performance, risk, etc. Ibbotson Associates has a system, but it's probably not cost effective for new planners, and Morningstar has become the industry standard.

a. Morningstar Principia Pro[155] ***Carol's Choice***

3. **Financial Planning:** This could be anything from a single "retirement planning" program to a comprehensive suite. If you're really doing financial planning, you need one software program that handles a variety of situations from budgeting to estate taxes. Add modules, but stick to one program.

a. MoneyTree[156]: Integrated programs that can grow with your practice, plus Monte Carlo Simulation. Competitively priced.

b. Methuselah[157]: Comprehensive planning that will focus on modules. Web presence makes it easier to work with geographically diverse clients. No initial capital outlay. Monthly fee. ***Carol's Choice***

4. **Asset Tracking:** This is the biggest choice and the hardest to learn, since most programs give you no clue as to "how" it's doing what it's doing.

a. dbCams+[158] from Financial Computer Support, Inc.: The most comprehensive, with a huge learning curve and the only asset tracking software available today that interfaces with financial planning software. ***Carol's Choice***

b. Centerpiece[159] from Performance Technologies, Inc.

c. Advent Software, Inc.[160]

d. Portfolio 2001 from TechFi Corporation[161]:

5. **Supplemental Educational Material** (Optional)

a. Text Library System[162] from Financial Planning Consultants, Inc.: A unique Client Relationship Management and Drip Marketing package containing

---

[154] See a demo of ProTracker at http://www.protracker.com. Created by Warren J. Mackensen, CFP® for his fee-only practice, ProTracker has recently added an on-line Knowledge Base to provide 24/7 support.

[155] Check it out by ordering a PrincipiaPro Explorer Kit from http://www.morningstar.com/products/clmppro.html.

[156] http://www.moneytree.com

[157] http://www.methuselah.com/

[158] http://www.fcsi.com/

[159] http://www.schwabperformancetechnologies.com/

[160] http://www.advent.com

[161] http://www.techfi.com/Products/

[162] http://www.financialsoftware.com Tell Judy Van Cleve, RFC you heard about TLS in "So You Want to Be a Financial Planner" and receive a discount on the purchase of the Text Library System.

hundreds of agendas, documents, letters, articles and checklists. ***Carol's Choice***

    b.   Kettley Publishing's Backroom Technician[TM163]: Simplified concept illustrations and reports covering popular financial topics and strategies.

    c.   Internet

6. **Asset Allocation** (optional)

    a.   Allocation Master from Frontier Analytics[164]: ***Carol's Choice***

    b.   Ramcap[165]:

Mitchell F. Keil, CFP®

"The motto for my company, Integrity Financial Advisory, is 'Helping Families Build & Preserve Wealth'," explains Mitchell. "Each word in my motto means something. Every word is active, carries weight and has value. I don't make any business decisions without first asking myself, 'Will this product/service help clients/families build and preserve wealth?' Before deciding on software, know exactly what you want it to do for your practice. Always go back to your mission statement. "

Ten to 15% of his budget every year goes to technology, with the knowledge that whatever he buys will change sooner or later. "It's frustrating," he says, "but the frustration will help you make a better decision the next time."

Mitchell feels financial planners must acquire software in the areas of contact management, portfolio management, financial planning and education.

He's partial to Junxure[166] for contact management, because of its built in wealth management assessor which enhances the system developed by Ross Levin in his book, The Wealth Management Index.[167]

TechFi[168] has a new integrated system utilizing the Internet, and is Mitchell's choice for asset management.

"You can really dig your teeth into Naviplan[169]," he says when asked about financial planning software. "But it's like an 800 pound gorilla with a learning curve equal to climbing Mt. Everest!"

---

[163] http://www.kettley.com/

[164] http://www.allocationmaster.com/

[165] http://www.software4advisors.com/ramcap.htm

[166] http://www.crmsoftwareinc.com

[167] The Wealth Management Index: The Financial Advisor's System for Assessing & Managing Your Client's Plans & Goals by Ross Levin, McGraw-Hill Professional, 1997.

[168] http://www.techfi.com/Products/

[169] http://www.emergingis.com/

Joel Bruckenstein, CFP®

Some of the most common sense, easy to understand information I've ever read on financial planning software comes from Joel Bruckenstein, CFP®. In June 2001, he published an article in MorningstarAdvisor.com[170] that sets forth what to consider before shopping for products. The editors at MorningstarAdvisor.com have graciously granted permission to reprint the article here:

A step-by-step guide to finding the program that's "right" for you

By Joel P. Bruckenstein, CFP®

When evaluating financial-planning software, there is one universal truth: No one program is "right" for everybody. Arriving at the proper fit for your practice requires a commitment from you. The more you put into the process, the better your chance of success.

Financial planners are not a homogeneous group. We may all adhere to the six-step process, but the similarities end there. There are legitimate philosophical differences among intelligent people as to how a plan should be designed and implemented.

Some planners favor detailed multiyear cash-flow-driven plans, while others prefer a goals-based approach. Some planners want to supply the client with extensive written documentation, while others believe that "less is more." Some place a high premium on charts and graphs, while others prefer text and tables.

Our client bases also differ. Those catering to middle-class clients will have different needs than those who deal exclusively with wealthy clients. Small-business owners present different challenges and opportunities than do middle-level executives.

Where to Begin

Before you begin your search, I suggest that you think long and hard about where your practice is today and where you want it to be in the future. What does your client base look like? Do you expect it to change? What types of services do you currently provide, and will you expand your offerings in the future?

Also, think about your approach to planning. Do you want to develop goal-based plans or cash-flow-based plans? Will you be presenting long, detailed, written financial plans or shorter written plans and action lists?

You should also think about whether or not you will be doing the data entry now and in the future. If you will be doing the data entry yourself, ease of entry may be less of an issue. If an assistant will handle the data entry, context-sensitive help and clearly laid out screens are a plus.

---

[170] http://www.advisor.morningstar.com (do an author search for Joel)

Capabilities You Need

Now, think about the capabilities that your program should possess. Whatever your approach to planning, your program should be capable of handling cash inflows and outflows, whether they are even or uneven. Typical cash inflows would include employment income, self-employment income, Social Security, pension income, and annuity income. Outflows would include fixed and variable living expenses, mortgages, taxes, and contributions to retirement plans.

The program should also allow you to invest excess cash flow in the investment of your choice and direct how short-term deficits will be covered. If assets are to be sold, which ones and in what order? If you intend to borrow, at what cost, and what are the tax implications?

In addition to the basics, think about what other functions are critical to your practice. Do you have clients with employee stock options? How about restricted stock? Investment real estate? Collectibles? Assets denominated in foreign currencies? Commodities? Certain types of assets require specific tax or accounting treatment. If your clients own such assets, you need a program that can deal with them. Just don't pay extra for capabilities that you don't need.

In the area of income tax, you probably want a program that can calculate both federal and state income taxes. If your clients typically own ISOs or other tax preference items, the ability to calculate and report AMT becomes essential.
 If most of your clients are young and middle class, they may not be interested in paying you for elaborate estate plans, so the ability to illustrate basic estate-planning concepts should suffice. Wealthier clients will obviously have additional needs. Can the software model the strategies that you typically recommend? Does it allow you to model multiple cash flows to or from an individual trust? Does it accurately compute estate taxes?

There may be other features that you desire, such as the ability to import or export to other programs, charting and graphing capabilities, etc.

Prepare to Compare

Once you have written down your wish list of capabilities, try creating a table or spreadsheet that will allow you to compare a number of programs. Then compile a list of candidates. You can start with a broad list (a number of publications produce a list of programs), or you can start with recommendations from reviewers, colleagues, and discussion groups. Check the MorningstarAdvisor.com[171] website for a list of my software reviews.

To learn more about the programs, contact the software companies by telephone or online. If certain features are essential to your practice, make sure those features are available, and ask specific questions about the strength of those features. Programs that don't meet your needs will be eliminated, leaving you with a short list.

---

[171] http://www.advisor.morningstar.com

Check Them Out

It's now time to request demos and look under the hood. Each company should supply you with a working program, not a scripted presentation.

Try installing the software. Does it load seamlessly on your computer? Do you get any error messages? Enter a case and play around. Hopefully, the program will not freeze up or cause other problems. As you work through the case, spot check some of the calculations, so you understand how the program operates. Print a number of reports. Can you control how reports are generated? Can you edit them? Are the calculations correct?

Request the telephone number for technical support and try calling them a few times. Make sure that you can reach them and that they can answer your questions. Find out if their hours of operation are convenient for you. Ask about support policies, frequency of upgrades, hours of operation, manuals, and training materials.

The Final Cut

By now, most contenders will have fallen by the wayside. At this point one final step may be necessary to arrive at a decision -- inquire about a live or on line training session. Many of the better companies are beginning to offer this option.

I recently attended all-day training sessions conducted by Net Worth Strategies (for StockOpter) and EISI (Naviplan Extended). Both were excellent.
Experienced instructors walked the class through an actual case study, one designed to use numerous program features, allowing the attendee a hands-on opportunity to use the software as one would in the office.

The training sessions allow you to ask questions as they arise. They also give you the opportunity to observe how other attendees react to the program, which may reveal facts that you overlooked. An added benefit of attending training sessions is that they force you to focus your attention on evaluating a particular software package for the allotted time, something that is often difficult to do at the office.

When you're making the final decision, spend as little as necessary to purchase the capabilities you need, but don't make price alone the deciding factor. If two programs can do what you want, but one produces a plan in significantly less time, they are not equal. The one that saves you (or your staff) time is probably the best buy.

If all of the above sounds like a lot of work, it is. But if financial planning is your bread and butter, then it is time and money well spent.

Joel has co-authored "Virtual-Office Tools for a High-Margin Practice" with David Drucker, published in 2002 and available at most online bookstores. If you're setting up an office, you need this book.

BOTTOM LINE ON TECHNOLOGY

There is no bottom line.
> Stay secure.
> Backup often.
> Budget generously.
> Watch for new systems and products.
> Check frequently for upgrades and patches.

RESOURCES

Most financial services publications and web sites have frequent articles on software, and often run comparison surveys. The August issue of Financial Planning® usually includes a software survey, which is updated throughout the year on their website at http://www.financial-planning.com → Adviser Centers → Software.

The Financial Planning Association lists a good sampling on their web site at http://www.fpanet.org/ → Resource Directory → Computer Software.

Joel Bruckenstein's regular articles on http://www.advisor.morningstar.com (→Article Search →Author) contain candid reviews of software and technology trends plus Advisor Tech Q&A.. Membership is currently free. You'll find exploring the site well worth your time. Joel is also the technical writer for *Inside Information*, http://www.bobveres.com, Bob Veres' newsletter.

Advisor Page has a comprehensive Resource Database on their page at http://advisorpage.com/, along with links to lots of products and services including a free newsletter. There is also a chatroom. Find out what others think!

Investment Advisor Magazine's annual software survey can be found at http://www.investmentadvisor.com/ → Industry Directories.

Bob Veres' **Inside Information** at http://www.bobveres.com contains Recommended Software/Web Services along with current product reviews. **Inside Information** is a subscription site. I think you're crazy if it isn't included on your *gotta' have it* list. Links to almost every other financial planning website you will ever need are here.

Chapter Six

Marketing 101

This will be a short chapter for two reasons:

1. I don't know much about marketing
2. There are entire libraries and degree programs on marketing

Don't interpret that to mean this isn't one of the most **important** chapters in this book. It doesn't matter whether or not you want to sell anything, or think you have anything to sell. You do. Before anything else can happen, you have to sell yourself: to an employer, a client, a lender, a landlord, etc.

Unless you can sell yourself and earn the trust and confidence of whomever you are dealing with, you will not succeed in this or any other service oriented business.

It is vital that you have a Marketing Plan as part of your Business Plan. Nothing will get you off the ground running faster than a well thought out strategy for bringing clients in the door. Whether you have a major brokerage behind you or are a one-person shop, ultimately it's up to you to bring in your own clients.

Before you can design a marketing plan, you'll need to make some fundamental decisions about your practice. You'll need a company name, of course, and a solid idea of what it is you can/will do (mission statement.) You should have a pretty good handle on what sort of clients you anticipate (middle-market, corporate, wealthy, retired) and the image you desire to project (casual, professional, academic, etc.) to clients and associates. Once you have a grasp on these things, it will be easier to proceed with marketing.

Christian Ramsey founded AdvisorPage.com[172] for the purpose of bringing together "PRACTICE MANAGEMENT AND BUSINESS DEVELOPMENT RESOURCES FOR FINANCIAL PROFESSIONALS." When I asked him if he would help lend some direction to this chapter, he graciously accepted the challenge and contributed the following:

---

[172] http://www.advisorpage.com AdvisorPage.Com is the electronic meeting place that supports the alternative marketing, research, recruiting and benefit needs of the financial services industry. Founded in December, 2000 Advisor Page provides meaningful business development and practice management solutions to some of the most well known individuals in the financial industry, as well as over 200 CEOs, Business Development and Marketing Officers from over 150 different companies.

What You Get Out of Marketing

By Christian Ramsey

What is the Purpose of Marketing?

Professional marketing, regardless of what industry you reference, involves setting up a system to both get the attention of your target audience and track the effectiveness of your marketing efforts.

It is accurate to say that you do not market yourself or your product; rather you identify a prospect's NEEDS by marketing. You are actually marketing 'PEOPLE'…specifically the people down the hall, in the office next door or in another state. THAT is why marketing is so important. Marketing is essentially a measure of how you identify with your target market and how well you are positioned to provide a service.

You can measure the attention you receive through careful marketing and you can use that information to further define your 'marketplace'. This is a fancy way of saying 'You learn how the PEOPLE you are providing service to like to think of themselves, what their needs are, and how those needs can be comfortably serviced by your company.'

Marketing is not selling. Marketing is interacting with PEOPLE to measure both the positioning of your company and the image you portray as a solution.

Marketing is designed to get people to come to you. That is how you measure the success of a campaign. It concerns YOUR relationship skills with the prospect. You (or someone in your office) need to be able to convince them to take action.

Getting tangible financial results from marketing is a bit trickier and requires an in-depth knowledge of your client's needs and how they respond to given situations. How do your clients identify themselves? How do they prefer to conduct business? How do they describe you and your office? This is incredibly valuable information because every financial professional has the ability to learn WHY people give them business. When you get this information, it is possible to quantify and solidify your appeal to the market place.

Most financial professionals think 'marketing=getting new clients' and measure the success of a marketing campaign by how many new clients they attracted. Getting new clients is a direct result of the personal interaction you achieve when you meet a prospect. This is where marketing takes its exit and your people skills enter.

What works best for Independent Financial Professionals?

What every marketing system provides is a way to track FLOW. Meaning: a marketing system will prescribe a series of events. Different marketing systems will track FLOW differently and in most cases stand a great chance of getting you attention. What works best for most independent financial professionals is referral-based marketing. Instead of focusing on attracting more attention, they focus on CONTACT MANAGEMENT with existing clients and actively pursuing referrals. The difference with this approach is that you focus on QUALITY rather than ATTENTION and let the quality you provide represent your firm. This is the best marketing that I can think of because it results in long-term relationships.

If you are an independent financial professional, I would focus on contact management systems that are or can be formatted to address the needs of your current clients and wait for the length of time it takes for your practice to reach the critical mass necessary for actual marketing/lead generation.

Instead of actual marketing you might focus on image-building tools like impressive sales kits or take up public speaking as a hobby. These types of tools will lend to your personal credibility and image so that the prospects that find their way to your door will be more inclined to give you their business.

How to Tackle a Marketing Plan

To start a marketing plan you need to first have a rough idea of how your service can benefit people. You should also have an idea of how people can distinguish your service from other similar services.

This is VERY basic market research.

Then you test your audience's receptiveness to your solution through some sort of action. This can be running an ad in a newspaper, or by purchasing a mailing list, or even having a prepared pitch you deliver in a conversation with your neighbor. You want to have a distinct image, an audience, a message and some basic system to track how effective your message is.

What you want to get out of marketing is:

1. Recognition: Do people understand what you do? Do they think of your firm differently than a competitor?

2. Interest: Do they have a need for your service? What service is it, and why does it appeal to them?

3. Action: Are these prospects willing to take some sort of action or to learn more or to give you their business? It is always good to understand WHY someone takes action so that you can give that same message to prospects.

In designing a marketing campaign, demographic statistics help. "The 2000 FPA Financial Performance & Compensation Study of Financial Planning Practitioners" has a plethora of information to help guide you in creating an effective marketing strategy. Beginning

October 30, 2000, Karin Stifler, writing for MorningstarAdvisor.com[173], reviewed the study and made some important observations. The article is in two parts under the title "The Marketing Edge."

Another good marketing resource which includes access to personal and business coaches and tips on insurance oriented material is the site hosted by the National Association of Insurance and Financial Advisors[174] (NAIFA.) Their "Gateway to the Internet" website, Financial Services Online,[175] offers a free e-mail subscription to "Financial e-News," a bi-monthly publication well worth perusing.

An absolute master at marketing is W. Aubrey Morrow, CFP®, President of Financial Designs, Ltd., a fee-based financial planning firm in San Diego, and host of "The Financial Advisors"[176], a weekly show on Money Talk Radio.

Aubrey, one of the most energetic people I know, always seems to have a zillion ideas that appear to come right off the top of his head. So I asked him for some help. He created a scenario: "I'm ready for a career change. Hey, money buys happiness and I like to be happy, it's therefore logical to work with money somehow. Since I would like the freedom and the unlimited income potential, I-want-to-be-a-financial-planner."

Thinking historically, Aubrey explained to me how stockbrokers and life insurance agents are trained:

"In the 'hiring process', the interview leaves them with illusions of becoming a 'financial planner' with great financial wealth to follow. In reality, the generally 'very good' training period includes teaching to gather the facts on how people earn a living, how they spend and what areas they commonly overlook. What is found, of course, is *inadequate* estate planning, poor risk management, wrong investment purchases, little retirement planning, excessive taxes, bad debt, etc.

"Before long, the honeymoon is over.

"During the stockbroker/insurance agent's training period, they are taught to maintain a list of 'whom do I know?'

"At the conclusion of the training period, it's now time to *MAKE CALLS*! Huh. 'Why don't people like me? Was it something I said?' During this period, most 'I want-to-be-a-financial planner's' self esteem is lower than whale shit on the bottom of the ocean (yes, you may quote me.)" Aubrey doesn't mince words.

---

[173] http://advisor.morningstar.com MorningstarAdvisor.com is a member site that is currently free. If you are not a member, join. Then perform a search for "The Marketing Edge" by Karin Stifler.
[174] http://www.naifa.org/sh_index.html
[175] http://www.fsonline.com
[176] http://www.moneytalkradio.com/

"Now comes the 'reality' of why so many people do not make it in this business: because they are not able to handle rejection -- know anyone who likes to receive calls from someone trying to sell them something? It's natural to react negatively.

"For the 'determined' I'm-going-to-be-a-financial-planner, it's time to map out your prospecting options. Keep in mind, as Michael Jordan sez 'Just Do It!' Success leads to more success."

MARKETING for the Determined
"I'm-Going-to-Be-a-Financial-Planner"

By Aubrey Morrow, CFP®

GETTING STARTED: First, evaluate your strengths and weaknesses. Ask a friend to confirm. Whatever you do, do it naturally; otherwise, you will come off as a salesperson sounding like a recording.

Then, in no particular order:

MAKE A LIST OF EVERYONE YOU KNOW: Create a letter or classy wedding-style card announcing your new profession. Describe briefly (in few words) how you help people "solve personal financial issues," etc. Enclose your business card. Don't mass mail to a zillion people. Mail selectively. On your list, categorize names which you feel are tops (like List 1, 2, 3.) Mail, for example, 25 per week, and CALL them for an opportunity to visit.

GET REFERRALS: This is absolutely the best source of new clients. One way to do it is to provide your client a sample letter (which your other clients have used to introduce you to their friends.) The letter can be on the client's letterhead with "copy" to you. Of course, you mail it when you want to meet new folks. (Note: don't date the letter in advance.) When you (the planner) mail the letter (from your client to their referral,) you send a copy to your client so they will be aware of it being sent (especially, if the referral calls to ask about you.)

You can also have a sample letter on your letterhead and simply mail your letter to the referral with copy to your client.

SEMINARS: These days there are an abundance of "instant seminar" materials – all pretty good. Companies like Emerald Publications[177] in Rancho Bernardo, California provides an extensive list of seminar materials for financial planners. The seminar topics vary from overall financial planning to specifics. This is an excellent way to break into the business!!! It's professional. Call for their catalogue. They also have 2-day training for planners covering A-Z on "how to do it."

---

[177] http://216.7.147.20/Seminars/WhySeminars.htm

These "instant" workshops can be used in many ways:

1. Send flyers in local newspapers announcing your workshops.

2. Team up with another professional to conduct workshops (split the cost of marketing.) You can do workshops on literally all the topics (tax planning, estate planning, retirement planning, long-term-health care, etc.) There are endless topics. To me seminars are the Number Two best way I have met clients. Number One is referrals.

CREATE A FLYER: About your services and distribute it everywhere. Offer a free consultation on something, such as a review of their life insurance policy, income tax return, etc. This is relatively easy and given lots of 'em, will get results. They're not always the best clients, but it's a start. Of course, once you have a happy client, you should get happy referrals (from your happy client.)

SPEAK: At service clubs, community organizations, etc. Most cities have companies who produce lists of clubs and organizations in their city. In San Diego, we have the "Source Book", a 3-ring binder listing all service organizations in the city by name and contact. A planner could use this list to advise them of the planner's availability to speak (using the Emerald and similar materials.) BTW – this is a piece of cake…is too easy! Service clubs are always looking for speakers, so it's a nice match. Of course, the speaker will make available handout information and an "Evaluation Form" for comments and future appointments.

NEWSLETTERS: Easy to do and makes you feel good about yourself. You can buy software and write your own (allowing you to say what you want) or subscribe to newsletters, which have your picture and contact information pre-printed. I use Emerald's newsletters. I buy 3 types: one for retirees, non-retirees and business owners. You can send them monthly, bi-monthly, quarterly, etc. Expect to pay in the neighborhood of fifty cents each (not including postage.) It's a nice way to keep your mug in front of clients and prospects. You can always offer a 6-month free newsletter to prospects. It's also a good idea to make it available when you speak. Otherwise, most folks do not want you to contact them. If they want your newsletter, they will provide you their contact information.

TEACH: Adult education classes. Most colleges have evening adult education classes. You can create a course called "Fundamentals of Financial Planning". The course could be taught over a 6-week period once per week for 2 hours per class. Guess how many modules Emerald's Complete Financial Planning Workshop has? You guess it -- six. Emerald also has workbooks available to go along with the program; great materials for "your" students. I did this and it works very well. And it's easy. For anyone who is interested, check with your local JC or college and get their catalog on adult classes.

COLD CALLING: Worse than a cold shower. The worst. However, that's how the brokerage firms and insurance companies train. After your classes, it's time to "dial for dollars" or an appointment that is. What's even worse is the person who says "yes" to your pitch does not know how to say "no" to anyone. However, the brokerage and insurance companies are noticeably successful, so I cannot argue with success. It's strictly a numbers game to start.

DROP BYS: Yep. For those of us who cannot handle calling a zillion people with no face, some of us (like me) decided to drop by businesses. In the old days, we did not have all the sources available today like instant lists in books and now the Internet. I actually planned cold calling going business to business. My "research" at the library with Dunn & Bradstreet lists showed me "SIC" codes on businesses and businesses by address. There were lists available of all the business listed next door to each other. I listed names of the owners / president's and literally "dropped by" and asked for the contact person.

This works…if you have the guts. Also, when you do land a good business owner, the referral letter idea on his/her letterhead is "the best"!

ASK: Other planners how they market and how they got started.

Remember: marketing is everything

Robin Vaccai-Yess, CFP®, a planner in Highland, New York, opened her independent fee-only practice on January 1, 2001. Prior to that time, she spent over a year working on her business and marketing plan, which has proved to be a tremendous help in attracting clients to her brand new practice. Robin has some straightforward, step-by-step tips on how to get your business up and running:

Marketing Your Financial Planning Practice

By Robin Vaccai-Yess, CFP®

Just like investments are only a part of a financial plan, a marketing plan is only part of your business plan. Marketing is the means and methods that get your name out to the public; advertising is only a part of marketing. Initially, you should have a plan for at least the first year of operations on a month-by-month basis. With a new practice, your marketing is about building a presence, name recognition, and credibility through various methods.

1. **Have a logo, business cards, letterhead, and a brochure** designed and professionally printed. Steer clear of perforated, self-printed business cards. Image is important and you don't want clients thinking you were up late the night before printing your business cards!
2. **Send a press release** to all newspapers (local dailies and weeklies) in your area announcing the opening of your new practice. If you've got a niche, stress it. Keep

the press release short, double-space it, and make sure it's grammatically correct. A typo in a press release is like cutting your own throat.

3. **Get a website**. Have it professionally done and make it an extension of your advertising and print materials. Prospective clients should be able to go to your site for more information than what they see in your print ads or get from your brochure. Revisit your website regularly to update and improve it. You don't need a counter on a website, but make sure your web hosting company provides a means for you to check traffic so you can monitor your marketing efforts.

4. **Get your name in the paper**. Write letters to the editor and send out regular press releases that include a professional press photo (readers love to associate a face with the name they're reading about). If you do something new like publish a newsletter for clients, join a board or professional organization or volunteer, use it as a tool to communicate with the press.

5. **Advertise in your local or regional newspapers**.[178] Here's the key to successful advertising – size isn't everything, frequency is. Don't put in the biggest ad you can afford if you can only afford to run it for 2 months. It won't do it. While in real estate, it's location, location, location, in advertising, it's repeat, repeat, repeat. Of course, your message has to solve a problem for the consumer or invite them to call you, but it should be regular. Always use your web address in your newspaper ads – remember #3 above, your website is there to give more information. Advertising doesn't have to be display ads; it can be a simple classified ad – as long as it's regular.

6. **Join the Chamber of Commerce** and go to meetings, luncheons, and fundraisers. Meet the business community and let them know what you do – networking is your best advertising.

7. **Volunteer** to join the library board, the arts council, or the school board. Get involved and get your name out there. It's the best way to meet people.

8. **Compile** a list of centers of influence and send them quarterly newsletters or problem-solving tools.

9. **Write articles** and send them to business editors. Business Journals are often looking for usable articles. If you can write, do it. You'll get your name in the paper as a credible source, which is a lot more beneficial than any size ad you can pay for.

Even with an aggressive and comprehensive marketing strategy, it'll probably take two to three years to build a practice from scratch, but it'll be worth it.

USING A "SYSTEM"

Whether it's a manual from your nationally known broker/dealer who spends millions advertising on the Super Bowl, or a book you borrowed from the library, a great place to

---

[178] After a year in practice, Robin claims she "Would limit my use of print advertising. The methods that work best are writing articles and teaching classes and workshops. New clients and/or referrals come from these but print advertising's results are limited. Naturally, the advertising sales reps tell you about keeping your name out there, but a word of mouth business is a better one." See more about Robin in Chapter Seven.

begin is with a wheel that's already been invented. Here are a couple of ideas to get you started.

Bill Bachrach

"My only regret is not doing this 5 or 6 years earlier," said Brian Fricke, CFP®, a financial planner in Florida and graduate of Bill Bachrach's[179] year-long Trusted Advisor Coach® program. Plunking down a hefty, non-refundable fee plus hotel costs and airfare to San Diego four times in the year 2000 brought his financial planning practice to an entirely new level.

Brian credits his pursuit of *Values-Based Selling* principles for a dramatic increase not only in revenue, but also in the character of his business. He says he "grew up in a commission based world, with all the problems inherent in serving 500 clients." When he switched from commission to fee-based planning a few years ago, he applied the 80/20[180] rule to slash his client base. He loved Bachrach's book and devoured the accompanying tapes, but blamed himself when the results weren't what the book promised. To determine what he was doing wrong, he signed up for the coaching program.

"It used to take at least a couple of meetings just to get a client to commit to working with us, and several more meetings to gather information, prepare and implement a plan. I learned interviewing techniques enabling me to establish a high trust relationship during an initial meeting with a potential client. Today, inside an hour, a client will turn over all the necessary documentation, sign my agreement and pay my retainer. Alternatively, we can determine that a potential client is not a match for our firm. That alone was worth every penny."

"Bill has this 'being done' part of the program. I determined how many clients I needed to get where I wanted to be, and when I reach that number in a few months, I'll 'be done'. My practice will have just the right balance of clients and revenue for me, and I'll stop accepting new business. I'm telling my clients if they have friends or family looking for a financial planner, let them know, because the doors will be closing."

Shortly, another planner in Brian's office will be attending the three-day *Values-Based Selling*™ Academy training, a course he highly recommends for any financial planner, no matter their years in the industry.

Keith Laibson, a planner in Charlotte, North Carolina, learned about Bill Bachrach from a senior partner with his firm. Keith purchased Bachrach's book, *Values-Based Selling* and was motivated later when he attended a conference where Bill spoke.

"I made a commitment to do the 'What is important about money to you?' question at the beginning of all my initial interviews. While it was difficult at first," Keith admits, "I got results and positive feedback from the clients. I use the roadmaps, which help me guide my

---

[179] Bill Bachrach's website is http://www.bachrachvbs.com/
[180] Pareto's Principle: 'In any series of elements to be controlled, a selected small fraction in terms of number of elements almost always accounts for a large fraction in terms of effect'

client to what I am trying to accomplish. It attracts a certain client to our firm: the type we want to work with!"

Text Library System

Ed Morrow's Text Library System[181] has a drip-marketing module that is marvelous. He has literally thousands of continuously updated articles in the Library, with a schedule for sending them periodically to prospects. Once a prospect is in the system, the work is done for you. When you log onto the program, the prospects or clients who are supposed to receive a contact that day or week pop up as a reminder. All you need to do is click on the processing to have pre-selected information prepared for each individual contact.

The Text Library System has come under fire in the past, but the problems cited appear to have been cleaned up. I've used the Text Library System, and found it to be a tremendous help with both contact management and as a prospecting tool.

High Probability Selling[182]

This is strictly a sales training process, touted as a "new paradigm for selling." Co-authors Jacques Worth and Nicholas E. Ruben explain, "In High Probability Selling the paradigm shifts from getting the prospect to buy to determining whether there is a mutually acceptable basis for doing business." The purpose is to teach salespeople hot to stop wasting time with "Low Probablilty Prospects". Makes sense…if your intent is to sell.

BRANDING

A logo. An image. A mark. A slogan. Something that says ***YOU!*** whenever it's seen. At some point, you'll need whatever it takes to set yourself apart. Even if you represent a huge conglomerate, you are special.

Dave Moran, CLU, ChFC, CSA[183] left the captive insurance agency scene in 1998 and set out to make a name for himself as a fee-based planner. Literally. One of the first things he did was to design a logo and motto, to stick on tee shirts and hats, which he gives to clients and influential people. "It's a real kick to see your own company logo & slogan on people," he says, "They love it!"

It was a deliberate move on Dave's part to name his company the RTA Group. "For anyone thinking of going independent I'd suggest giving a lot of thought to the name of your business - don't just blindly call it 'John/Jane Smith Financial Planning, Inc.' If you want to build a business, then having your name attached may hurt when it comes time for you to pull back in later years.

"The idea is to build an image, or a brand that people associate with you, not the other way around. For example, my company name is 'The RTA Group.' The obvious question is,

---

[181] http://www.financialsoftware.com
[182] http://www.highprobsell.com/
[183] http://www.rtagroup.net

'What does RTA stand for?' That's exactly what I want people to do. Stop me. Ask that question and then listen. It's up to me to have an excellent, rehearsed response. I say, 'Risk Transfer Action Group: I show people how to transfer the risk of outliving their money - that's what financial planning is all about!' The logo is very nice and my slogan is 'Your Wealth. Your Security.' It's on everything I do."

Millennium Advertising[184] has built an entire industry around helping advisors promote themselves. Founder Peter Montoya[185] has written a book entitled *The Brand Called You"* with co-author Tim Vandehey, available through all the usual places.

Andy Gluck's Advisor Products, Inc. offers "one stop for all an advisor's marketing needs" and incorporates branding, newsletters, brochures and web site construction at http://www.advisorproducts.com.

INTERNET

The Internet is here to stay, and if you want to stay in business, you'd better be on it. You need a web presence, preferably one from which prospects can learn about you and your business, and can contact you through an e-mail link. Having your own domain name is a big plus. Register a great company name for yourself at Network Solutions.[186]

When Andy Gluck, president of AdvisorSites, Inc.[187] virtually invited me to see the etchings and other things in his workshop, I had no idea what an exciting time I was in for!

I was in my office in California on the phone with Andy, who was out there in cyberspace somewhere, when he gave me a web address to log onto. A few keystrokes and secret passwords later, I was behind the scenes at AdvisorSites, Inc., wandering up and down aisles of logos, photographs, artwork, and all manner of templates. He asked me to pick one, and had this been for real instead of research, I would have had a dicken's of a time making up my mind!

As it was, I selected a nice scene from the photographic area, and at Andy's prodding, invented a company "name" and wrote a couple of quick comments loosely resembling a marketing campaign. Then I sat back stunned as my "company" jumped to life on the monitor before me. "I sorta' like orange," was my reply when Andy asked if I was satisfied with the letters and colors on the screen, and suddenly the words scrawled over the picture were in orange -- a terrible color for words on a web page, by the way!

Next, I was presented with a menu of stuff just like I've seen at the web sites of some very impressive companies. Andy told me to check boxes if I wanted them on my web page. I could have stock market data, links to client portfolios, newsletters (written by me or others – whatever I wanted,) links to interesting sites and a whole bouquet of innovative ideas from

---

[184] http://www.milladv.com
[185] http://www.petermontoya.com/home.asp
[186] http://www.networksolutions.com
[187] http://www.advisorproducts.com

which to choose. Happily checking several boxes and clicking OK brought me to a fairly finished product that, in spite of the orange letters, looked really neat!

"This," said Andy, "Is what your clients and prospects could see if they clicked on your website. They could see the news of the day, find out what the market was doing, check their personal portfolio (if you wanted them to) and e-mail you, right from the site."

"Oh, sure," I replied. "Like I could afford this." I was amazed at what less than $50 a month could buy! When I mentioned I already had my own logo, Andy said it was no problem to incorporate it into my website. What's more, once my website was up and running, all I had to do was use my new password to get back into that fascinating workshop of Andy's, go to my own special room, and play around with my choices to my heart's content! First thing to go would be the orange letters.

There is no question that you need a website if you are in business today. If you have a Broker/Dealer, compliance dictates that you'll need to play by their rules and do what they tell you. AdvisorSites has created sites for reps at dozens of different Broker/Dealers. If you're independent and have no Broker/Dealer, Andy's company specializes in helping you create your own brand and can make your company look like a financial services giant.

NICHE MARKETING

In his controversial White Paper entitled "The Future of the Financial Advisory Business Part II: Strategies for Small Businesses," Mark Hurley[188] insists independent advisors will not survive without developing a successful niche business. The first step to creating such a business is to develop specialty services, by focusing on client problems shared by a select group of people.

Dr. Lynda Falkenstein is the *Niche Doctor*. Her niche is helping others find their niche. Her book, "*Nichecraft*: Using Your Specialness to Focus Your Business, Corner Your Market and Make Others Seek You Out," is filled with worksheets and ideas to help you do just that. Dr. Falkenstein was the guest speaker January 18, 2001 on Financial Planning Interactive Live Forum[189]. Check the Chat Transcripts.

When Andrew F. Hylton, LUTCF[190], ChFC signed on, American Express Financial Advisors had a winner. In 1994, in search of greener pastures, Andrew researched new opportunities. He was swept off his feet by what American Express offered, and the romance hasn't ended.

---

[188] Mark P. Hurley is President and CEO of Undiscovered Managers Funds. His first Undiscovered Managers white paper was "The Future of the Financial Advisory Business and the Delivery of Advice to the Semi-Affluent Investor."

[189] http://www.financial-planning.com/

[190] Life Underwriter Training Council Fellow, The LUTC **Fellow** designation is conferred only upon those individuals who meet or exceed the qualification requirements determined by LUTC and The National Association of Insurance and Financial Advisors (NAIFA), joint sponsors of the designation. http://www.amercoll.edu/mainlutc/

Andrew is Black (African-American.) He looked around his community in Southfield, Michigan, and saw too many African-Americans weren't utilizing the services of financial planners. "There are a lot of successful black people who only know about CD's and real estate," said Andrew. "As a whole, our community is not educated about what comprehensive financial planning is and what it can do, nor the financial tools of the general securities market. People fear what they don't know." Today, thanks to Andrew and the niche he has developed, that is changing.

A planner in Southern California, Scott Dauenhauer, CFP®, was appalled at the choices available for his wife's 403(b) plan. Determined to do something about it, he became an expert in education benefits. Today he publishes a newsletter entitled "The Teacher's Advocate: Protecting Teacher's Financial Interests", and has found his niche.

Before he retired from his job as Sr. Vice President of Operations for a division of a large computer company, Stephen J. Fazio, CFP® sought out a financial planner to advise him on his pension portfolio. "I ended up with 30 and 40 year olds telling me what to do with my money," Steve told me. "It didn't take long to realize that they were working to be where I already was and that I could do this for myself!"

Steve enrolled in a CFP® program, began attending FPA meetings, and signed up with Financial Network. "Retirement is when you do what you want, when, where and with whom you want." His niche is dealing with clients that were just like he was approaching or beginning retirement. He provides credibility that was lacking in the corporate environment when he needed a financial planner. "My God!" he exclaims, "I wish I'd found this thirty years ago!"

I have a suggested starting place if you're looking for a niche. There are some incredible resources available through the Society of Certified Senior Advisors[191], and the certification course is filled with important information. In 2000, I earned the CSA designation and while that is not where the emphasis on my practice lays, the education I received has been invaluable. Consider structuring educational seminars on senior issues and taking your show on the road to senior citizen centers.

NETWORKING

The American Heritage Dictionary[192] defines the verb network: "to interact or engage in informal communication with others for mutual assistance or support."

What a wonderful concept, particularly for one just starting out! Think about the benefits you both might derive from a conversation with someone who understood your motivation, related to your marketing concept and may share a mutual need.

---

[191] http://www.society-csa.com/
[192] The American Heritage® Dictionary of the English Language, Fourth Edition Copyright © 2000 by Houghton Mifflin Company. Published by Houghton Mifflin Company. All rights reserved.

Nearly 100% of this book came from, was driven by, or completed through contacts I have made during my career as a financial planner. What contacts I didn't have in place from networking, were introduced to me from associations directly evolved from years of networking within and without the industry.

Long before I became a financial planner, I was a member of the American Business Women's Association[193]. I attended monthly local chapter meetings and was active on the board. The organization was supportive as I made the transition from real estate to financial planning. My first several clients were almost all referrals from members of ABWA. Yet, it was years before a single member of ABWA became a client. Much of the value I add to my practice is the huge referral source I can be for my clients. I frequently refer to ABWA members for services and information. Networking is not a tit-for-tat thing. It is the act of acquiring and nurturing valuable contacts and resources. As your network grows, so does your opportunity to know someone who is able to help, or who can put you in touch with someone who can help, or someone who needs your help, whatever the circumstance.

Network to expand your horizons, and to improve your general knowledge base so you can provide more benefit to existing clients. Be discriminatory. It is said that if you want to soar with eagles, you shouldn't hang around with turkeys. There are eagles in every profession and at every level of society. Find out where they congregate.

You may find yourself networking in different arenas. If you are "niche" marketing among professional bowlers, you'll want to join a bowling league, subscribe to bowling journals, attend bowling conventions, and know where to buy bowling shirts. Eventually you will develop a fine network where you will know someone who introduces you to someone that will add to all you already know about bowling. All those people will know you are a financial planner.

Before long, you will be an expert in all the things that professional bowlers need, where they go, what they spend their money on, how much they save and who holds the accounts. Professional bowlers will recognize you as "one of them" and you will be their source for information on which bowling journals have the best information, where to buy the nicest bowling shirts, and, of course, obtaining excellent financial advice personally tailored for professional bowlers.

One of the organizations to which I belong is the National Association of Estate Planning Councils[194]. I was looking for a place to meet more attorneys, life underwriters and CPAs who understood the intricacies of estate planning. After attending my first meeting, I knew I had found the right source. When I inquired about membership, I was told that the membership consisted of 30% each in the disciplines I sought and 10% of "others", which included trust officers, financial planners, foundation directors, etc. There was a waiting list for the "other" category.

"You need more financial planners," I explained, "to pull the teams together. Financial planners should be right up there with the attorneys, CPAs and life underwriters." I

---

[193] http://www.abwa.org
[194] http://www.naepc.org

petitioned for membership. Ultimately, the Association has changed their bylaws and today financial planners are on equal footing in chapters across the country. Originally, I simply wanted to be around professionals who could enhance my estate planning capability. The attorneys, underwriters and accountants I network with have taken my business to another level. I like being around the eagles. My clients like it too, and enjoy the benefit.

MEDIA

A few years ago, I set as my goal to become "known" to the media. I tried all sorts of things, but by far the easiest was simply signing up on the CFP Board Media Resource[195] list. This benefit is only open to CFP® practitioners, but it's certainly something to strive for.

When I first signed up, I was daunted by the list of over eighty categories. I checked general and relatively safe things, like "retirement" and "financial planning for middle income families". Soon I realized how stupid that was. Everyone else was checking those same things. I started doing "niche" stuff – checking categories that are more esoteric. For instance, when the rules changed and it looked like "529 Plans" would become an important part of college planning, I set out to make myself an expert on them.

The first year I signed up, it wasn't very long before I began getting calls from places I'd never thought of, like "The Tenneessean" with a specific question. I treated the reporter with respect and enthusiasm! Shoot! My name in a newspaper in Tennessee! Yippee!

Early on, I received a call from a free-lance reporter on the east coast. She happened to be doing a story on real property, and how it fit into an investment portfolio of mutual funds. Right up my alley! We hit it off personally, and spent an enjoyable half hour discussing the topic over the phone. A few months later, we had a flurry of calls from people wanting to make an appointment for a free consultation. I had been quoted in Southwest Airline's Spirit Magazine. Southwest flies into Ontario, and people read that magazine!

I responded with a sincere thank you to the reporter, and we have kept in touch. She writes regularly for different publications and quotes me somewhere about once a year. There is absolutely no way on earth to buy this sort of relationship!

After a year or two, the calls started coming from more prominent consumer publications, such as The Los Angeles Times, Money Magazine, Worth and finally, the Wall Street Journal. These days, hardly a week goes by that I don't get at least two or three calls from the media.

Start with your local paper. Introduce yourself to the business editor. Suggest feature articles covering topics in which you have expertise. Remember, readers aren't experts, and they don't want esoteric stuff. They love lists, like "Ten Things to Do with Your Tax Refund" for an April edition, or "Six Steps to a Sexier (or Safer) Portfolio", depending on what the market's up to.

---

[195] http://data.cfp-board.org/pressroom/nd_media_list.asp

Learning to deal with the media is not difficult, but I've learned from seminars and experience some things that work.

1. Prepare a "media" kit for yourself. Have all the pertinent data pertaining to your name, company name, credentials, location, etc. handy.

2. When a reporter calls, ask what the story is about. If it's not a subject you can talk about, admit it right up front. Don't waste their time.

3. If you **can** talk about it, use real examples. Think of a client situation. Embellish if you need to get a point across, but make it interesting. Consumers enjoy reading about realistic situations. Think of neat sound bites or tag lines for a variety of situations.[196]

4. Ask when the reporter's deadline is. If you can call them back, it will give you time to get your thoughts together and come up with something pithy to say.

5. Find out when the article will be published. Watch for it and send the reporter a brief note thanking them for mentioning you, and commenting on something terrific that the reporter has said. Perhaps suggest a follow-up piece or another topic altogether.

6. ALWAYS return a reporter's call! Even if it's just to tell them you're leaving for Tahiti in five minutes. Establish the contact.

7. Start your book of clippings! Don't forget to reference your quotes on your web page and in your public relations folder in your office waiting room.

SEMINARS

There are some wonderful seminar presentations available commercially[197], but if you're starting on a shoestring, call the sales reps from some of the mutual fund companies you work with. Not only do they have great literature, but they are also trained to help you promote their funds. Many major mutual fund families will have reps that will actually prepare and sometimes deliver a seminar for you.

Mutual fund companies have developed some of the best consumer educational materials I've seen. Oppenheimer Funds[198] have some great kits that include 35 mm slides, marketing materials, and workbooks. A I M Funds® [199] have PowerPoint presentations available on many generic topics. Independent advisors can order a CD that includes a complete seminar package.

---

[196] "…keep socking it away." Well, it was ok for the Wall Street Journal, when they asked what should be done with extra money once a debt was paid.
[197] Successful Money Management® Seminars have set the standard in the industry.
[198] http://www.oppenheimerfunds.com → Investor Education will give you an idea of what's available through your Broker/Dealer.
[199] http://www.aimfunds.com/ Used with permission of A I M Management Group, Inc.

Larry Goto, a financial planner in Honolulu, HI invites seniors to a free breakfast seminar at a local restaurant every month, where he discusses tax-advantaged investments or other financial planning topics. "I invite senior citizens or retirees because they are the ones who have the money and the time to see me during the days and not nights," he explains. "I purchase a mailing list of retirees in my area aged 62-80 with income over $25,000, and send out about 2000 fliers for each seminar. Average monthly attendance is about 40. Winners of gift certificates to area eateries are drawn from the evaluation forms I receive at the end of the seminar. All this costs me about $700 per month."

I don't exactly use seminars any more as a marketing tool, but if the purpose is to bring in new clients then the result is the same. One Saturday each quarter I invite clients to a breakfast get-together at a nearby university. We try and vary the program utilizing educational and entertaining topics. My portfolio designer from Boise is always there to give a brief economic overview, and the private money manager we work with, Stan Kiefer, talks about the market. I'll take five minutes to introduce my staff and mention new happenings in the office, and we'll have a 20-30 minute presentation on a topic of general interest — everything from how long to keep old tax returns and other records to the hottest things to do during retirement.

The invitation goes out to every client and center of influence. Postage for the event is incidental, since I would be mailing some sort of contact information to that list every quarter anyway. The university, which lends credibility with an appropriate setting, serves a delicious hot breakfast. We usually accommodate 40-50. The room is always animated and the thing I hate most is having to break in and quiet everyone when it's time to introduce the speakers. The cost is under $500 a quarter, and clients often bring highly qualified guests who later call for an appointment.

There's not a marketing expert out there with half a brain that won't agree client retention is incredibly more valuable than finding new clients. Of course there will be attrition, but if your objective as a financial planner is long-term relationships with existing clients, then you'd better spend time nurturing the clients you have!

Nancy Note: I don't think there is anything I've ever done in marketing to better cement my client relationships than sending my clients post cards.

Yes. I said post cards. Whether I'm attending a conference, convention, seminar, or simply on vacation, if I'm gone more than a few days, I send post cards. Before I leave the office, I print out transparent labels for every client, and bring enough 20¢ (whatever the current rate is) stamps for the labels. Upon arrival, I purchase the requisite number of post cards. They cost a lot less at tourist centers than at the hotel. The first night, while watching TV or just relaxing, I slap on the labels and stamps.

When I have a few minutes during the conference, awaiting the start of a session or quiet time after a meal break, I scribble (usually the same) something on the card and include a personal comment if possible. It might be something like, "Picking up some interesting ideas from a panel selected by Louis Rukeyser at the Morningstar conference here in

Chicago! Look forward to discussing them with you when we get together in June! Hope your mom enjoyed the cruise!"

When we meet in June, more often than not, the opening dialogue from my client is, "How did you like Chicago? We were there in..." Our relationship reaches an entirely new level through this simple, personal contact.

SUMMARY

Never underestimate the importance of marketing!
Include a marketing plan in your business plan
Read everything you can on marketing in a service industry[200]
Think "outside the box" for marketing ideas
Maximize your special talents in marketing efforts
Nurture existing clients for they are your greatest source for referrals

---

[200] Appendix E includes a book list with a section on marketing.

Chapter Seven

From Plotter to Planner in Less Than Five Years

Nancy Langdon Jones, CFP®
NLJones, Inc.
Upland, California

Back in the early eighties, I was a Realtor struggling with my conscience every time a young family with a baby would want to buy a house I felt they couldn't afford. Lenders would squeak their loan applications through with double-digit interest rates and I worried the family would go bankrupt if they had another child or were laid off. On the other hand, if I didn't sell them the house, I couldn't afford to put food on my own table.

When the College for Financial Planning put on a presentation for the Board of Realtors, they got me all excited about the prospects of it being my **job** to tell people whether or not they could afford a house! I signed up on the spot. Half way through the course, I left real estate and began working as a financial planner.

I'll never forget being wined and dined by a large broker/dealer, who promised to send me to New York for training and painted a glamorous picture of my exciting future with the firm! Stars were in my eyes, but I hadn't even made it to my car, when I realized that what he had actually promised was, "If it's Friday and you haven't made your quota, get out there and sell something to someone whether they need it or not, or you're outta' here!"

It was quite a disappointment to learn that most financial planners really got paid by selling stuff. But hey, I got to do the financial planning part on the way to finding out how much money the client had.

Some of my study group went to work for a small, regional independent Broker/Dealer, and I followed suit. I sold mutual funds and limited partnerships to friends, family, and eventually a growing clientele. After a few years, a large, national Broker/Dealer bought out the company I was working for. At the first annual seminar with the new firm, the Chief Compliance Officer gave a wonderful talk. Right up until the close, when he reminded us all to, "get out there and sell…sell…sell!" I thought, NO! I want to plan, plan, plan!

I stuck it out for a few years, but finally went to my manager, John Jackson, and explained that I really just wanted to write financial plans for a fee. He gave me a big hug, said he'd miss me, and wished me success. John's still on my list of all time neat people, and I'll always be grateful for the solid training I received under his tutelage.

The next few years were spent proving people wouldn't pay a financial planner just to write a plan. Why should they? Most Broker/Dealers would give consumers a "free" plan (so they could find out how much money the client had!)

Things have changed.

Today, people entering the financial planning industry have some solid choices and options. Other chapters have dealt with compensation issues, and my personal experiences are terribly outdated, thank goodness! What follows are case histories of financial planners who have made it during the past five years.

Victor Guettlein, CFS
BluePrint Financial Services
Denver, Colorado

In 1993 a friend in the insurance business told Victor, "You should do this!" Victor was earning a modest living as a records manager for a government facility and getting a degree in Finance and Business Administration at the time. "This" was go to work for an insurance company, which he did, after graduating magna cum laud. The first year he matched what he had made as a records manager, but the next year income was down, and cash flow erratic.

"I didn't like the pressure of selling the product du jour," so in January of 1995, Victor opened his own business with about $50,000 in savings, used to pay living expenses while building a revenue base.

Did you have a business plan?

"I should have, but I didn't. I probably could have used it! Ninety percent of the small business owners I work with don't have a formal business plan. Now I have an informal written plan."

What were the biggest obstacles you faced?

"Head trash! You need confidence in your abilities. Even friends can be an obstacle if they don't support you. I make it a point to limit depression to one hour.

"I didn't realize there's a big difference between sales and marketing. Marketing is still a foreign concept to me."

What did you do right?

"Married my wife! She's my cheerleader! And I quit my job while I was still young enough to weather the lean years."

How did you get training? Did you have a mentor?

"The insurance company provided good training while I got my feet wet. You can't just start from scratch. You've got to learn the ropes even if you don't like the material the rope's made out of. "I'm still struggling with getting the CFP®. I'll probably break down and go after it within a year or two. I wish I'd had a good mentor."

How long did it take to start making money?

"The bills were paid and we started to make decent money in the third year. The first two or three years are brutal unless you have sizable capital resources. It's a lot of sweat equity. I drove around seeing clients. Now I have an Executive Office Suite to see clients, and spend 75% of my time at home with administrative stuff. I plan to bring on part time staff to free up time to see more clients."

If you had it to do over again, what would you do differently?

"Marketing! I'd get help. I've changed my name and logo several times. I'd develop a corporate identity concurrent with opening my door if there were a next time!"

Where do you see yourself in five years?

"I'm at a real fork in the road, torn between staying small, with just two or three employees and doing a great job for my clients, or building a "brand name" business. I know I can't compete with Schwab or Merrill Lynch's marketing muscle, but they can't do what I can for my clients!"

What's the best advice you could give someone just starting out?

"If you're in it just for the money – stay out! Make a three-year commitment. Don't let yourself give up after a year – it'll take longer than that to make it work. Read. I read a ton of books."

Jim Williams, CPA, CFP®
J. F. Williams Co., Inc.
Denver, Colorado

Jim's been a CPA since 1978, beginning with a national public accounting firm, and for the eight years prior to becoming a financial planner, he was director of taxes for a NYSE listed utility company with a sizeable organizational staff. He was aware, however, that his career progression was determined primarily by the politics in the organization and that his career progression was almost entirely in the hands of two or three people.

Feeling he was stalled with his current position and wanting to go further, Jim re-hired a career counselor he had worked with in the past. The two worked together to validate Jim's choice of the Financial Advisory field as his new career direction. Then, Jim started putting things in place for an exit plan a couple years before leaving the company. Jim reactivated his CPA license that had been inactive while employed with the utility company. He even thought about starting a CPA practice for all of about 15 minutes, but after 18 years of preparing taxes didn't find it fun anymore.

Though he could have challenged the CFP® exam, Jim enrolled with the College for Financial Planning and took all the courses while still working full time.

Today he heads up J. F. Williams Co., Inc., with the help of one full time administrative assistant (who he could only afford to hire part time after his first two and a half years in business as a fee-only financial planner.

Did you have a business plan?

"Yes! If you don't put a business plan together, you're whistling in the dark! I was wildly optimistic. Thought I could put a financial plan together in two or three hours and gather assets. I go over my business plan every year – both dollars and time."

What were the biggest obstacles you faced?

"There's a big misconception that you can put numbers in a software program and come up in a few minutes with a financial plan!"

What did you do right?

"My business is a reflection of who I am. My values. There's real satisfaction in doing it yourself. Financial Planning is a 'calling' – a manifestation of my own personality and values.

"I started marketing to CPA firms a year and a half before leaving the corporate world. I made contact with CPAs that had clients needing someone to help them on a fee-only basis. It was a good tactical move. Most of my referral sources are CPAs. They're trained to identify situations where there's a conflict of interest, and they understand about working on a fee-only basis."

How did you get training? Did you have a mentor?

"I took all the CFP® courses. I felt an obligation to have a level of expertise. Exposure to the material would benefit my clients. I was strong in tax, but had no insurance background."

How long did it take to start making money?

"Starting a fee-only practice takes at least four years and a working spouse!"

If you had it to do over again, what would you do differently?

"I thought I wanted to get into an established firm. Now I'm glad I started on my own!"

Where do you see yourself in five years?

"I'm not pessimistic about the big firms taking over. They're selling a picture. But small firms will have the relationships and enact that picture. People want to sit down and look their advisor in the eye. It's a trust-based relationship. That's where I'll be."

What's the best advice you could give someone just starting out?

"Look at your motivations. Approach it as a calling. If you're looking at financial planning simply as a way to make money fast, you'll be disappointed.

"But don't overlook the fact you **need** to make a profit! Experience is critical! The CFP® course can't possibly teach you everything you need to know!"

Mike Ling
Berkeley, Inc.
Boise, Idaho
Michael@berkeleyinc.com

Mike joined the Navy right out of high school, so was late getting started in college.

He had no clue "Financial Planning" existed as a profession when Mike graduated with a BA in economics from the University of California at Berkeley. He set off for Boise to make his mark in the world, but was disgusted with the job market in the early 90's. Scrambling to make ends meet and hoping to make contacts that would jump-start his career in economics, Mike took a job marketing for a Berkeley alumni, but soon realized he wanted more control over his own destiny.

His drive and determination, coupled with a strong background in economics, secured him a position with American Express Financial Advisors, where he feels he received excellent training. But he felt from the beginning that he wanted to emphasize the financial planning for his clients, rather than use planning as a loss leader to sell products. In November of 1995, Mike left AMEX and all his clients to start a small fee-only practice of his own.

Did you have a business plan?

"No. I had an idea of what I wanted, but it wasn't written down. I just did anything I could to survive!"

What were the biggest obstacles you faced?

"Credibility."

What did you do right?

"I started to look for organizations where I could become known. First stop was the Cal Berkeley Alumni Association of Idaho. I developed contacts with Estate Planning Attorneys and CPAs. I took them to lunch, and asked them to tell me what they do, and how. I focused on them, and helped them to believe in what I do. There are no reciprocal arrangements. I need competent people to refer my clients to."

How did you get training? Did you have a mentor?

"I've completed the course work for my CFP® through Florida State's program on the Internet. There was truly great training with AMEX, and I was assigned a mentor. But only 3 out of 10 of the people who started with AMEX at the same time I did are still there."

How long did it take to start making money – and how did you survive?

"It took three incredibly long years and a working spouse – who has since divorced me! Rent and software were the biggest expenses. I netted less than $6000 my first year. This is my 5th year in the business and I expect to net nearly $100,000."

If you had it to do over again, what would you do differently?

"Not much. I would have been willing to work as a paraplanner in an independent office – but there's no such thing in Boise."

Where do you see yourself in five years?

"I'll be acquiring a practice in California within that time frame. The deal's already started. I expect my net income to be around $175,000. I'll have a personal assistant (my new spouse), a couple of Paraplanners and a receptionist in both Boise and California. I expect to max out at about 70 clients in Boise and twice that many in California, with a couple of Investment Advisor Representatives already being groomed to become partners.

"I plan to retire at 55 – when I'll probably hire someone to do my investing, so I'm not emotionally involved."

What's the best advice you could give someone just starting out?

"I'm amazed at the number of advisors who really don't know what they're doing! You have to specialize, because you can't do everything. You must know comprehensive planning, but use expertise in other areas where you can't independently evaluate the situation. Build a good professional network! You must like doing things independently. Be confident and work with conviction."

Fall 2002 Update:

"The past year or so have been solid years for my firm and me. While business growth has been a goal, I've also wanted to better balance my personal and professional lives. I've spent more time with my new wife and we play golf regularly. I'm happy to report that my handicap has reached seven. And during the same time, my business has increased by 30%. During bear markets, clients appreciate the extra services provided such as ongoing comprehensive financial planning and ongoing tax planning in their accounts. I have also been involved in establishing a new not-for-profit in Boise that provides training young adults in the food service industry as well as helping to feed the local underprivileged population. It reminds me of the Old Milwaukee beer commercial that concludes by stating, 'It doesn't get any better than this'."

Brian Sells, CFP®, CPA
Peak Financial Advisors, LLC
Denver, Colorado

Right out of college, Brian was hired as a staff auditor for Arthur Andersen, where he remained in the tax division for six years. He entered Arthur Andersen's personal financial training program, and was hooked on financial planning, though he felt the accounting firm wasn't really pursuing an entrée into financial planning. He left in 1995 for a financial planning firm in Cleveland, where he worked with Fortune 500 clients for a couple of years, until his wife became homesick for Denver.

In June of 1997, Brian and an accountant bought half of each other's practice and opened a tax and financial planning partnership in Denver. About the same time, he successfully challenged the CFP® certification exam.

Brian started with two clients from the Cleveland firm, but it only took two years to realize the partners were at odds. The accountant felt Brian wasn't billing enough hours, and Brian thought the accountant wasn't taking the time to build relationships. The 'divorce' was final in 1999 and Brian took on the overhead in a solo practice with a full time assistant.

"Please," pleads Brian. "Just one more year like 1999!" Client assets were up only about 1 ½% in 2000.

Did you have a business plan?

"I certainly did! It's great looking back at the original projections and tracking my progress! It also helped me focus."

What were the biggest obstacles you faced?

"Too much grunt work. You do **everything** yourself when you're first starting on your own! This business is different from tax and accounting. You have to build relationships, not bill hours."

What did you do right?

"I knew enough to be patient. I'm just now getting business from someone I met 3 years ago!

"And I started out allowing myself flexibility. I work more hours than I ever did before, but it's for **me**. I set my own hours, and they include playing golf with clients.

"My CPA background was invaluable! I also joined a Country Club which has helped me make some important contacts."

How did you get training? Did you have a mentor?

"My father, although he is not a financial advisor, is the most brilliant businessman I know. I wouldn't be in business today without his help. Harold Evensky's 'Wealth Management'[201] was immensely helpful as well.

How long did it take to start making money?

"I was lucky. Just after the partnership fell apart, I earned a large account I'd been working on for months.

"My wife, the Director of Communications for The American Institute of Architects, was very supportive, financially and otherwise."

If you had it to do over again, what would you do differently?

"I'd have a book of business before I started!"

Where do you see yourself in five years?

"I expect to have two employees, a paraplanner and an administrator, and just enough clients to keep me busy. I'll only be working with people I like. I have no ambition to make millions, only to be comfortable."

What's the best advice you could give someone just starting out?

"Read! Read everything! If you don't like to read, you're getting into the wrong business. And be careful about picking partners! Get out of the office and meet people. One person you meet will make all the difference in the world to your practice. You just have to find that person."

Barry L. Kohler, JD, CFP®, CLU
NorthStar Retirement Strategies
Portland, Maine
BKohler@bdmp.com

As clients in his law practice began to age, they became more concerned about how the pieces fit together, so Barry set out to find a client-focused financial planner to work with— especially someone who would take a really comprehensive view of his client's situation. What he found in his area were what he calls "one-trick ponies"—advisors who were really trying to sell insurance, mutual funds, or some other "product." He is outspoken in his opinion that, "most planners don't have a clue about their clients' whole picture and woe to the client who falls into the hands of those few who are "highly competent and totally unscrupulous."

---

[201] Evensky, Harold: Wealth Management. Irwin Professional Pub, 1997.

Barry is no ordinary attorney. He actually wanted to **solve** family law problems instead of add to them. Tired of having to work in an adversarial setting and charge in six-minute increments, he went to a vocational counselor. Testing revealed a high degree of autonomy coupled with an interest in people, and financial services popped up.

The founder of NorthStar was used to working with attorneys and approached Barry to help launch the financial planning firm. Barry left his law practice after 22 years to join NorthStar in 1997. In April 2000, he challenged the CFP® certification exam and became the financial planner he couldn't find.

Although both Barry and his partner Barbara Appleby are "recovering" attorneys, they are careful not to practice law and do not draft documents. They work with the client's legal counsel or refer them to competent counsel. "We get so many referrals from lawyers, we'd be foolish to compete with them!" he says.

Did you have a business plan?

"No. But the founder of NorthStar did. He knew exactly what he wanted to do. We've modified the basic plan."

What were the biggest obstacles you faced?

"Wondering how to eat in the meantime! I watched others trying to transition with no outside income. A few 'ran out' of family and neighbors as clients and didn't know (and worse, did not want to learn) how to prospect. Others spent too much time on very detailed planning and were not able to make a living because they could not work in a cost-effective fashion.

"It's still hard to explain what it is we do. We try to help clients reconcile their values with their financial situation. People hunger for this service, but many don't know exactly what it is they hunger for."

What did you do right?

"From the beginning, I was committed to doing the right thing for each client, whether I made money or not."

How did you get training? Did you have a mentor?

"I had a *de facto* mentor (that is, *he* didn't know I thought of him as my mentor.) He taught me that clients typically come with cares and concerns, and rather than tying to impress them with how much you know and how much skill you have in preparing comprehensive plans, what the clients want is a process that will end with their having 'peace of mind.' In other words, they just want to feel better."

How long did it take to start making money?

"As we discovered, the founder's plan had a major flaw. He thought bright, articulate people who care about doing the right thing for their clients would have prospective clients beating down the door. No matter how good the business plan and the practitioner, in my experience it still takes three to five years to build a practice.

"I was fortunate in that I had accounts receivable from my law practice, the founder gave me an advance against future income, and my spouse worked."

If you had it to do over again, what would you do differently?

"Nothing. Well…I might have negotiated a longer safety net; a more gradual transition. But I was fed up with practicing law."

Where do you see yourself in five years?

"One of five or six professional planners in a firm. The original model for NorthStar was traditional: everybody does everything. We're now heading toward substantive specialization, with each planner having expertise in a particular area or areas. Our business is a relationship business. Almost any of the individual "parts" can be outsourced! It is the knowledge and advice we offer that is the key."

What's the best advice you could give someone just starting out?

"If all you want to do is make lots of money, then forget it! Win the lottery and engage in financial planning until it's all gone.

"Coming from another career is a terrific thing to do, but there are no shortcuts— we all have to pay our dues. I think the most effective planners are in their 40s and 50s, with life and family experience."

Fall 2002 Update:

"After our founder left the company in January of 2000, Barbara and I acquired the company. Almost from day one, we had offers coming in 'over the transom' to affiliate, to form a strategic alliance, to sell or be acquired, etc. Almost all were from product vendors seeking yet another distribution outlet.

"Then, in late 2000, we began discussions with the largest independent accounting firm in New England: Berry, Dunn, McNeil & Parker, with 100 CPA's and offices in Maine and New Hampshire. In April 2001, we sold our independent planning firm, and became an affiliated firm, now known as 'BDMP Wealth Management.'

"It has been an interesting time for a couple of former lawyers turned financial advisors to find themselves in the heart of a large regional accounting firm! The acquisition was not without tradeoffs. We now have help with infrastructure costs, which were keeping us from reaching the next level of planning sophistication, and introductions to business owners, professionals, and other high net worth clients. On the other hand, we are a part of a bureaucratic organization with all that implies.

"Our work with clients continues unaffected by our new affiliation: we continue to help them integrate the various aspects of life into a cohesive plan that reflects the values and goals of each client or client family. The accounting firm exerts no influence on how we do business (other than supporting our fundamental view to continue to do what is in the client's best interest, regardless of short term compensation issues). Next step of my personal plan: encourage the firm to open the long-talked about Florida office so I can split my time between Maine and Florida, working with our 'snow bird' clients in the winter and our Maine clients in the summer!"

Jason Gongaware
Chapel Hill Investment Analysts, Inc.
Greensburg, Pennsylvania

Making a comfortable income and at the top of his career as a highly regarded trauma nurse, Jason looked around one day. What he saw were people 20 and 30 years his senior who couldn't wait to leave. Though committed to his challenging work, he realized it was only a matter of time before he, too, would burn out.

That's when, in 1995, he walked away from his burgeoning career and enrolled in the University of Pittsburgh, intent on earning a degree focusing on economics, political science and history. "My wife, and everyone else, thought I had lost my mind," he laughs, "leaving such a high paying job that I truly loved."

He was married to a registered nurse, and their income was great until Jason started school. Frustrated when he couldn't find a financial planner to work with his family, he began to consider the industry for himself. The family scrimped and saved while Jason studied. A short-lived relationship with an insurance company disillusioned him for a brief period. Then in 1998 he went to work for a company that is now Chapel Hill Investment Analysts, Inc. as a service assistant, preparing applications and making appointments.

In 1999 his wife quit working and the couple's first child was born. Today Jason coordinates the investment policy committee for his firm, and it doesn't look like his wife will have to return to work any time soon.

Did you have a business plan?

"No. At first, I didn't realize I was going to be a financial planner. However, once I decided to work in this field I knew that integrity and education were the key to success, so I focused my energy on learning the business, providing objective advice, an becoming an advisor, not a salesperson."

What were the biggest obstacles you faced?

"It was hard to go from being a respected professional in nursing to being an entry-level assistant. Suddenly I was the low man on the totem pole."

What did you do right?

"The effort I put forth let me build something partly my own. In the hospital I was more of a cog in a wheel. Once I decided on financial planning, I went to FPA meetings, took short courses, everything I could to enmesh myself in the business. Now I have a flexible schedule. It's long hours, but I have control."

How did you get training? Did you have a mentor?

"There was a certain amount of training with the insurance company, but it focused on generating commissions. I wanted to be an advisor. I had a good background in economics, but after getting my degree, it was mostly self-taught. I'm a voracious reader! Also, the owner of the company I work for now has been instrumental in my education."

How long did it take to start making money?

"I was lucky in that I didn't have to generate income at first. For the first 2½ years, I was salaried. Now I'm working for a percentage of the firm's profits plus a salary, and I now earn more than I did as a nurse.

If you had it to do over again, what would you do differently?

"I would have skipped the cookie-cutter insurance company training program, and I might have gotten my CFP® while still a trauma nurse with a good income."

Where do you see yourself in five years?

"I expect to help my firm grow substantially while having a larger leadership role in the company. I'm currently enrolled in the CFA[202] program, and expect to have my MBA within six years "

What's the best advice you could give someone just starting out?

"Act as an advisor right from the beginning, not a salesperson. Focus on education, objectivity, and service."

Fall 2002 Update:

"The corporate structure at Chapel Hill Investments changed, and the company was split into smaller divisions, but has maintained its focus on financial planning and asset management. I'm definitely on track to take a more active leadership role, and my title is now Vice President and Portfolio Manager for the Investment Analysts, Inc. division. I still expect to finish the CFA program within the next three years, and follow it with my MBA."

---

[202] Chartered Financial Analyst: Designation given by the Association for Investment Management and Research (AIMR) to those who pass multiple exams in the areas of accounting, economics, money management and security analysis.

Tom Davison, MA, PhD, CFP®
Summit Financial Strategies, Inc.
Columbus, OHIO

Utilizing his Doctorate in Cognitive Psychology, Tom spent 20 years as a technical manager for AT&T before accepting a buy-out offer in 1998. He was ready for a change, though the offer accelerated what he had in mind by six months.

Always interested in the numerical side of things, Tom's awareness of financial planning goes as far back as 1972 when he first started investing on his own, and he has researched the industry for years. To get an idea what the business was like, he read not only trade publications, but also technical journals.

Back in the '80s he had a couple of different firms do a financial plan for him, to see how they approached it. In 1992, after reading John Sestina's book "Fee-only Financial Planning: How to Make it Work for You"[203], Tom did a financial plan for his parents.

While working full time at AT&T, Tom enrolled in the College for Financial Planning's CFP® Certification course and supplemented the home study materials with one day a week classroom study at a local university. At the same time, he wrote in depth notes on a variety of planning topics. These came in handy in demonstrating to potential employers that he was serious and capable. One set of notes dealing with Net Unrealized Appreciation of Employer Stock in Qualified Plans has been published in CCH journals.

In 1998 Tom went to work for Summit Financial Strategies, Inc., and is still incredulous at "how much risk this little firm was willing to take by letting me work with them!"

Did you have a business plan?

"I felt a written business plan was more helpful to a sole practitioner. I always wanted to be in a firm – part of a team."

What were the biggest obstacles you faced?

"Culture shock! Things are done a lot differently at a firm with six people than they were at AT&T where there were 100s of people to interact with everyday. Here we have to take our coffee cups home to wash them! The hardest part for me was getting clear on which business model I'd be comfortable with. I know I'm not cut out to sell products. I'm way too analytical."

What did you do right?

"Preparation. Finding the right fit is much more important than the technical stuff. Making the switch wasn't easy, but I did it with confidence because I knew what the field was like and my goal was clear. All that time and energy I spent going to FPA meetings, reading

---

[203] J.K.Lasser publishes Mr. Sestina's book. Similar material is covered in Sestina's newest book, "Managing to Be Wealthy: Putting Your Financial Plan and Planner to Work for You"

trade journals and talking to others in my classes helped me sort out the business model I wanted."

How did you get training? Did you have a mentor?

"One of the members of the firm took me on as a project."

How long did it take to start making money?

"I started out making one-sixth of what I was making with AT&T. Lucky for me I'm not the primary breadwinner! My wife is an Information Technology Director. I'm not in this business for the money. More than anything else, I'm doing this for amusement. I like it!"

If you had it to do over again, what would you do differently?

"Very little. Information about financial planning is hard to get. For instance, what is a financial plan? The answer's different depending on whom you're talking to."

Where do you see yourself in five years?

"In five years, I'll pretty much be doing what I'm doing now, but I'll be getting really good at it!"

What's the best advice you could give someone just starting out?

"Do everything you can do to find out what it would be like in the final position. Be an intern! Approach it like you would approach moving to another city."

Fall 2002 Update

"Still doing what I was doing before. Haven't gotten really good at being a financial advisor yet, but keep getting better. I feel good about working with clients – that's so rewarding, and what this business is all about. The clients I probably work the best with tend to be corporate folks – that ties to my AT&T experience – and retirees. The team environment at our firm has been wonderful; personally, I can't imagine making as much progress if I were a solo practitioner. I'm blessed to have found such a supportive environment.

"I need variety, and like to have a new 'extra' project every month or two. Volunteering for professional activities is welcomed even from a newcomer – I've reviewed several things for the FPA, written articles for myStockOptions.com and the local press, got little pieces in trade journals and participated in exam question reviews for the CFP Board of Standards. I've done a lot in some particular areas, such as employer stock options, and have been appointed to the Advisory Board of myStockOptions.com. Each thing that comes up is a learning experience, and forces me to continue to develop depth and breadth, as well as a broader set of contacts to turn to. All of these things circle back to the client work. I'd really encourage everybody, especially those of us new to the profession, to try out different ways of participating – it is hard to imagine that you can be helpful until you jump in and work through whatever comes up."

Rich Chambers, CFP®
Investor's Capital Management
Palo Alto, CA
richc@feesonly.com

Though interested in personal finance and helping friends and family make investments for over 30 years, Rich spent his entire career in the technology industry. While working his way up the corporate ladder, he began putting money in real estate. Dealing with tenant problems soon dictated a switch to the stock market for his personal portfolio. Early success with his own investments brought co-workers seeking advice and the realization there were a great number of people who either didn't like to invest or weren't good at it. They needed help.

In 1992, as a software engineering manager at 3Com, Rich enrolled in the CFP® course at the College for Financial Planning, determined to take at least one course per year. In 1998, he began his own company, garnering a few investment clients.

When he passed the comprehensive exam in 1998, Rich left 3Com and spent time with a fee-only financial planning firm as an intern, in order to gain experience. There, over an eight-month period, he learned, "stuff not taught in books!" He also learned he couldn't survive on such a small, erratic income.

To supplement his income, he spent a year with a high tech start up company, and was finally ready to strike out on his own with Investor's Capital Management, the company he had started a few years earlier.

Did you have a business plan?

"Sort of – on the back of an envelope. It was more like knowing my goals: 1. Have my own business (just like my dad.) 2. Help people with financial issues (because I'm good at it.) The revenue goal was easy: I knew I could do better in the future on my own than employed as a software engineer."

What were the biggest obstacles you faced?

"I didn't have a sense of the reality of the business. Compliance, registration, the SEC…it's all scary! There's so much beyond the classroom: producing reports, the practical applications, finding resources, tools, etc."

What did you do right?

"Early on, I began holding workshops on employee stock options. In Silicon Valley, everyone has stock options. You can really hurt yourself with those things!

"I was smart to get my CFP® right off the bat, even though I didn't know what I was doing at the time. It was lucky for me that the CFP® is the designation that came out on top. There was so much to pick from at the time!"

How did you get training? Did you have a mentor?

"I was lucky to have landed an intern job where I could use my technology background to help bring income. Those eight months with a financial planning firm were very instructive. There are two friends I can always ask, who are great resources. Nothing formal, just strong professional relationships."

How long did it take to break even?

"Well, I'm making much less than I did at 3Com, but I expect to break even this year, my third. Within 18 months, I expect to see annual revenues of $150,000. My office is in my home. I hate paying rent, so when we look for a new home, I'll look for one with an office that has an outside entrance. Software, research, and conferences are my highest cost items."

If you had it to do over again, what would you do differently?

"I should have started sooner! I didn't because of the money; waited until I could afford it."

Where do you see yourself in five years?

"I'll have built up a good asset base and have one or two partners. We'll keep administrative staff to a minimum with technology, and will probably hire an intern to service the smaller clients.   Smaller clients need so much help! I'll be spending the majority of my time with a small group of wealthy clients I really know and like."

What's the best advice you could give someone just starting out?

"Get your CFP® and join the FPA to enrich the whole experience. Get a job and start earning the experience requirement as soon as possible."

Fall 2002 Update:

I expect to be profitable this year (finally). We did move to a larger home that has an external building I am using for my office – there's even room for an associate or two. I have an intern now – someone I met at a CFP® retirement class that I teach at UC Santa Cruz Extension.

Working with Allied Professionals has been a big help in attracting new clients. My best contacts have been with a Wealth Management firm, a mortgage loan officer, and a CPA.

More than I had expected, I am concentrating on middle-income clients. Partly because I joined the Garrett Planning Network, Inc and liked the business model and partly because I really enjoy helping people more like me.

Currently there are just over 100 clients and ¾ of them are hourly consulting clients who are self-directed investors. Most of them subscribe to a monthly investment service that I offer to keep their portfolios up-to-date and we meet twice per year. The other ¼ of the clients choose to delegate the investment management to me. For all clients, I charge an hourly fee for financial planning.

The typical new client wants to rationalize their investment portfolio and understand the how's and when's of retirement. I offer a Basic Financial Plan that covers both of those topics. Clients can add on financial planning modules as needed to the Basic Plan, e.g., income property analysis and estate planning.

Cecil Provost
Waddell & Reed
Saratoga Springs, New York

In 1982, Cecil graduated from the State University of New York in Potsdam and went to work for Raytheon as a software engineer, moving on as a system specialist with Digital Equipment Corporation, only to follow his own entrepreneurial spirit and enter the residential real estate field in 1987.

Cecil was named "Rookie of the Year" by his local real estate board in 1988, and commenced purchasing investment property for his own portfolio. Thirteen years later, with a successful career as a Realtor, he became restless and looked forward to a new challenge. Financial Planning seemed logical, since he had always considered himself a Real Estate "Advisor", rather than a salesperson. He thought about business consulting, purchasing different franchises, other businesses. But he kept returning to financial planning.

He talked to a number of large financial planning and insurance firms, researched job fairs, the Internet, Monster.com[204]…and finally decided on a major insurance company trying to reinvent themselves as a financial planning firm, where he received a salary and benefits. But five months after joining, Cecil became very disappointed in the training, micromanagement and captive agent atmosphere, and left for the planning focus, more independent culture and strong management support he found in the local office of Waddell & Reed. He has since obtained his CMFC designation and begun the CFP® course on his own.

Today, although he maintains his Realtor's license to service former real estate clients, he is focused on expanding his financial planning clientele with Waddell & Reed. Cecil and his wife, Sarah, a speech therapist in private practice, hope to start growing their family, as well, within the next year.

Did you have a business plan?

"Absolutely. I'm an entrepreneur at heart, but realize that success is dependent on having a solid plan. I knew how I would build my business, by working my extensive network of former clients and business associates, but first needed the education to service them. I just had to find the right system to support me in my education and growth in this business."

---

[204] http://www.Monster.com

What were the biggest obstacles you faced?

"I'm a classic case of not knowing enough up front about how the business works to know what questions to even ask. I wish I knew 'then' what I know now. I'm still learning! I expect to thrive, not just survive, in anything I do. When I first entered the field, I didn't realize how much more education, mentoring and support I would need to really excel as a financial advisor." I knew how to prospect and service clients, and how to market myself, but in this field there's a huge learning curve of specialized knowledge – investments, insurance, compliance issues, etc. That was my biggest challenge, becoming competent in a very complex new field."

What did you do right?

"I got my Series 7 out of the way first, I tried to find a company focused on planning instead of sales, I developed a comprehensive business plan, and I marketed myself well.

"Well, having owned a business before, the idea of no overhead is one I'm getting used to pretty quickly!"

How did you get training? Did you have a mentor?

"I already know how to manage clients and run a business. But I found quality education, training and mentoring with the manager at my Waddell & Reed office." I also took it on myself to enroll for the CMFC at the College for Financial Planning, completed that in my first 3 months at Waddell, and now am working on my CFP®."

How long did it take to start making money?

"I started off strong in my first couple of months, but once I became frustrated with my first company and decided to make a change my productivity fell off until I made the move and got settled at Waddell & Reed. Now business is going great.

"Since I continue to operate my real estate business, this wasn't a factor for me, only an enhancement. I like someone else to have the overhead!"

If you had it to do over again, what would you do differently?

"First and foremost, I would begin the CFP® program while still working in my previous career. Get the basics so that you can hit the ground running in this field. As far as choosing a place to work, I should have done more thorough research. I was swayed by 'friendships', and didn't make good business decisions. Personal relationships clouded my judgment. I should have explored financial planning sites[205], vault.com[206], and broker/dealer sites."

---

[205] Financial Planning Interactive: http://www.financial-planning.com
[206] http://www.vault.com/

Where do you see yourself in five years?

"I'll expect to stay with Waddell & Reed, but if something changes there I would consider setting up my own practice. I anticipate having at least 400 clients, with several paraplanner/assistants to do the background work. I'll be planning for the employees of organizations, such as medical groups and the Board of Realtors."

What's the best advice you could give someone just starting out?

"Start with what you know. For me it was Realtors. My local Board of Realtors has 2000 members. I do workshops for them, offer planning services at a discount, act as a resource for them, and look for referrals.

"I believe that prospecting and personal marketing are two critical skills for success in this business.

"Find a manager with a good track record of developing first year associates, and one with a well structured training program. You'll need good training."

Fall 2002 Update:

"I set up an independent practice affiliated with Raymond James in February, with offices at a local bank. I love the unlimited variety of solutions that I can offer my clients, and it's nice to have some business come to me through the bank (fewer referrals than I expected, but generally good quality).

"Of course, I'm faced with the additional challenges that come with running your own practice. I've spent a lot of money this year on computer equipment and software, hired a fantastic licensed assistant 20 hours/week doing admin stuff and some plan prep, and may hire a second part-time clerical person after the new year to let Lin focus on paraplanning.

"I'm still working on my CFP®. The plan to take the test in November got pushed back because my wife and I had our first child in October. I'm now shooting for the March exam. I've been teaching quite a few seminars, and am getting published with articles in some local publications. I love the career, feel like I've established a solid foundation, and expect to see my practice really take off in the next couple of years."

Robin Vaccai-Yess, CFP®, President
Center for Financial Wellness, Inc.
Highland, New York
robin@financiallywell.com

Robin was a stockbroker for five years before quitting to have a family, and participate in a variety of odd jobs from her home over the next five years. She worked as a graphic designer, did marketing for other firms, worked on restaurant menus and ran a temporary agency. From 1996 until 1999 she was engaged in the College for Financial Planning's CFP® self study program, simply because the industry excited her.

At 35, she went to work for a small financial planning company with a Broker/Dealer affiliation, and left after a year and a half to establish her own fee-only firm. She opened her doors on January 1, 2001, and feels like a kid in a candy store. "There's nobody around here like me! Every year I get older and my life gets better!"

Did you have a business plan?

"Yes! And I keep looking at it. It's 23 pages long and took me six months to plan. A business plan is extremely important! You must outline what you need to do and what it'll cost to get started!"

What were the biggest obstacles you faced?

"Worry! Fear that I was cutting off my income. I had sleepless nights a full month before and after opening my office!"

What did you do right?

"Because of my business plan, I knew I could do it! Part of the business plan was marketing. I bombarded the local press. There are no fee-only planners within an hour of my office, and that intrigued the press. They wrote about me. My involvement with the press led to a call asking if I would teach a financial planning class in the local school. I got paid, have a new credit on my resume, and I get to meet people! All this within weeks of opening my office!

"I joined the Chamber of Commerce, and teach Personal Finance through Adult Education classes."

How did you get training? Did you have a mentor?

"No mentor. My training was disciplined self-study. I watched how things were done in the firm I was working for. I kept visualizing how I would do it differently. And I read!"

How long did it take to start making money?

"I paid all my bills in the third month from cash flow. I took out a home equity loan to get started, but I'm taking care of all my bills, including the loan payment, from what the business is bringing in already. Next thing is to start paying myself."

If you had it to do over again, what would you do differently?

"Set more cash aside instead of borrowing."

Where do you see yourself in five years?

"I'll be living comfortably in this small town, serving the middle class, helping people who need it get unbiased advice. My clients want financial planning. I'll be managing assets on retainer. And I expect to be netting $100,000."

What's the best advice you could give someone just starting out?

"Write a business plan! Know your market and competition, and know how they are marketing. Read Harry Beckwith's *Selling the Invisible: A Field Guide to Modern Marketing*.[207].

"You have to be a 'Jack of all trades' when you work in financial planning. Having a bunch of credentials and spitting out numbers doesn't cut it. Be a good listener, and good with people. If people feel you're not listening and understanding them, all the facts in the world won't matter."

Fall 2002 Update:

"Yes, I am still in the business. At the end of my 2nd year in fee-only practice, it is finally just getting to be a self-supporting practice. (The surge in cash flow I experienced in March 2001 turned out to be temporary!) If I had to do it all over again, I still would, but I'd be more realistic in how long it would take to turn positive cash flow and I wouldn't spend so much on advertising, but would teach workshops and write articles - both of these have been the biggest source of new clients for me. My advice to anyone starting is to plan on at least two, if not three, years to really see steady cash flow.

If I had to do it all over again, I...

- Wouldn't purchase ProTracker because I've never really used it and I ended up buying ACT! a month ago, which is more than useful for my type of practice, not to mention a hell of a lot cheaper.
- Didn't and still wouldn't purchase Centerpiece. I don't call asset management the main focus of my practice so that would have been more money (and a lot) thrown in the toilet.
- Would establish a niche right away. My first is in divorce planning and now the second is working with non-traditional couples, which is less stressful and more rewarding!
- Would have more cash available up front and would plan on cash flow not being positive until into the second or third year. I was way too optimistic with that!

Jim Skrydlak, CFP®
Independent Contractor
Mountain View, California

Jim's claim to fame is that he was the first man ever to play the banjo in Bishop Auditorium at Stanford Graduate School of Business. That and the fact he wrote his first software program in 1968 while he was a high school senior and most of us didn't even know what software was.

After earning his MBA from Stanford in 1975, he went to work as a financial analyst for the data processing department of a Chicago bank during a bad job market and record cold.

---

[207] Beckwith, Harry: Selling the Invisible, Warner Books, 1997.

Having enough of that, he returned to California and worked as a pricing analyst with various high-tech hardware and software vendors for the next 23 years.

In 1989 he met financial planner Curt Weil while watching the fourth (and, as it turned out, final) World Series game between the Giants and the Athletics on television at the apartment of a mutual friend. They learned they had something in common. Each had donated gallons of blood to the blood bank. Later, Curt would pique Jim's interest in financial planning.

His aptitude for the industry can be seen in Jim's own dealings with money, which has allowed him to enter a new career with no income worries. He was in the habit of saving 35% of his pay every year.

Jim started maintaining financial planning software for Carolyn Bell and the Stanford Investment Group in Mountain View early in 2001, and contracted to develop software for financial plans with his second client, Weil Capital in Palo Alto, the Monday after I interviewed him.

Did you have a business plan?

"No. I've spent my life preparing business plans for new products. In spite of the fact I hate working for big corporations, I always felt I would be an employee, not an entrepreneur, and wouldn't need a business plan for myself."

What were the biggest obstacles you faced?

"I have no resilience. I could never be in sales. If a client were to tell me, 'no', I'd just go away. It seemed to me the financial planning firms were all looking for sales people, not planners. And my own fear, that I wouldn't be able to live my current lifestyle without dipping into my savings."

What did you do right?

"Developed a broad and deep set of skills: math, finance, programming. And I can talk to people! The fact that I can talk to financial planners and translate their need into a computerized tool places me in high demand now in my area. I set out to get the CFP® as soon as I realized I was going to enter the industry. I completed the program while I was working full time and received the designation in 1996."

How did you get training? Did you have a mentor?

"Curt Weil. We're sort of 'blood' brothers."

How long did it take to start making money?

"I'm astonished at the demand for people like me – more and better geeks! I'm not doing this for the money, but firms are willing to pay for what I have to offer. My savings are a safety net."

If you had it to do over again, what would you do differently?

"Maybe I should have jumped in a little earlier. But I didn't realize at first how to position myself. When it dawned on me that I should be using my computer and quantitative skills rather than more generalized financial planning skills, it became clear that I could go out on my own."

Where do you see yourself in five years?

"Semi-retired somewhere in Iowa. I'll be doing financial planning and teaching accounting part time."

What's the best advice you could give someone just starting out?

"Know what you do well. Remember it's increasingly important to bring computers in to do things that haven't been done before. Be computer savvy and know how to develop your own tools."

Fall 2002 Update:

"No big changes. Curt Weil has sort of re-organized his business to be, as far as I can tell, more of a money-management business, so he didn't have any more work for me. I'm now positioning myself as a software developer with financial skills, rather than a financial planner with software skills, but that's just a matter of which skills I emphasize. I continue on track for retirement in rural Iowa in the second half of 2004."

Joseph J Ponzio, President and CEO
Meridian Financial Management
mfmcorp@attbi.com

Did you have a business plan?

"Yes. This was, without a doubt, one of the most difficult and crucial steps in the creation of my firm. It helped me, and continues to help me, identify my "ideal" client, my surrounding competition, my professional and financial goals, and my strengths and weaknesses as a business owner."

What were the biggest obstacles you faced?

"The absolute biggest obstacle was an internal one. Namely, "Am I ready to venture on my own and be an advisor, a CEO, a CFO, a marketer, a portfolio manager, a compliance officer, etc., and still be a good husband, son, and friend to those I care about?" Once I had decided that the answer to this question was an emphatic "yes," I came across my second greatest obstacle – convincing my family that I was ready. The third great obstacle was, and still is, managing my time to allow for all of this responsibility and work, and still find clients and service clients the way that they need to be serviced."

What did you do right?

"For lack of a better description, I lined my ducks up before I knocked them down. I made sure that I did intense research on my market, my competition, and the required rules and regulations. I created a business plan and I stick to it. I consulted with at least eight other advisors across the country, as well as clients of fee-only advisors, to get a clear understanding of the business and expectations on both sides of the fence. I relied heavily, but not solely, on the FPi web boards for information and advice. I ensured that my family and friends were supportive. I have read, and continue to read, everything and anything remotely related to the industry and my practice."

How did you get training? Did you have a mentor?

"After college, I went to work for a well-known insurance agency. I had no knowledge of insurance and felt I needed the training before I could ever advise on the subject. Also, I felt it was important to know what insurance agents would be telling my future clients. When I felt comfortable, I left the agency and became a stockbroker at a large national firm. Because of my passion for investments and portfolio management, I learned very little from my firm in comparison to my self-study. I did have a mentor at both firms, but learned the most through my professional associations with attorneys, CPAs, and CFP®s, and through my own research. It was probably a longer process than most people can afford, but it was the method with which I felt most comfortable."

How long did it take to start making money?

"Because of my home office and low overhead, and the fact that I am an aggressive cost-cutter, I was able to turn a profit in five weeks. So as not to inflate others expectations, this is extremely rare. However, I am not, by any means, drawing a large salary at this point. The profits that the firm has made up to now have been rolled into set-up and training for the two CFP®s that I have on staff to date. As of today, we have been accepting clients for just over three months, and I expect to be drawing a comfortable salary, according to my needs, at the six-month anniversary."

If you had it to do over again, what would you do differently?

"The only thing that I would change would be to go back to day one and set a time at which I stop working. Though there are days that I finish by 3:30 pm and relax the rest of the evening, I find myself more often than not working until 10 pm or 11 pm, breaking only for dinner and coffee with my wife. Also, I work every Saturday and many Sundays. Because I had not set a "quitting time," I have created a workaholic routine. Luckily, it is one that I can, and plan to, change in the near future."

Where do you see yourself in five years?

"I see a physical office apart from my home office that houses me, four to five CFP®s, two secretaries, a paraplanner/intern, and a part-time technology/compliance consultant. I expect one or two of these on staff to have earned ownership in the firm. I will no longer be accepting clients, as I will balance my limited number of clients and the business itself. The firm will have large community presence, through both active involvement and charitable gifting. What I foresee are great things for my firm, my employees, and the clients. When I have achieved this, I will be a success. As a side note, my business plan extends well beyond five years, looking forward to my retirement and exit strategy, which is decades away."

What's the best advice you could give someone just starting out?

"Decide, and be honest about, what it is that you hope to achieve throughout your career as a financial planner. Many people try, and fail because they are focused on the "unlimited income potential" and the successful planners they meet. Create a business plan and stick to it. Identify a target client and work your business around him or her – the money will come regardless of whether they are high net-worth or not. Whatever you do, do it in your client's best interest, even in the beginning when you are struggling. Every person you help, even if you are not compensated monetarily, will repay you ten-fold in referrals and advertising. Determine what it is that you love to do and become a specialist. Finally, talk to other planners. I have found that they are extremely receptive to strangers calling and asking questions. I did it and still do it. If you would like additional information, feel free to contact me as well."

Angie Herbers
The Garrett Planning Network
Shawnee, Kansas

Did you have a business plan?

"In college, my most dreaded class assignment was writing a Business/Career Plan. At the time, I felt that I had no direction and I was more comfortable just taking it day-by-day and waiting to see where the wind blew me. As it turns out, once I began to write my Career Plan, I knew exactly where I wanted to go. In addition, I found out that some of the things that I was doing were NOT taking me there."

What were the biggest obstacles you faced?

"I am what the industry calls a 'newby' planner as apposed to a 'career changer'. The only obstacles were getting through school and finding the job I wanted."

What did you do right?

"My first interest in financial planning was inspired by a nationwide, collegiate competition hosted by American Express Financial Advisors. In April of 2000, I was one of a team of three selected to participate in the First Annual Collegiate Financial Planning Invitational, which required me to be enrolled in a CFP®-Registered program. An accounting major at the time, I enrolled in the CFP® program and our team went to New York City and won the national title. As a result, our team, Kansas State University's CFP® program and other participates were featured in major industry publications. After that, I dropped my accounting degree and dove head first into financial planning."

How did you get training? Did you have a mentor?

"I had both an internship and a mentor. Following the American Express competition, I received a student scholarship to attend the National Association of Personal Financial Advisors (NAPFA) annual conference. Networking at this conference turned out to pave my career path in financial planning. This is where I meet Wayne Cassaday of Covenant Financial, a fee-only financial planning firm in Charleston, South Carolina, who provided me with an incredible internship experience. This is also where I met my mentor and current employer, Sheryl Garrett."

How long did it take to start making money?

"In May of 2001, I earned my Bachelor of Science degree in Personal Financial Planning from Kansas State University and joined Sheryl as a salaried employee, dividing my time between being a staff planner in her small, independent financial planning firm, Garrett Financial Planning, Inc., and providing member support in The Garrett Planning Network, Inc."

If you it to do over again, what would you do differently?

"Without a doubt, I would have taken the CFP® comprehensive exam the first available date after graduation! The greatest benefit to graduating from a CFP®-registered program is fulfilling the educational requirement to take the CFP® exam. Now that I am deep into my career, I have a hard time dedicating myself to study."

What's the best advice you could give someone just starting out?

"There are three pieces of advice that I would give to someone who is just staring out in the financial planning industry – whether you are starting your own business or seeking a job in a planning firm:

1. Learn to market yourself effectively.
2. Develop a Long-Term Business Plan or Career Plan.
3. Accept the TRUTH: Develop a realistic inventory of your strengths and weaknesses."

Where do you see yourself in five years?

"I plan to just keep learning and gaining experience in the financial planning industry. I believe that my youth is my most valuable asset because I have the time to grow with a dynamic industry. As consumers become more aware of the benefits of financial planning, I believe career opportunities in financial planning will expand. All this leaves the doors completely opened for exploration, and *that* is really exciting!"

Summary

How should the novice financial planner approach the business? According to those I interviewed, there is a definite pattern. Below is a summary of the advice they impart:

Did you have a business plan?

Most planners who didn't have a business plan wish they had!

What were the biggest obstacles you faced?

Misconceptions about what the financial planning career encompasses, and fear of the unknown, especially of not being able to support oneself in the transition.

What did you do right?

Patience, preparation, commitment. Knowing what it is you want to do, as well as who your initial market is!

How did you get training? Did you have a mentor?

Self-confidence, discipline and early attainment of the CFP® course work, coupled with strong industry relationships. Join the FPA and network.

How long did it take to start making money?

Three to five years. Having an income source in the meantime helps!

If you had it to do over again, what would you do differently?

Research the industry. Set aside capital. Get started while current income is available.

Where do you see yourself in five years?

Most planners want to continue on their chosen path, with established relationships and more definition.

What's the best advice you could give someone just starting out?

Get the CFP® designation. Prepare a business plan.[208] Be confident with goals. Read! Begin marketing with resources you know and do well.

One Person's Path to the FP Holy Grail

What follows is a bonus from someone currently in transition, who has asked to remain anonymous:

I am in my middle years and have a successful career now, but I find myself strongly drawn to the field of Financial Planning, and I believe after I come up to speed I can really help

---

[208] MS Office has a business plan template. Business Plan Pro software by Palo Alto is an easy to use program. View a demo plan at http://www.paloalto.com/ps/bp/

people and make a contribution to society in this field. Like many others, I plan to start on a part time basis.

First Step: I enrolled in the CFP® course offered by the College for Financial Planning[209]. I have completed the first of 5 modules successfully (General Financial Planning, Risk Mgmt and Insurance), and am part way through the second (Investing & Asset Management). The other 3 modules are Income Tax Planning, Estate Planning and Retirement Planning. Each module takes up to 4 months to complete, although you could easily do it quicker if you were willing/able to put in the time. Excellent program - I highly recommend it. I may also take their Chartered Mutual Fund Counselor course, partly to be able to use their CMFC designation, but also because I will be doing a lot with mutual funds in my planning work.

Second Step: Took the Series 65 Exam because it is required to be registered with the State of Maryland. Anyone who holds himself out as a financial planner in MD must be registered with either the SEC or the state. But the SEC won't let you register without having at least $25M of assets under management. I want to register now so that I can legitimately set up a financial planning business and start gaining hours toward my CFP® experience requirement. Also, there is the psychological aspect that I will take the whole program more seriously and get more out of it if I begin to practice while I am studying.

My current Financial Planning Career Goal: I want to be independent, not work for a broker-dealer or a large company. I want to be a fee-only planner, at least to begin with. I want to work first primarily with young singles and families, and eventually with middle class older families and those close to or in retirement. I'm not currently interested in working with "high net-worth clients" (nor do I expect they would be interested in working with me.)

Problem: Who would hire a rank beginner like myself?

Solution: I'll begin working with friends and family. I have several adult children for whom I will be doing a financial plan, and a couple of close friends. All this meshes with my career goals. I will charge very modest fees -- not primarily for the money, but for the experience. (Added benefit: Hopefully my kids won't sue me when I foul up.)

As I gain more confidence & knowledge, I will gradually begin to market myself to others. Many planners don't seem to be interested in the middle class, since they aren't willing/able to pay very much. So there is a need I think I can satisfy. (Needless to say, I'm not getting into this primarily for the money.)

Once I complete the CFP® course, in about 18 months or so, I will consider leaving my current job if I can afford to. I will be eligible for early retirement, and have a growing 401K, which may be enough. Otherwise I will keep on doing the financial planning work part time. I will also consider, however, going to work for a planning firm for a couple of years at that time to get jump-started and get the CFP® experience requirement out of the way more quickly than I could do it part time. I will make the decision on which route to take after I complete the CFP® course.

---

[209] College for Financial Planning offers the courses leading to the CFP® Certification Exam at http://www.fp.edu.

I have also subscribed to Financial Planning[210] magazine, and I plan to join the FPA[211] this year. I find Financial Planning to be an excellent publication, and I think this publication plus membership in the FPA will be invaluable in learning first-hand how experienced planners think and what they do. I bought -- and highly recommend -- Katherine Vessenes' book *Protecting Your Practice* [212] along with her diskette of forms, letters, contracts, etc. Katherine's book is an excellent introduction to many of the legal/compliance issues as well as having many helpful tips on keeping clients happy. Two other books that I have found very helpful in getting oriented and learning how to think like a Planner are *The Excellent Investment Advisor* [213] by Nick Murray, and *Best Practices for Financial Advisors* [214] by Mary Rowland.

Next step: file Form ADV with the Office of the Attorney General, Securities Division, State of Maryland, to register with the state[215].

Next step + 1: set up shop -- probably as a sole proprietorship; figure out how to set up record-keeping and accounting, etc., all on a shoestring budget. I will freely admit the thought of registering is a mite scary -- once I register, I am then bound to comply with all of the record-keeping and other compliance requirements, even if my clients ARE friends and family. Being a born do-it-yourselfer and an engineer, I'll probably try to do this with a minimum of legal and accounting assistance -- just enough to keep myself out of trouble.

Warning -- all of this costs money (not to mention time): $2295 for the CFP® course in digital format, including print curriculum, $350 for the comprehensive review exam course, $595 for the Certification Exam (plus transportation, food and lodging if required), $65 for the Series 65 Study Guide, $85 for the Series 65 exam, $300/year to register with the state of MD, $59/year for the FP magazine subscription, $100 for Katherine's book & diskette, $275 to join the FPA (student rate, for students enrolled in the CFP® course, $95,) $$ for computer, $$ for home accounting software, $$ for home office setup, etc., etc.

Bottom line: all this is a big investment in both time & money. If you're serious, I think it is well worth it. If you're not willing to make these kinds of investments, in my opinion you're not serious enough to succeed.[216]

Digression on financial planning software search: After evaluating six or seven software packages, I have decided to start without one. I think it's best to develop my own style first. So I'm going to create my own questionnaire, and use spreadsheets for the calculations. Eventually I may revert to a commercial financial planning software package if I find one that fits my style (and that I can afford.)

---

[210] Financial Planning Magazine is a Thompson Financial publication and a trial copy can be ordered through http://www.financial-planning.com/subscribe.html

[211] Information about the Financial Planning Association can be found at http://www.fpanet.org.

[212] Vessenes, Katherine, "Protecting Your Practice", Bloomberg Press, 1997.

[213] "The Excellent Investment Advisor" by Nick Murray, The Nick Murray Company, Inc., 1996.

[214] "Best Practices for Financial Advisors" by Mary Rowland, Bloomberg Press, 1997.

[215] Information on the process of State Registration can be located at http://www.nasaa.org. Most states have registration forms and instructions available for downloading.

[216] Prices current as of 11/30/2002

Well, that's my plan, for what it's worth. I don't recommend it for everyone. Perhaps you young'uns out there may want to take a different path -- get yourself hired by a small firm that operates in a style you're comfortable with, get them to pay for some of the training, courses, etc., and get the experience requirement out of the way quickly. But I hope some of my thoughts will be useful to some of you.

Chapter Eight

Get a Life!

Financial planning may well be the world's most rewarding career. Where else can helping others realize their hopes and dreams bring not only personal satisfaction, but also your own financial freedom? I have never heard of a retired financial planner. Most planners tell me they will never retire. They love their profession and intend to keep on doing it for the rest of their lives.

Colin Benjamin Coombs was an inspiration to me when I was starting out. Ben built an incredibly successful practice and his clients adore him. At a time when other people his age consider retirement, Ben simply moved his office to Three Rivers, California, got out his fishing pole, and began conducting review meetings with clients out on beautiful Klamath Lake. The guest room is always ready and the food's great. After a day or two, everyone is up to speed and the next client arrives to kick back and talk with Ben.

I'll be the first to admit experiencing serious problems in my life when it comes to balance. Quite literally, because I love doing what I do so much, nearly everything is wrapped up in my business. My hope, with this chapter, is to remind people entering the profession to do some planning with their own lives right from the beginning, so they're not consumed by their work as I, and countless other planners, tend to be. Don't wait until it's too late to remember that you have a family, a hobby, and a life after five o'clock.

The Roger Reaction

This was brought home to me in spades during the FPA Master's Retreat in 2001. Early in my career as a financial planner, I attended a conference session on asset allocation given by Roger Gibson. His ideas seemed, to me, pretty esoteric. Observing Mr. Gibson in his suit and tie, academic to the core, showing hieroglyphics on an overhead, I somehow knew this was an important presentation, but frankly, I was bored. My perception of the man was that of someone so wrapped up in numbers and scientific research that I wondered how on earth he could ever have any fun.

Fast-forward fifteen years or so, and perched on a stool before me sat a highly regarded author, whose work explained one of the most valuable analytic concepts in the financial planning world. That day in 2001, he was just a relaxed guy, in an open sport shirt and Levi's, casually telling an intimate audience about a turning point for him, and giving us each a powerful lesson in life.

In the mid-1980's, Roger Gibson had finally achieved a modicum of success in an independent financial planning firm that was proud of his concentrated effort in developing an asset allocation model. The talk I heard so long ago was his first foray into the speaker's arena and he was feeling pretty good about it. So good, in fact, that he had planned a few

days after the conference to spend time with his wife in celebration of their achievements —
two children, a respected position with his firm, a decent income at last, a little savings. He
actually purchased a ring for his wife, unaffordable before, to commemorate the occasion.
Her response: "I want a divorce."

Suddenly everything was gone. Focus on his career was instantly changed to a desperate
struggle for custody of his son and daughter. Eventually he was granted 50% custody. He
joked about being, "half dad and half bachelor, not such a bad thing!" But the battle he
won had been an enormous setback, and the life he had anticipated and planned for, was
permanently shattered.

Shaking himself loose from the remnants of his previous existence, Gibson took the lemons
he 'd been handed, and made the proverbial lemonade for his kids and himself. In an effort
to establish a healthy environment for his children, he reduced his client load from 65 to six,
left the firm he was working for, created a home office and, simply as a way to stay home
with his children and keep food on the table, began writing what was to become a
cornerstone for every serious financial planner's repertoire.

Now there was time. Time to consider stuff there'd never been time for in the past. Gibson
picked up a clarinet for the first time in years and joined a local band. Never mistaken for
Charles Atlas in his prior life, he took his son for Tae Kwon Do lessons, and today he and
his son each hold a black belt. Fireworks are fun, so Gibson pursued a childhood dream and
now he's a licensed pyrotechnics expert, or whoever it is that lights the match setting off
those spectacular 4th of July shows. That quiet academic I saw giving his first public seminar
is flying high. Really! He even earned his pilot's license, another forgotten childhood dream
brought to life, in his spare time.

It may have been an unexpected and unwanted turn of events that prompted it, but today,
Roger Gibson has a life! You need one too. Don't wait until you get kicked in the ass by an
unfortunate event. Take a holistic approach with your future, just as you'd do with a client.
Build in the fun times, right from the get go!

Many of your clients, particularly during the first few years, are likely to come from friends
you meet with socially, during family get togethers, or while engaging in your favorite hobby
or pastime -- if not the exact people you're associating with, then often from their referrals.
Be careful not to neglect current activities and relationships because they're not obvious
sources of business for you. I belonged to the American Business Women's Association for
more than a year before getting my first referral from a member. After the first one,
referrals came frequently. Early on, at least 50% of my business was from ABWA referrals,
yet not one single ABWA member was a client.

On the other end of the spectrum, however, far too many planners are caught up in the lives
of their clients and what's going on in the industry, to the detriment of their own family and
future. Precisely because it is so personally rewarding (and often, fun), financial planning
work has a tendency to become addictive. There is certainly nothing wrong with having
passion for the work you do, but it's important not to let your work become an addiction.
Here are some suggestions to help keep your life on an even keel.

Get a Calendar

One sure-fire way to schedule time for yourself is to simply put it on your calendar. For the past ten years, I've spent the first Tuesday of every month in absolute ecstasy. It began when I won a free session with a massage therapist. Thinking a massage was a sort of kinky thing to do, I initially ignored the prize.

Eventually I was coerced into making an appointment. I still remember lying half naked and stiff as a board while Debbie spread oil over me and tried to get me to relax. Once she was finished, I couldn't wait for my next appointment! Everyone who knows me, including clients, friends and associates, is aware I never, ever see anyone but Debbie on the month's first Tuesday. I'm such a fanatic about it, if you looked on my calendar you'd see Debbie already scheduled on the first Tuesday for the next ten years!

Franklin Covey Co. has built an empire, combining time management with the Seven Habits concept. Stephen Covey's seventh habit is taking time to "sharpen the saw." In *The Seven Habits of Highly Effective People* [217] he tells the story of the woodsman who appeared exhausted after spending five hours sawing. When asked why he didn't take a break and sharpen his saw so things would go faster, he emphatically answered that he was too busy sawing!

I suggest programming regular saw-sharpening times in your calendar. With the terrific assortment of electronic schedulers, personal data management devices, web sites that coordinate with personal organizers and paper planners, there is no excuse for not making the time for fun and balance in your life!

Local chapters of the Financial Planning Association meet monthly for breakfast or lunch in most areas. Schedule the meetings on your calendar for the next year or two. Block out the times you'll be on vacation, well in advance, even if it's just a couple days away from the office. Make plans to attend national conferences and conventions where you can share ideas with your colleagues. Combine vacation time with your family around out of state industry events by adding a week or two for leisure. Put the kids' recitals and sports events down, and the PTA meetings.

After pre-arranged meetings, massages, vacations and conferences, I block out afternoons or even whole days every week without appointments to play catch up, or just to reflect. One evening a week and one Saturday a month, I save for clients who can't make it into the office during normal business hours. This alleviates the guilt from taking a day off during the week! If someone asks to see me on the first Tuesday, I simply whip out my planner and say, "Sorry! I'm booked!" No need to explain that I'm booked on a table where Debbie will pour warm oil over my poor aching shoulders and work her magic.

---

[217] Covey, Stephen R., The Seven Habits of Highly Effective People (Simon & Schuster, 1989)

Get a Financial Planner

Yes, I know. You **are** a financial planner. Have you heard of the cobbler's family who ran around barefoot? A surprising number of financial planners are living examples of that analogy and forget to take time to set goals and objectives for themselves and their families. In their zeal to improve the lives of their clients, planners often neglect their own investment portfolio, become too emotionally involved to make prudent financing decisions, or forget to update their own wills and trusts. As you begin your new career, walk carefully around this career trap. Interview some planners. See what it feels like to sit on the other side of the desk and talk about how you spend money and what your plans are for the rest of your life. You will be glad you did!

Brent J. Beverly, CFP® and Christian Li, CFP®, both with The Advisory Group in Diamond Bar, California are financial planners for each other. Brent has been a financial planner since retiring from the U. S. Marine Corp. Reserves in 1984. Recently he fell in love with an expensive new car, but before committing to the purchase, he consulted with Christian, to make sure he wasn't sabotaging his goals.

Christian, bit by the financial planning bug in 1985, just six months after graduating from college, went right to the basics. The two sat down and discussed cash flow and assets, setting aside the emotional aspects long enough to determine how the car could best be acquired.

Mike Ling, my portfolio designer and owner of Berkeley, Inc., an investment advisory and financial planning firm in Boise, Idaho, only works with clients he likes. I guess he likes me, because when I asked him to be my financial planner he agreed. Even after he told me he wants his clients to be comfortable and excited about coming to see him, I was anything but comfortable during our first few meetings. That's how I discovered how incredibly difficult it is to bare your financial soul to someone, even if he likes you! This awareness is as important, in my opinion, as knowledge of the technical aspects of estate planning.

To get my own financial plan, I had to fill out a lengthy questionnaire and face some tough questions. Believe me when I tell you the questions are easier to ask than answer. Of course I zeroed in on retirement, and it didn't take Mike long to learn things about me that I didn't even know myself. I realized that my idea of retirement is pretty much doing the fun part of what I'm already doing. It would be nice, I told him, if I could spend more time meeting with my clients and traveling. I mentioned what fun I had working with the financial planning discussion boards on the Internet, helping would-be planners get started, and how one day I'd like to write a book, something I'd never really thought about until he got me focused.

For some reason, it seems to me I'm spending a lot of time traveling recently, and enjoying being with my clients. You're reading the book. Occasionally I wonder if I wouldn't still be caught up in the rat race if Mike hadn't insisted on getting me to focus on what my successful future would look like. I hope my clients are half as pleased with what I do for them, as I am with the way Mike has freed me so I can stop worrying and start thinking about what really matters.

Get a Grip

I'm very fortunate to know, personally and in many cases intimately, some of the most successful members of America's top-rated career. Let me share with you a few of their words of balancing advice.

"For the past four or five years, I've been sneaking off to a little three bedroom house called the Lindley Institute for Conflict Resolution on the ocean front at Rincon Point," confesses J. Michael Fay, CFP® of the Claremont Financial Group in Claremont, California. Mike's daughter discovered the retreat while studying at the University of California at Santa Barbara and working part time for her father. She suggested the office staff spend a weekend there, doing some strategic planning.

These days Mike won't allow himself to take work with him on visits to the Institute. Sometimes he goes alone, other times with his wife and daughter. But when he's there, he's reading spiritual books, cooking vegetarian meals or just lazily wandering the deserted beach. "I try and break away for two or three days every quarter. It's a stress reducer...a centering experience," he says.

One of the busiest planners I know is former Co-Chair of the Financial Planning Association, Elissa Buie, CFP®, from Falls Church, Virginia. "I don't go to the office on Fridays but, rather, sit on my deck or take a drive or do something else," she explains. "It gives me the space to think big thoughts, dream big dreams, think about my clients and my staff in terms of what is important in their lives and to just be. I am much more productive on the days I am in the office for having had this time and space to focus on the spirit of life."

"I go off to a wildlife refuge in the Oregon high desert with 5 or 6 women friends for a week each spring," says Laurie McClain with Socially Responsive Investing in Eugene, Oregon. "We stay in an old double wide trailer, cook lots of good food, and get up early each morning to go birding. Sometimes we're organized enough to use the local park naturalist as a tour guide. We also sleep, gossip, hike, meditate and do yoga. I get nice womanly energy, good exercise, Zen practice in sitting still and watching birds, mammals and scenery, and a very spiritual connection to the universe."

"I ~ laugh!" admits Gayle Coleman, with Coleman Knight Advisory Group in Carlisle, Massachusetts. "I am most relaxed and full of Aloha when I am laughing, happy and smiling.

"I consciously and intentionally think about my happiness (and those around me) and how to maintain it in this sometimes chaotic/frenetic world," she continues. "I relieve stress by simple practices of breathing, finding clarity in the situation and trying to find the humor. If I can laugh, I know I have succeeded in processing 'the stress'. Life is just not as serious as most of us make it out to be. Though these words may seem rather feeble, my father used to say: 'Gayle, you're not going to fall off the face of the earth.' And, I haven't.

"Laughter is part of who I am and luckily it takes me to a less stressful place. Knowing my clients need help finding ease and peace of mind, if I can't walk my talk as I practice financial planning, it is pretty hard for me to be counseling and advising others."

Once a month, Patti and I get together. She's not a social acquaintance, nor a professional colleague. I only see her once a month, when we have breakfast together. I wouldn't miss that breakfast any more than I'd miss my appointment with Debbie, or Christmas! I hand-picked Patti, from a number of candidates, to be the person to whom I'm accountable. She's the sort of person I can count on to tell me I look like the dickens in that dress I paid too much for.

When we first decided upon this alliance, we agreed to be ruthless. We promised to listen to each other, and that we wouldn't hold back when we felt too depressed, or ashamed, or embarrassed, to tell anyone else. I can tell Patti how excited I am that I made a difference in someone's life…and how frustrated I am that a favorite client decided to move her account to a different planner. She pats me on the back, reprimands me like a Dutch uncle, and patiently lets me get it all out. Of course, I don't tell her names or specifics, but it's terribly important that she's there for me, and it's rewarding for me to be there for her. Everyone needs a Patti. She is intelligent, nonjudgmental, and trustworthy -- and she demands those qualities in me.

Get a Hobby

"What puts me back together is writing. I write fiction," says Bev Chapman, CFP®, who's been a planner since 1994 and has a fee-only practice, Values: Financial Counseling and Education, in Newton, Massachusetts. "Just give me a little time alone to write fiction, and the nectar of the gods' flows in my veins. That and being in nature, in one way or another. I love to walk, bike, kayak, canoe and hike. As long as it's in pristine beauty or rugged beauty or pastoral beauty, I'm one happy woman. Bubbling over, actually!"

Tony Shostak, in Woodbury, Minnesota, reads. He reads Harry Potter, when he's not walking the dog, playing tennis, or out on a month long jaunt in his RV. "I also work with clients about four hours a day on the phone from my home office, and continue to do that on our travels," he says. "I'm semi-retired and love it! Relaxing is so good, I almost feel guilty about it." Tony actively helps his clients get to where he is now. "Learning and education are the main drivers in life," he feels, so he has organized men's retirement groups that delve into all aspects of aging. "I did it to learn what's up ahead," he says. "It's different when you actually make it! Balance is always a challenge."

"My passion is photography," insists my new friend Naguib Kerba, CFP® who hails from Mississauga, Ontario Canada. "It seems that my camera is always the first item packed if I'm going anywhere. No subject is too boring, but I do have my favourites – I love exploring anywhere I go AT SUNRISE. Maybe I'm looking at life as – '**You wake up and the rest of the day is a bonus.**' There is a certain sense of renewal and being at one with the world. There's nothing like the peace of being out on a northern lake in a canoe when the only sounds you hear are the droplets of water falling from your paddle as they hit the glass like surface of the lake. My heart's core is to capture that on film AND SHARE IT, maybe even publish a book someday."

"Eating is my hobby, my passion," admits Rick Kahler, CFP®, who has the distinction of being South Dakota's first CERTIFIED FINANCIAL PLANNER™ practitioner. "Dining is an event; something that has long been celebrated by the European culture and never embraced by us Americans. I can think of nothing nicer than enjoying an excellent meal with great friends that lasts for hours.

"It was my passion for food that caused me to start a restaurant guide, which rates our local cateries," he continues. "Because of my high profile in the community, I published the guide anonymously. Following our first two publications, we moved the guide to the web. After a hard day's work helping my clients plan their financial futures, there is nothing more rewarding than retreating to one of our finer restaurants...and then writing it up in the guide!

"I also enjoy wine collecting." Rick claims he was a teetotaler, "until I met my wife, who introduced me to the finer things in life. Since then, I have become a compulsive wine investor. I began the day I discovered that some of the 1990 and 1991 Silver Oaks that I had purchased had tripled in value. Being a value investor, there is no way I could drink a bottle of wine that had a Parker rating of 91 and was selling for $95! Instead, I sold them at an Internet auction, and purchased some French wine rated 92 by Parker for $15 a bottle. I have traveled that road ever since, investing in the cult wines, selling them when they triple in value, and buying equivalent wine for a fraction of the price!"

Get Exercise

One day a week, I don't go into the office until noon. The morning is spent at the gym with my personal trainer, David. When I embarked upon a fitness program in 1998, I decided to do it right, and hire someone to show me the ropes. David's a real slave driver, and I don't dare not work out the rest of the week, because David has a way of knowing if I've sloughed off! I'll have to confess, I sometimes read trade journals while I'm on the treadmill, but the rest of the time I'm concentrating on the physical stuff. The result is a level of energy much higher than I had years ago! The real advantage is feeling good about me! Taking good physical care of yourself is vitally important when it comes to serving your clients. Don't think for a moment you don't have time to stay healthy!

Mark P. Tolan, CFP®, a 25-year veteran with American Express Financial Advisors, Inc., keeps in shape by coaching year-round. Whether it's basketball, baseball or his 12 year old daughter Caitlin's softball league, he's at practice two or three days every week. Active in sports since his youth, and coaching since 1984, Mark uses the sports world to impart business principles to his kids. "It's important to keep in touch with them," he says, taking great pride in the fact son Kevin is now working beside him as an advisor.

Get Away

"Getting away to me means not thinking about matters financial, says William K. Dix, creator of Fortune Management Group in Raleigh, North Carolina. "So I ride a motorcycle (across country if possible) with my bride." Bill says his bride of more than thirty years has "been on the back of the bike from the moment I first began riding. Our Honda Goldwing is a large six cylinder touring bike.

"Motorcycling is an acquired skill that can be done well," he continues. "It is also an activity that rewards concentration and punishes inattention. It is absolutely the best way to see, hear and smell the countryside -- especially with Bach playing through the helmet speakers from the cassette player. Maybe one day we'll do the Alps!

"I bought my first bike in the spring of '81, after a several week riding course at a community college in California. All the riding tests in the California Department of Motor Vehicle's arsenal was our final exam. I have sought recurring training so that I don't have to learn everything by painful experience. You see kids today riding in shorts and tee shirts, which just tells you they have never fallen. Once they do, and find out how uncharitably asphalt treats skin, they will wear long pants and a jacket every time they ride...if they continue riding. It's risky and fun. Paying attention and building skills helps manage the former and enhance the latter."

"I relax by taking long hikes in the mountains with my faithful dog, Mancha", says Judith Goldman, CFP®, with JG Associates in Walnut Creek, California. "It's rejuvenating, re-creating, and peaceful. Sometimes I realize I'm thinking about work, or a client. Most of the time, I find myself just taking in the trees, dirt, chipmunks, and wonderful wind sounds as they move through the pine trees. If I come upon a stream, I might sit with my feet in the water and just simply watch how the sunlight plays on it."

Judy admits, with only a modicum of guilt, "I also will bring up financial planning magazines and sit on my deck, able to focus on the subject much better here than at my office with the multitudes of distractions."

It's easy to get away, and encounter new and wonderful experiences at professional events. Just by attending industry conferences, retreats and educational sessions, I've heard terrific presentations by Colin Powell, John Wooden, Michael Gerber, John Glenn and Stephen Covey, just to name a few. I've attended classes at Yale, spent a week in my very own apartment just off Times Square, tasted antelope at a winter Olympics resort, had my picture taken with Willy Mays, helped pull an Amish family's wagon from a ditch, ridden a tiny capsule to the top of the arch in St. Louis, cruised the Caribbean, seen the Terracotta Warriors in Xian and wandered New Orleans' French Quarter.

Most of this was beyond my wildest dreams until I became a financial planner. Opportunities abound to learn from the best minds, in the most exciting cities, under advanced technological systems. And much of it's tax deductible!

162

Get a Backup

"It seems workaholism is especially prevalent among people in the financial services industry," wrote Leslie Rosenberg for Ticker Magazine in October 1999. She goes on to quote financial planners who are "shifting their priorities to make room for their personal lives – and their businesses are thriving as a result."

Whether your office is the corner of the dining room table or a suite atop the World Trade Center, you're going to need help. There are forms to fill out, phones to answer, records to keep, things to file, appointments to schedule and letters to write. You may think you have superhuman powers and know you can do these things better than anyone else, and maybe you can. But you're crazy if you don't bring in someone to free you from these tasks and put you before clients, which is where you should spend your valuable time!

Some of the more popular excuses include:
1. I can't afford to hire any help.
2. I can do this faster and better myself.
3. I need to handle all the details if I'm going to build my practice.
4. I love this business and want to do it all myself!

Whoa! It's terrific to have such enthusiasm, but stop and think why you wanted to be a financial planner in the first place. Did you picture yourself filing statements at 2 a.m.? Were you anxious to spend hours at the computer researching airfare to your next conference? Perhaps you wanted to show off your writing skills composing appointment letters. My guess is it had nothing to do with any of these things. Prevent burnout by making it a top priority to get help.

I had amazing luck! My best friend, Ronnie, a chief cost analyst for General Dynamics, took early retirement when the company was sold to Hughes in 1993. Since I was beginning to feel a time crunch, I asked if she would consider coming in to help me out one day a week and was thrilled when she accepted. Ronnie went to the College for Financial Planning and earned her Paraplanner certification. She now puts in about thirty hours a week.

Someone asked me recently what Ronnie does. I went on and on about how she knows all my clients, keeps the books, makes travel arrangements and a million other things. When I took a breath, he said, "You have no idea what she does, do you?" I had to stop and think, but the fact is, I don't. I just know that when a client comes for an appointment, the completed report is on my desk. If I tell her I'm going to Chicago next month, I know that when it's time to go, she'll hand me my ticket, hotel reservation and itinerary. If the securities auditor comes calling, she'll produce the file he asks for.

It makes me laugh to think there was a time when I felt I couldn't afford help. Now I wonder how I ever managed, even during the early days, without her! Aside from the obvious, knowing that someone is there when I'm not is a huge load off my mind. Whether I'm across the country on vacation, in the next office with a client, or home in bed with the flu, I'm confidant things will be taken care of in my office.

Get a Perspective

"My personal 'respite' is found in the air," explains Beverly Fogle, CFP®, with Cambridge Financial Management Corp. in Vancouver, Washington. "I'm a pilot, and flying requires me to actually leave my ground-bound concerns behind and seriously concentrate on the task at hand. When I was active as a primary flight instructor, I sometimes had to tell certain students that they'd better give up the idea of flying because they couldn't shift psychological gears, so to speak. This can literally be a matter of life and death."

"Since I do fly in serious weather, and sometimes to remote and foreign destinations, it is imperative that I train regularly," she continues. "I have a training partner with whom I've had a great relationship for about fifteen years now. We work each other over aggressively, doing the difficult stuff in the airplane including the things you hope to never actually need. When we get through, I know that I've definitely been concentrating and working very hard. It does keep one sharp. Plus, it's a great change of pace.

"The really beneficial part," adds Bev, "is that when I haven't been flying much, for whatever reason, I find myself getting tired, cranky, impatient, and entirely too intense. Then someone will say, 'you need to go flying.' They're right. Amazing how just an hour or even less in the air can change my whole mental state. The airplane is truly a necessity in my life, my tranquilizer, so to speak."

Get a New Interest

Ever tried belly dancing? Lena Mandelis, CFP®, from Wellesley, Massachusetts, does it every chance she gets. When something exciting happens in her office, it's not unusual to see Lena doing the shimmy for her associate! In fact, taking belly-dancing lessons is practically a requirement for her staff at Mandelis & Associates. "I find it gets me out of my head and back into the rest of my body. It allows me to connect with my spiritual self. Every woman should experience it!" she claims.

"My business partner started playing the piano," relates Dennis Means, CFP®, with Financial Services Network, Inc. in Denver, Colorado. "One night, we were at his house for a dinner party and he sat down and began to play. I had taken lessons as a child way back in the dark ages, and had remembered that I actually liked it as a kid and had quit when it wasn't 'cool' to play the piano. That night at my partner's house brought back the desire to play again. I ended up buying a used piano, just to see if I would like it. I started taking lessons. It is one of the most relaxing things that I do. I can sit down and play for 2 hours and it doesn't even seem like a moment. I get totally engrossed in it. It causes me to forget everything except the focus on playing a particular piece. It is really fun and enjoyable. I am far from concert quality yet, but I expect in about 30 days, you will be able to schedule to hear me play as I begin to tour the country. Yeah, right," He laughs. (Knowing Dennis, it wouldn't surprise me in the least!)

"Five years before our 25th wedding anniversary, my husband and I started planning for a trip to Italy," enthuses Cynthia S. Myers, in Sacramento, California, who writes a column entitled "Myers on Money" for her local newspaper. "We researched the Renaissance and took Italian lessons. We thoroughly enmeshed ourselves in Italian culture and had an incredible time doing it. It's how I do everything! I make it all a part of my life."

A shy young woman, Cynthia took voice lessons in the early 80's to help build her confidence. She ran from her first audition, petrified. But performing at Senior Citizen Centers helped her gain self-assurance, and led to participation in community theatre.

"One day," she recalls, "a client in her late 60's came into the office really soured on life. We started talking and she let slip that she had always wanted to sing. I invited her to come with me to a community musical theatre audition and she won the part. It changed her life! She's still acting," Cynthia laughs, "but I'm not. I'm too busy with my Italian lessons!"

Get Outside of Yourself

"I boss people around with a hammer in my hand," jokes Kathleen Parks, CFP®, with Greenbrier Capital Management. "Working with Habitat for Humanity has taught me new skills. I can build a house!"

"In 1995 when we moved to Tennessee, my husband and I wanted to do something together for the community," she says. "We knew no one in Knoxville. I had just left my job as treasurer for a medical consulting firm and hadn't started my financial planning practice yet." Kathy picked up the phone book and looked for volunteer organizations. "It's consumed us," she said, of their work building homes for those in need. "We're together two Saturdays a month, managing crews on construction sites!"

When she first contacted Habitat for Humanity, they asked her to teach a budgeting class. That led to development of an entire curriculum for the other teachers on simple skills such as balancing a checkbook and making a spending plan. Kathy 's involvement has extended from teaching budgeting classes to serving as president of the Knoxville Habitat Board.

"What we do for a client is so cerebral," she says. "It's mentally and emotionally draining. Habitat construction is physical. When I'm directing a crew of eight or ten volunteers to raise a 28' gable that weighs a few hundred pounds, I'm really concerned about setting it on the wall safely and not dropping it on somebody! This kind of focused activity gives me a mental rest from the hundreds of details swirling around in my head. I come away from the experience physically exhausted, mentally refreshed, and spiritually exhilarated!"

Get Your Priorities Straight[218]

"I sat down one day and did a little arithmetic. The average person lives about seventy-five years. I know, some live more and some live less, but on average, folks live about seventy-five years.

---

[218] From a story passed around from time to time on the Internet

"Now then, I multiplied 75 times 52 and I came up with 3900, which is the number of Saturdays that the average person has in their entire lifetime. It took me until I was fifty-five years old to think about all this in any detail, and by that time I had lived through over twenty-eight hundred Saturdays. I got to thinking that if I lived to be seventy-five, I only had about a thousand of them left to enjoy. So I went to a toy store and bought every single marble they had. I ended up having to visit three toy stores to round up 1000 marbles. I took them home and put them inside of a large, clear plastic container right here in my workshop next to the radio. Every Saturday since then, I have taken one marble out and thrown it away.

"I found that by watching the marbles diminish, I focused more on the really important things in life. There is nothing like watching your time here on this earth run out to help get your priorities straight.

"Now let me tell you one last thing before I sign-off with you and take my lovely wife out for breakfast. This morning, I took the very last marble out of the container. I figure if I make it until next Saturday then I have been given a little extra time. And the one thing we can all use is a little more time."

Appendices

Who would have thought this was the hard part? I began with the desire to put everything there is to know about financial planning into the Appendix, but finally came to my senses and realized everything is already out there. Throughout this book, there are links to much of what you need to know about entering the financial planning profession.

If you're going to be a Financial Planner, you'd better know how to navigate the Internet and research on your own. The Financial Planning Association[219] or the CFP Board of Standards[220] website will get you started.

In lieu of a normal appendix, which I initially thought should include samples of Form ADV, the CFP Board's Annual Report, extensive data gathering forms and completed financial plans; I've come up with a very short list. I suggest a few books, and a couple of other things you won't easily find without asking.

If you're looking for more stuff, like copies of engagement agreements and business plans, post a note at http://www.nancysbooks.com or the FPi Getting Started Discussion Board at http://www.financial-planning.com/wwwboard5/. Simply ask.

Appendix A: "Sensitive Financial Services" by Frank Sisco, CPA, PFS

Appendix B: Recommended Reading

Appendix C: Complimentary Interview Form for Prospective Clients

Appendix D: Cambridge E&O Insurance Application and Checklist

Appendix E: Setting Up Shop Shopping List

Appendix F: Nancy's Marketing Piece

Appendix G: The Paperless Office

---

[219] http://www.fpanet.org
[220] http://www.cfp-board.org

Sensitive Financial Services

By Frank Sisco, CPA, PFS

An article about the new "sensitive" approach to personal financial services.

Can my financial planner and advisor truly help me get what I really want? Is "sensitive" financial services the next big thing or just another sales gimmick in different clothing?

It seems like it came out of the blue, but the "sensitive" approach to personal financial services has been boiling under the surface for several years. It now has exploded on the scene to be perhaps the most radical change in financial services since personal financial planning became a legitimate profession two decades ago.

A. What is it and why does it seem like the next big thing?

1. "Sensitive Financial Services" defined

Sensitive Financial Services (also called "SFS") are personal financial advisory and planning services which are provided to clients in a manner that is openly very sensitive to the client's feelings, needs, goals, temperament, past experiences, emotional and family issues, values, philosophies about life and financial context. Compared to traditional services, sensitive financial services have a greater likelihood of satisfying the client's innermost desires, including goals, which are not apparently money-related. Clients often attain a higher level of peace, security, balance and self-expression. In brief, they get happier. Providers of sensitive financial services (also called "sensitive advisors") usually have a never-ending supply of qualified clients. Such advisors recognize that a client's feelings are not necessarily right or wrong, and that these feelings often run a person more than their intellect. The heart often rules the head. Often, the advisor and the client reach an understanding of the feelings-based thinking and behavior, and then progress to either surmount it or work within its context. SFS is not for every client. Also, it takes special temperament, skills and experience to be a sensitive advisor.

2. How are "SFS" different from traditional services

Sensitive financial services ("SFS") have many practices similar to more traditional services including comprehensive financial planning, estate planning, retirement planning, and investment and insurance services, but there are certain key differences. For SFS, unlike predecessors:
- The consumer usually initiates the request for help. Rarely does the provider solicit clients, primarily due to a very high demand.
- All facets of personal finance are considered, not just a narrow band
- Family relationships are center stage instead of mere context
- Time-efficiency and simplification have veto power
- Money is quantified in order to measure its influence
- Fees and other costs to the consumer are often based on "extra money" realized by the consumer as a result of implementing certain strategies
- The performance of investments is a factor but plays a minor role
- Consumers sometimes experience an emotional and psychological breakthrough as a result of the process. Emotion-based obstacles often get overcome.

Art vs. science

Traditional services look more like science. The recommendations from the advisor often are universal and applied in a wholesale fashion. Input from other advisors is rare. The advisor usually pushes strategies on the client. The process is businesslike and detached; something necessary which appeals to the mind.

Sensitive services look more like art. The recommendations from the sensitive advisor often are very personalized and applied to one unique client. Recommended strategies vary greatly from client to client, even those with what appear to be similar characteristics. Other advisors are often consulted. The advisor and client work together in a joint effort. The process is enjoyed by the clients, lifts the spirits, feels good, and appeals to the heart and soul, as well as the mind.

3. Here are some examples of why Sensitive Financial Services eliminates problems often associated with traditional services.

1. A sensitive advisor probes deeply when a client has significant concerns about safety and security, and will develop an investment allocation, which is truly more stable and contains a larger amount of principal-assured investments, like bonds or principal-protected equity investments.

2. When the advisor is very sensitive to a client's desire to remain in control, the advisor will often suggest an estate plan whereby a smaller amount of their estate is given away during their lifetime, even though the future estate taxes might be quite substantial.

3. In cases when the client is not easily trusting, the sensitive advisor builds trust gradually, implementing strategies in stages with a high level of disclosure so that the client always feels in control and understood.

4. For a client who feels a great weight of responsibility for their elderly parents, a sensitive advisor could empower the client to get siblings motivated to all share the expenses of long-term care policies, which ordinarily might be shunned due to limited resources of the parents.

5. A sensitive advisor recognizes when a client has limited financial knowledge and then creates simpler strategies even if they result in less financial gain, and the advisor spends more time explaining in order to gradually enhance the client's knowledge. Then the advisor builds more complicated strategies as the client's knowledge and comfort level increases, and reviews progress with the client more frequently to help the client understand cause and effect relationships of financial transactions.

6. A client who is obsessive about details and organization is handled by a sensitive advisor much differently than a client who is more laid back. The sensitive advisor will provide more information to support or corroborate strategies, often including very detailed projections of cash flow and investment growth. In many cases, several what-if scenarios are developed. Additionally, the ongoing relationship with the client is usually more hands-on. Sometimes, the high level of client involvement in the details necessitates that the framework be established at a simpler level at the outset to keep advisory time and fees to a minimum.

7. A sensitive advisor recognizes when a client is driven to be efficient with time and with money. The advisor should continually check with the client on ways to streamline financial affairs and to streamline the advisor's services. Sometimes, a client will forsake many thousands of dollars in potential extra money from a complicated strategy because it will take too much time or fees to implement, even if a significant net benefit. The sensitive advisor must recognize these situations and handle them with the client, either overcoming concerns through open discussions or not proceeding at the client's request.

B. What caused Sensitive Services to come into vogue?

The most significant developments and the related trends leading to the emergence of Sensitive Services are the following:

1. Stultifying information

Computerization and the Internet has bestowed wondrous gifts on us. We can be more efficient with mundane tasks and spend the saved time on more humanistic and spiritual endeavors. However, too often we fill our time with other mundane tasks and leisure activities, which leave us unsatisfied. But for sure, the easy access to so much information, through a search engine on the web or by clicking away at the TV remote device, or the scan button on our car radio, we do not get more secure but less so. In fact, we get frazzled and fried. It is tougher to make a decision because we feel guilty if we do not check at least five sources where one was fine in the good old days. And to save $20, we will go to extremes often spending hours. Our trust of specialists is reduced because we trivialize the importance of the knowledge they have, since a search engine like Google gives us hundred times as much for free, and at three in the morning if we want.

The information revolution has brought great benefits, but for us individuals seeking financial well-being, it has only confused matters. Financial advisors have gotten carried away with the info explosion too. If you have stock options to sell, the typical advisor will recommend running the numbers with tax impacts 10 ways to Sunday. If you are thinking about evaluating your investments' performance and voice it to a caring financial advisor, then before you know it you are knee deep in Morningstar mutual funds and stock reports, prospectuses, mounds of data on alternative investments such as 17 different money managers, news articles from far-out mags, etc. We've all got caught up in the info bubble, which is now bursting.

2. Stressed-out baby-boomers

For an 18-year old in the Summer of '67, like me, the summer of love was exhilarating and the future was rich with promise. Let's face it boomers, most of us still haven't found what we're looking for. Those of us who had kids later, now have teenagers who are driving us crazy with their rebellious attitudes and blatant contempt for authority, namely us, with no let up in sight. Do the 2 million kids on prescription antidepressants like Ritalin really have Attention Deficit Disorder or do parents and children find drugs the only path to cope. Those baby boomers with children in college are up to their eyeballs in education expenses, often paying with home-equity funds. Those boomers with children out of college are sometimes supplementing their children's income or still providing them with a place to sleep. Making matters worse for many baby-boomers, also called the Sandwich Generation, is that there are parents and sometimes grandparents needing help in their retirement years. Who cares if you can afford a pleasure craft because there just is not an hour to spare to even take it out into the harbor! And the 3-day get-away weekends just do not do enough to expunge the stress.

3. Prolonged lives and their meaning

There is a growing trend of people seeking more meaning and spirituality in their lives. One causative factor is a greater awareness of the preciousness of life and to live it as fully as possible now. We have been seeing people around us live into their 90s and 100s. Some age gracefully, some with major medical problems, and some kept alive artificially. Also, thanks to the shrinking world and globalization of media, we are reminded of lives cut short around the world due to disease, poverty, war, and natural catastrophe. Barraged continually by these images and messages, we cannot help but believe it is important to treat life as quite precious, and to live it fully, and live it now. We are driven to live it fully because we may live to 120, God willing, and who wants to be stuck in a dead-end job for the next 70 years. Also, we want to live fully because we may die next year and what a shame to have wasted so much time not doing what had always been our passion.

170

Another reason for the additional emphasis on life's meaning and importance is that the idealistic generation of the 1960s, the baby boomers, are now in middle age and have the resources, sheer numbers, and influence that can shape the world. With this power comes a feeling of responsibility to do meaningful things. The men's weekend retreat I attended last January was emblematic of this trend. Forty men, most in their forties and fifties, in a mutual quest for truth, shared life stories with each other, openly, and often quite emotionally.

4. Feminization of money

Women have become, if they were not already, the main financial decision maker. It is true that the man might open the discount brokerage online trading account, but it is often the woman who calls the shots on major purchases like cars, homes, home improvements, retirement plan investments, which college for the child, etc. In the last 30 years, women have taken a much greater role in family financial planning. In addition, women on average live much longer than men, and women head up more single-parent families and thus are forced into being the decision makers. This may account for the fact that many financial advisors, myself included, serve more women than men. In divorced or separated situations, women have had to retool, become better income earners, and be more diligent in getting the estranged husband to pay his share. Watch 50 television commercials and skim through 10 general interest magazines and newspapers and you will see who are being appealed to - it's the women. In my financial planning sessions with couples over the years, I find women participate much more actively and often contribute the greatest insights.

5. The individual is better than the group

Hurray for the entrepreneur! So many deca-millionaires and billionaires have been created by the entrepreneurial boom and by the internet revolution, giving more ammunition to the argument that true innovation comes from small packages not big. As the individual start-up man or woman takes their risks and are successful, more people join the crowd and shun the status quo, and then big emulates small and the related benefits for flexibility and growth. However this sometimes leads to an unfortunate bubble but for now seems to lead to greater prosperity for all. This focus on the individual has been brewing for decades and not just in the business arena. Positive developments in the movements for more equal rights for races, religions, genders and nationalities have fostered a greater appreciation for the individual, no matter how different from the group. In fact, many firms now seek out unique individuals because of the greater insights, which a diverse group often brings to the mix. Many years ago the slogan was to "Adapt or perish" and now more and more it is "Viva la difference!"

C. Who are the Sensitive Advisors?

1. Personal

You cannot find Sensitive Advisors in planning departments of the leading wirehouse brokerage firms, nor in separate kiosks at the neighborhood bank. You will not find ads for seminars in the papers nor will you get an invitation in the mail. The mutual fund companies will not be mailing you a Sensitive Financial Services Compact disk or tout the best website to do Sensitive Financial Services online. Why not? Because SFS cannot be done efficiently by large organizations. It takes an individual who has at least most of the 12 traits listed below, and those individuals are usually not working for such large organizations. They usually work on their own or in very small groups, sometimes partnerships and sometimes associations.

2. Caring vs. knowing

You've heard the expression "People don't really care how much you know, but they really know how much you care." For us in the financial services industry, if we are to maintain the trust of clients we already have, and gain the trust of new clients, we must pay more attention to how much we care versus how much we know. If we do not genuinely care, we should find other work, and quickly before we do damage. If we do genuinely care, we need to continually demonstrate it by providing great service tailored to the particular client. We must see the financial planning and advisory function as a process of distilling the enormous array of products and services into a manageable set which relates to the client's unique situation and then keep shaping it as the client changes in the ever-changing world around them. Wherever we lack skills, we must get them or network with others who do have them. We are more than change agents, helping clients cope with change. We are also change portals - channels through which the clients can see their future and step into it.

3. Profile of the sensitive advisor
The people getting the most recognition as Sensitive Advisors seem to fit the following profile:
1. Caring
1. Experienced in several facets of financial services (e.g. was a stock broker and insurance agent, was a full-time CPA or attorney or start-up incubator manager with a yen for personal financial services) and experienced in several facets of other industries, providing sharp financial acumen, learned in the trenches where the knowledge sticks
2. Passionate about serving people as individuals
3. Female or male with a keen awareness of female aspirations and attitudes and comfortable in female company as well as in male company
4. Seasoned with life experiences to draw from. Age-wise this often means 45 or older
5. Successful financially in the overall, but with several failures, which led to greater appreciation for risk and understanding of complexities
6. Very creative and innovative, often bringing new perspectives to the issues
7. Networked well, knowing many people she can call on to get their knowledge and opinions
8. Impatient with bureaucracy but tolerant of it until changed
9. Glass half-full vs. half-empty
10. Excellent at communication and spurring discussions of important issues
11. Solid citizen with good character and community-minded
12. Leadership strengths to be a quarterback, marshaling the services of other professionals

D. What are the attributes of sensitivity?

Research shows that decision-making about financial services has many aspects in common with decision-making about other endeavors and activities in life. Thus, if the provider of financial services is sensitive to these attributes, and tailors financial services and products accordingly, then there is a much greater likelihood that they will indeed meet with success and that the client will benefit.

These are the 11 key attributes of sensitivity of clients, which impact significantly on SFS:
1. Secure and safe
2. Free and not burdened or controlled
3. Not left out and in-the-know
4. Not taken advantage of
5. Understood
6. Respected as an individual
7. Efficient
8. Responsible and not too risky
9. Young at heart, fresh, innovative
10. Successful financially and successful life-wise
11. Loving, harmonious, spiritual, and not controversial

172

All clients have these attributes, but the prioritization greatly differs with each individual and is impacted very differently by the scores of aspects of financial services. For example, one client might feel she is being responsible by saving 20% of her salary for her 12-year-old daughter's future college education by investing in a mutual fund of large capitalization stocks, whereas another client would feel responsible only if the money was invested in bank certificates deposit. Because empirical evidence about market volatility could be interpreted to support either view, it is important for the advisor to appreciate the client perceptions and help shape them into an actionable plan in line with client feelings. Another example is that one client might feel he is more loving and considerate about his children by setting aside money into irrevocable trusts for their benefit so that future estate taxes could be reduced and that more money will be available for them. Another client might see the situation completely differently and believe the children should not get large inheritances, which might spoil them and cause them to be less high-achieving and entrepreneurial in their lives.

The Sensitive Advisor not only must be mindful of these attributes as they show up in their clients but also be mindful of how the advisor's attributes show up for the client, affecting the process. Often the greater the alignment of attributes, the greater the success of the relationship.

E. The process of Sensitive Financial Services

1. The main phases are simple:
1. First contact is through a referral from the prospect to the sensitive advisor
2. Setting the context
3. Building rapport and developing understanding
4. Identifying real needs and goals
5. Creation of financial strategies, holistically and sensitively
6. Implementation of key strategies
7. Follow-up, empowerment, referral

For each phase, the sensitive advisor gathers information about the client's 11 sensitivity attributes, and what influences them most. Completing specially-designed questionnaires is one way to get information about the attributes and their ranking of importance for the client. Throughout the process, another important way for the advisor and the client to communicate is through the telling of stories and of their views about matters of the day, always protecting the confidentiality and anonymity of the parties involved. The advisor should tell stories of cases where the client's lives were impacted significantly and how it happened. The client should tell stories about their own lives, successes and failures, and stories about the lives of others they respect and emulate and of those who they do not.

2. Details about each phase

1. The first contact is through a referral from the prospect to the provider
Providers of Sensitive Financial Services make it a practice not to actively solicit new business through conventional means of seminars, mailings, radio, internet, letter-writing or calling. Instead, such providers rely on satisfied clients to spread the word of their satisfaction with SFS to their family, friends, business associates etc. who will then call or write to the providers if interested. In this way, the providers can focus on doing their work rather than marketing which is really unnecessary due to the very high success rate of converting an interested prospect to a paying client, due to the referral basis.

2. Setting the context

At the outset, there must be frank discussions between clients and providers about the expectations, steps in the process, time and cost considerations, reasonable short-term and long-term goals. Here are examples of the detailed steps:

a. Family tree - Clients and advisors complete this chart together, discussing relationships, the financial resources of family members, the expectations of responsibilities, the quirks as well as successes of family members, etc. As the chart is built, the uniqueness of the client's situation becomes apparent. Many financial strategies are identified during this step. Often the conversations cross into the other areas mentioned below. The advisor is mainly a listener, asking open-ended questions to trigger deeper discussions. (e.g. Tell me about how your father with a limited income was able to provide for you and your siblings and pay for all your education through college. How did your mother or your father approach big money decisions?)

b. Explore past - Many clients have strong views about certain money issues as a result of past experiences (e.g. lost money in a business, gambling problem of a relative, cousin who hit it rich with an IPO, etc.). Discussing the past helps everyone see what is driving the present and helps distinguish what is real and what is drama, and what is steadfast and what is changeable.

c. Map future - Discussions of the future need to be as visual and specific as possible. For a vibrant 40-year-old successful English professor, writing and publishing short stories during retirement is a more realistic goal than just playing golf. If so, perhaps a small income can be assumed during retirement that augments investment income and social security.

d. Focus on key strategies - Establish what is most important. Develop a list of the 4 or 5 essential issues to resolve, and discuss tentatively sample strategies to deal with these issues, evaluating sensitivity attributes.

e. Discuss key elements of the process - There must be a clear discussion of fees (and the type of fee structure such as value-based fees), the steps to gather information (including completion of various forms and questionnaires, schedules of expenses, assets and cash flow,) the methods of reporting results, the use of computers and the internet, the advisor's network of associates and clients and the client's network of other advisors such as attorney, insurance agent, investment broker and accountant.

3. Building rapport and developing understanding

If there is not chemistry, mutual respect and a clear appreciation and trust of each other after the first meeting, it is strongly suggested that the advisor and client should openly discuss this matter, and if there is not resolution immediately, then the process should not go forward, and the advisor should not accept the engagement. If the process does move forward, it is important for both the advisor and the client to take steps to bolster the rapport and understanding, such as additional meetings, phone calls and emails, clarifying discussions, sharing of stories, and attending certain dinners or events together. For example, the way a client reacts to a waitress serving her during a dinner can speak volumes about the client's consideration of others, expectations, self-centeredness, etc. Likewise, the client should note that an advisor who knows no one at a professional gathering is probably not well networked, and this can spell limitations of financial strategies. The process is helped when the advisor and the client take part in conferences (e.g. conference phone calls) with other advisors such as CPAs, attorneys, insurance agents, etc. and with other family members. Of course, attending events such as plays, movies, sports, etc. can further the relationship; however these events should not be too frequent which could cause a blurring of the client/advisor relationship and a fostering of a relationship that is too cozy and comfortable, making it difficult for either party to stand ground when needed.

Because sensitive advisors usually get more involved with more emotional and psychological aspects of a client's life, there are often more matters for which a client requests the sensitive advisor's help. Sensitive advisors must be careful not to get so involved as to taint the advisor's objectivity or render the client over-reliant.

4. Identifying real needs and goals

It is one thing for a client to express a goal like retiring at age 60. It is another thing to delve deeper to find out why at age 60, what is there planned after age 60, will there be sufficient resources to make it happen, what will the spouse be doing, does the client have hobbies or other interests to occupy time, etc. Often it is important to prepare a detailed projection of cash flows and investment growth (e.g. using electronic spreadsheets going out many years) in order to test and refine the goals. Looking ahead to identify other events that might impact the goals is an important step in the process. For example, children may be getting married, parents might die or get ill in advanced years possibly leading to more or less money, income might not grow as quickly, a mortgage might get paid off, etc. Once the needs and goals are discussed, evaluate them in terms of the 11 sensitivity attributes, and refine them again. For example, a client who wants to be in control might not really be able to handle emotionally the downsizing of a house and move into a retirement community.

5. Creation of financial strategies, holistically and sensitively

The sensitive advisor must have the skills and experience to survey the information obtained in a holistic manner and then create the best few financial strategies which can help the client achieve their goals and satisfy their needs. The advisor must be sensitive to the client's attributes in developing the strategies. For example if the client is not very analytical and prefers broad concepts, the advisor should not inundate the client with detailed analysis but rather summarize it clearly for the client, perhaps not even sharing the analytical methods used, whereas for another client who might like analysis, the advisor might walk through all the analytical steps, sharpening the strategy with the client's input. If the client is loath to spending current cash flow on insurance like long-term care insurance, the advisor might propose that the client pay premiums by using the build-up within tax-deferred annuities, which are in excess of future needs. This could save future estate taxes and also future income taxes, by paying taxes at the present income tax bracket rather than the beneficiary such as a high-earning adult child paying taxes at a much higher rate.

As part of the creation process, the advisor should review all typical strategies, decide which ones are the most worthwhile and then determine ways to creatively combine them or enhance them. The advisor should refer to manuals and checklists for traditional strategies, supplemented by strategies discussed in publications and the media. The advisor should also use financial websites and search engines to explore potential strategies.

The advisor should look for opportunities to simplify the client's life, and sometimes zero-basing in this regard helps. For example, let's suppose that stagnant low salary income is interfering with the client's ability to save for retirement. Instead of recommending that she drastically cut personal expenses which could be disempowering, the sensitive advisor might suggest that the client should seriously consider her own business, using some of her invested money for start-up capital, assuming the risks when reviewed are not significant (e.g. the client has very good skills, great network of potential customers, solid business plan, etc.)

The advisor should request colleagues to review the basic information and findings to see if additional strategies can be created. Each strategy should be evaluated in terms of the client's sensitivity attributes, and if helpful ranked from 1 to 5 on a grid.

6. Implementation of key strategies

The advisor's role in the implementation should depend not only on the advisor's skills, licenses and powers, but also should depend on the client's sensitivity attributes. For example, an advisor who can easily implement investment allocation recommendations by purchasing and selling securities should not do so if the client is the type of person to question the advisor's objectivity even if the advisor is very objective in reality. Also, the advisor must be sensitive that some clients want to have a very involved role in implementing strategies and using their existing network as much as possible, while other clients may want one person, the advisor, to be responsible for everything. Of course other key areas of sensitivity involve the matter of time (e.g. implement all strategies right away, or do gradually) and money (e.g. each client will view the advisor's compensation, the amount and type, differently). In some cases, the advisor might be able to reshape the client's views and feelings, but usually not. Thus, the advisor is often better off identifying the sensitivities and adjusting her ways of doing business, or else run the risk of a client being dissatisfied over one point, spoiling the entire batch.

7. Follow-up, empowerment, referral

Client relationships can be lifelong with the right follow-up which can keep the client empowered to continue the improvement of their financial health and attainment of goals and objectives. Look again at the 11 attributes of sensitivity. Efficient cost-conscious self-starting clients will probably want an expeditious schedule of follow-up, perhaps quick reports and discussions on a semi-annual basis. Other clients who want to be more in control of the information and perhaps are less trusting of the overall plan will want more frequent follow-up, and perhaps in greater depth. Those clients who closely intertwine life and money may desire the advisor's involvement in many endeavors and events throughout the year, planning often to make the life event as rich and meaningful as possible. For example, a client evaluating the purchase of a new house may involve the advisor not only to advise on lending and tax implications but also on the other implications on one's life (e.g. on family, on cash flow, on school selection, on future needs) of buying an expensive home requiring high maintenance situated far from one's employment.

Finally, some clients will easily refer friends, associates and relatives to the advisor, and other clients will shun such referrals, often having little to do with the degree of excellence of the advisor's services and more to do with the client's feelings and attributes. Yet, there will usually be many more referrals when an advisor uses the sensitive approach to financial services. It is more likely that the feelings that might have been obstacles to a referral get a chance to be seen by both the client and advisor, addressed by them in an ever-growing mutually-respectful relationship that is often seen as emblematic of each other's life mission, which is to grow as a good person, serving others to the benefit of all. The client gets an opportunity to serve the advisor by making a referral, and the referred person becomes an eager open new client for the advisor to continue his or her mission to serve, and to serve in a sensitive manner.

F. Conclusion

Sensitive personal financial services represents a quickly-growing trend, which often results in services which are better suited to the client, and lead to greater fulfillment for the advisor. The trend is in harmony with societal trends of individualism, diversity appreciation, and emphasis on life's more important issues including self-actualization, love and inner peace.

For more information, contact Frank Sisco at 914.381.3737 or visit his website at
http://www.thirdthousand.com

Appendix B: Suggested Reading

Getting Started:

Fee-Only Financial Planning by John E. Sestina, CFP®, ChFC, John Wiley & Sons, Inc., 2001, Hardcover 235 pages ($49.95)

Getting Started as a Financial Planner by Jeffrey H. Rattiner, Bloomberg Press, July 2000, Hardcover 304 pages ($34.95)

Getting Started in Financial Consulting by Edward J. Stone, John Wiley & Sons, March 2000, Paperback 304 pages ($18.95)

How to Become A Successful Financial Consultant by Jim H. Ainsworth, John Wiley & Sons, January, 1997, Hardcover 221 pages ($29.95)

Practice Management:

Virtual-Office Tools for a High-Margin Practice: How Client-Centered Financial Advisers Can Cut Paperworrk, Overhead, and Wasted Hours by David J. Drucker and Joel P. Bruckenstein, Bloomberg Press, October 2002, Paperback 249 pages ($50)

Rattiner's Financial Planning Bible: The Advisor's Advisor by Jeffrey H. Rattiner, John Wiley & Sons, August 2002, Hardcover 304 pages ($34.95)

Your Clients for Life: The Definitive Guide to Becoming a Successful Financial Life Planner by Mitch Anthony, Barry LeValley, Carol Anderson, Dearborn Trade Publishing, April 2002, Hardcover 272 pages ($35)

Tools and Templates for Your Practice by Deena B. Katz, Bloomberg Press, 2001, Softcover + CD-Rom 296 pages ($50)

Keeping Clients for Life by Karen Caplin Altfest, John Wiley & Sons, April 2001, Hardcover 240 pages ($49.95)

Getting Clients Keeping Clients: The Essential Guide for Tomorrow's Financial Advisor by Dan Richards, John Wiley & Sons, April 2000, Hardcover 400 pages, ($59.95)

Deena Katz on Practice Management for Financial Advisers, Planners, and Wealth Managers by Deena B. Katz and Ross Levin, Bloomberg Press, September, 1999, Hardcover 308 pages, ($50)

Protecting Your Practice by Katherine Vessenes, Bloomberg Press, October 1997, Hardcover 491 pages ($50)

Marketing:

Garrett's Guide to Financial Planning: How to Capture the Middle Market and Increase your Profits! By Sheryl Garrett, National Underwriter, October 2002, Softcover + CD-Rom ($39.99)

Building a World-Class Financial Services Business: How to Transform Your Sales Practice into a Company Worth Millions by Don Schreiber, Jr., Dearborn Trade Publishing, July 2001, Hardcover 304 pages ($40)

The Personal Branding Phenomenon by Peter Montoya, Tim Vandehey, Paul Viti, Peter Montoya & Tim Vandehey, April 2002, Hardcover 235 pages ($24.95)

Storyselling for Financial Advisors: How Top Producers Sell by Scott West and Mitch Anthony, Dearborn Trade Publishing, June 2000, Hardcover 246 pages ($30)

High Probability Selling by Jacques Werth and Nicholas E. Ruben, ABBA Publishing Company, http://www.highprobsell.com, 2000, Paperback 178 pages ($19.95)

Effort-Less Marketing for Financial Advisors by Steve Moeller, American Business Visions, October 1999, Paperback 395 pages ($44.95)

Get Media Smart! By Lisbeth Wiley Chapman, Ink & Air, http://www.inkair.com, 1998, Paperback 67 pages + 50 minute Tape ($49.95)

Selling the Invisible: A Field Guide to Modern Marketing by Harry Beckwith, Warner Books, 1997, Hardcover 252 pages ($19.95)

The Excellent Investment Advisor by Nick Murray, The Nick Murray Company, Inc., November 1996, ($42.50)

How to Succeed Selling Life Insurance in spite of being a nice person by Athena Ghion, http://www.selling-well.com/index.html (not sold in stores) 219 pages ($24.95)

Values Based Selling: The Art of Building High-Trust Client Relationships by Bill Bachrach, Bachrach & Associates, May 1996, Hardcover 368 pages ($34.95)

Business and Personal Development:

Successful Business Planning in 30 Days by Peter J. Patsula, Patsula Media www.businessplan30days.com, 2002, Paperback 212 pages ($19.95)

The One Page Business Plan^{SM} by Jim Horan, The One Page Business Plan Company, 1998, Paperback 97 pages ($19.95)

The E-Myth Revisited: Why Most Small Businesses Don't Work and What to Do About It by Michael E. Gerber, Harperbusiness, Updated Edition April 1995, Paperback 288 pages ($16.00)

The 7 Habits of Highly Effective People: Powerful Lessons in Personal Change by Stephen R. Covey, Fireside, Reprint Edition August 1990, Paperback 360 pages ($14.00)

What Consumers are Reading:

Facing Financial Dysfunction: Why Smart People Do Stupid Things with Money! By Bert Whitehead, MBA, JD, Infinity Publishing.com, August 2002, Paperback 167 pages ($24.95)

Spiritual Finance: The Relationship between Spirituality and Your Financial Planning by Sheldon Zeiger, JD, CFP®, Cypress Publishing Group, 2002, Paperback, 241 pages ($21.95)

The New Retirementality: Planning Your Life and Living Your Dreams…at Any Age You Want by Mitch Anthony, Dearborn Trade Publishing, April 2001, Paperback, 241 pages ($16.95)

The Right Way to Hire Financial Help by Charles A. Jaffe, The MIT Press, 2nd Edition February 2001, Paperback 352 pages ($19.95)

Robbing You Blind: Protecting Your Money from Wall Street's Hidden Costs and Half-Truths by Mark Dempsey, William Morrow and Company, Inc., 2000, Hardcover 274 pages ($25.00)

Get A Life: You don't need a million to retire well by Ralph Warner, Nolo, Third Edition August 2000, Paperback 336 pages ($24.95)

Seven States of Money Maturity: Understanding the Spirit and Value of Money in Your Life by George Kinder, Dell Publishing, April 2000, Paperback 369 pages ($12.95) also in Hardcover.

Appendix C: Complementary Interview Form for Prospective Clients

NLJones, Inc.

Financial Planning

2485 Mesa Terrace•Upland, Ca 91784
Phone:909.985.5550•Fax:909.985.9500
nancy@nljones.com
visit our website: http://www.nljones.com

Complimentary Interview Form

Appointment Date:_____ **Time:**_____   **Referred by:**_____

Your Name:_____   Date of Birth:____/___/____
Employer/Profession:_____   Bus.#:_____

Spouse/Partner's Name:_____   Date of Birth:____/___/____
Employer/Profession: _____   Bus.#:_____

Home Address:_____
Home #: (_____)____-_____   Fax #: (_____)____-_____   Pgr/Mbl: (_____)____-_____
E-mail: _____   What is the best way to contact you:_____

Child: 1._____   Date of Birth: _____/_____/_____
     2._____   Date of Birth: _____/_____/_____
     3._____   Date of Birth: _____/_____/_____

1. How did you hear about NLJones, Inc.?_____

2. What is your primary motivation for contacting a financial planner at this time?
_____
_____

3. What are your most important financial concerns?
A)_____
B)_____
C)_____

4. What are your most important *non*-financial concerns & objectives right now?
A)_____
B)_____
C)_____

5. Do you or your spouse/partner have any of the following?

Wills_____   Trusts_____   Life Insurance_____   Disability Insurance_____

Family Owned Business_____   Investment Real Estate_____

6. Who makes important investment decisions in your family?_____

7. Have you ever worked with a financial advisor before?   Yes_____   No_____

What was good about that experience?_____
_____

Unsatisfactory?_____
_____

8. What changes do you expect in the future that you wish to plan for?

FamilyObligations: _____
_____

Inheritances:_____

Other: _____

9. What would you like to accomplish through this engagement?_____
_____
_____

10. Is there anything else we need to talk about? _____
_____
_____

Please bring this completed questionnaire along with copies of the following with you for your appointment:

    Cash Flow Statement (list of income and expenses)
    Net Worth Statement (list of assets and liabilities)
    Most recent Income Tax Return

(Internal Use)

Summary of
Concerns:_____

_____

_____

_____

Summary of benefits we can
provide:_____

_____

_____

Next step:_____

Appendix D: Cambridge E&O Insurance Application and Checklist

...E&O Insurance for Registered Investment Advisers

9. Indicate professional services by approximate percentage. Must equal 100%. Indicate **all services** provided by the practice regardless of whether the revenues are declared in Question 8.

%	NATURE OF PRACTICE	%	NATURE OF PRACTICE (Continued)
	Modular/Comprehensive Financial Plan Preparation/Advice		Timing Services
	Divorce Planning		Pension Fund Consulting
	Discretionary Asset Management(LPOA)		Business Management Consulting
	Non-Discretionary Asset Management(LPOA with Prior Consent)		Tax Preparation
	Asset Monitoring (No Limited Power of Attorney to Direct Trades)		Accounting Services Other Than Tax Preparation
	Investment Management Consulting (No LPOA)		Third Party Pension Administration
	Product Sales Based On Financial Plan		Hourly Advice
	Product Sales Not Based On Financial Plan		Wrap Accounts
	Other:		Other:

10. If you receive commissions, indicate the breakdown of total commission income by percent. Must equal 100%.

%	TYPE OF PRODUCT	%	TYPE OF PRODUCT (Continued)
	Mutual Funds		Commercial Paper
	Variable Annuities		Private Placements
	Life / Health / Disability / Accident Sales		REITS
	Viatical Agreements		Limited Partnerships
	Listed Stocks		Unregistered Securities
	Unlisted Stocks		Foreign Securities / ADR'S
	Investment Grade Bonds		Hedgefunds
	Junk Bonds		Options / Futures / Tangibles/CMO's/Derivatives

11. What % of revenue is derived from **professional** entertainers, celebrities, athletes and musicians?

12. Does the applicant provide personal management services (e.g. sport management / bill paying) to any client?

13. Do you render advice to mutual funds, REITS, limited partnerships or private placements? _____ If yes, provide details.

14. Please **CIRCLE** yes or no. All **YES** answers, please supply details. Has the Applicant or **any** associated professional:

Yes	No	Had a professional license/registration denied, suspended, revoked, non-renewed or restricted?
Yes	No	Been formally reprimanded by any court/administrative/regulatory agency?
Yes	No	Had a complaint filed with consumer agencies, applicant's broker-dealer, the SEC, NASD, the IRS, state securities dept., insurance dept., or other regulatory agency?
Yes	No	Been audited by the SEC, NASD, state securities dept., or other licensing or regulatory agency? **If yes, please supply audit letter and firm's response to regulator.**
Yes	No	Been formally accused of violating any professional association's code of ethics?
Yes	No	Been convicted of a felony?
Yes	No	Been involved in or is aware of any fee disputes including suits?

15. If you have client **assets under management**, do you:

A. Use a written Investment Policy Statement for other than ERISA accounts?   ☐ YES   ☐ NO

B. Have Limited Power of Attorney to direct trades in the client's account? If yes: please answer: ☐ YES   ☐ NO

    ☐ I use full discretion to trade without prior consent of the client
    ☐ I use discretion to trade within an Investment Policy Statement or written parameters
    ☐ I decline to exercise the discretion and obtain prior consent for each and every trade.

D. Excluding advisory fees, do you have power to withdraw/disburse funds in the account?   ☐ YES   ☐ NO

E. Do you use limited partnerships, options, futures, derivatives in your portfolios?   ☐ YES   ☐ NO

F. **On a separate sheet**, please briefly describe your investment philosophy.

G. **On a separate sheet**, please list the types/percentages of investments used in portfolios.

H. Number of Discretionary Accounts: _____   Amount of Assets Under Management: _____

I. Number of Non-Discretionary Accounts: _____   Amount of Assets Under Management: _____

Applicant declares and warrants that the statements, including additional sheets, are true and that no material facts have been suppressed or misstated, that Applicant understands and agrees this application will be made a part of any policy issued and any such policy is issued in reliance upon the representations made herein. Applicant further understands and agrees that failure to provide a true and accurate response to any of the foregoing questions may, at the option of the company, result in the voiding of insurance issued in reliance on the application and / or denial of claim asserted.

NOTICE TO APPLICANT: Any person who knowingly files an application for insurance or statement of claim containing any materially false information, or conceals for the purpose of misleading, information concerning any fact material thereto, commits a fraudulent insurance act, which is a crime and also punishable by civil penalties in certain jurisdictions.

Print Name: _____ Title: _____
                                                   (Owner, Partner, Senior Officer)

Signature: _____ Date: _____
SIGNING THIS FORM OR REMITTANCE OF DEPOSIT DOES NOT BIND FSIC OR THE APPLICANT OR THE UNDERWRITER TO COMPLETE THE INSURANCE CONTRACT. YOU WILL BE NOTIFIED WHEN COVERAGE IS ACCEPTED AND BOUND.

PROFESSIONAL LIABILITY INSURANCE FOR FINANCIAL ADVISORS / PLANNERS
NEW BUSINESS APPLICATION CLAIMS MADE BASIS

THE POLICY FOR WHICH APPLICATION IS MADE, SUBJECT TO ITS TERMS, APPLIES ONLY TO CLAIMS FIRST MADE AGAINST THE INSURED DURING THE POLICY PERIOD. THE LIMIT OF LIABILITY AVAILABLE TO PAY DAMAGES IS REDUCED BY THE AMOUNTS INCURRED AS DEFENSE EXPENSES AND DEFENSE EXPENSES ARE SUBJECT TO THE DEDUCTIBLE.

Applicant's Legal Name	
Address	
Telephone	Fax
Email	Web Site

1. List all **employed (W-2)** financial advisors **including self**. Independent Contractors (1099) are **not** covered under the firm's policy and require separate applications or, if requested, can be added as additional insureds. **CPA firms** should list **only** those involved in financial planning / investment advisory services.

NAME OF ALL EMPLOYED FINANCIAL ADVISORS	PROFESSIONAL DESIGNATIONS	NASD SERIES LICENSES	NASD CRD NUMBER	PROFESSIONAL ASSOCIATION AFFILIATIONS

2. Do you have any independent contractors (**non-employees**) giving investment advice on behalf of your RIA? ☐ Yes ☐ No
Please   list   names:
_____

3. List all **professional liability** insurance carried (e.g. accountants, tax preparation, group broker-dealer, life agent)

INSURER	LIMITS	DEDUCTIBLE	POLICY PERIOD	RETROACTIVE DATE

4. Select **Standard** Limits and Deductibles   **OR**   **Higher** Limits and Deductibles

Per Claim / Aggregate	Deductible		Per Claim	Aggregate	Deductibles
☐ $ 50,000 / $ 100,000	$ 1,000	☐	$1,000,000	☐ $1,000,000	☐ $ 5,000
☐ $ 100,000 / $ 200,000	$ 1,000	☐	$2,000,000	☐ $2,000,000	☐ $ 10,000
☐ $ 250,000 / $ 500,000	$ 2,500	☐	$3,000,000	☐ $3,000,000	☐ $ 15,000
☐ $ 500,000 / $ 1,000,000	$ 2,500	☐	$4,000,000	☐ $4,000,000	☐ $ 20,000
☐ $ 1,000,000 / $2,000,000	$ 5,000	☐	$5,000,000	☐ $5,000,000	☐ $ 25,000

5. Has any professional liability claim, complaint or proceeding been made against the firm or any associated professionals or is the applicant **aware of any circumstances** which may result in any claim being made against the applicant, its predecessors in business, or any of the applicant's present or past partners, officers, directors, employees or associated professionals? ☐ YES ☐ NO If yes, please **attach complete details** on a separate sheet.

6. **Conflicts of Interest – Do you or any member or associated person of your firm:**

A. Act as trustee to an advisory client?	☐ Yes	☐ No
B. Advise clients to invest in any enterprise in which a firm member has material ownership interest?	☐ Yes	☐ No
C. Advise clients to invest in any enterprise owned by client?	☐ Yes	☐ No
D. If a CPA, do you perform advisory services for any client for whom you do any attest work?	☐ Yes	☐ No

7. Do you use a Compliance Attorney or Consultant? ☐ Yes ☐ No Name: _____

8. Indicate **gross** annual revenues **derived from financial planning, advisory activities, commissions and/or product sales. Do not** include professional accounting services revenues.

YEAR	GROSS REVENUES (100%)	% FEE ONLY REVENUES	% COMMISSION REVENUES	NO. OF FINANCIAL ADVISORS
1999				
2000				
2001				

FPA001NB(04/86)   PAGE 1

© Copyright 2001 The Cambridge Alliance, LLC   TELEPHONE: (800) 691-1515

184

Appendix E: Setting Up Shop Shopping List

	Item	Expected Cost	Actual Cost	Notes
Real Estate				
	Executive Suite			
	Home Office			
	Rent			
	Shared Space			
Registrations				
	ADV Registration			
	Business License			
	Permits			
Education				
	CFP® Course			
	Series Exam Course			
	Testing Fees			
Insurance				
	Casualty			
	Errors & Omissions			
	Service Agreements			
Staff				
	Bookkeeper			
	Clerk			
	Coach			
	Computer Consultant			
	Office Assistant			
	Paraplanner			
Furniture				
	Bookcase			
	Computer Station			
	Conference Table & Chairs			
	Desk			
	Desk Accessories			
	Executive Chair			
	Filing Cabinets			
	Lighting			
	Office Chairs			
	Wall Décor			
	Waste Basket			

	Item	Expected Cost	Actual Cost	Notes
Hardware				
	Computer			
	Desktop			
	Laptop			
	Copier			
	Monitor			
	Overhead Projector			
	PDA			
	Printer			
	Laser			
	Ink Jet			
	Safe			
	Scanner			
	Shredder			
Supplies				
	Binding Machine & Supplies			
	Brief Case			
	Brochure			
	Business Bank Account			
	Business Cards			
	Calculator			
	Card File			
	Computer Disks			
	Copy Paper			
	Desk Organizer			
	File Folders			
	Labels			
	Logo			
	Message Pads			
	Paper Clips			
	Paper Products			
	Paper Trimmer			
	Pens, Markers			
	Postage Scale			
	Printer/Fax Cartridges			
	Reference Books			
	Scissors			
	Staplers			
	Stationary			

	Item	Expected Cost	Actual Cost	Notes
Software				
	Accounting			
	Allocation			
	Analysis			
	Asset Tracking			
	Contact Management			
	Education			
	Financial Planning			
	Office Suite			
	Presentation			
	Regulatory			
	Word Processing			
Telecom				
	Answer Machine/Service			
	Domain Name			
	E-Mail			
	Internet Service Provider			
	Telephone			
	Desktop			
	Extensions			
	Cellular			
	Headset			
	Web Site Design			

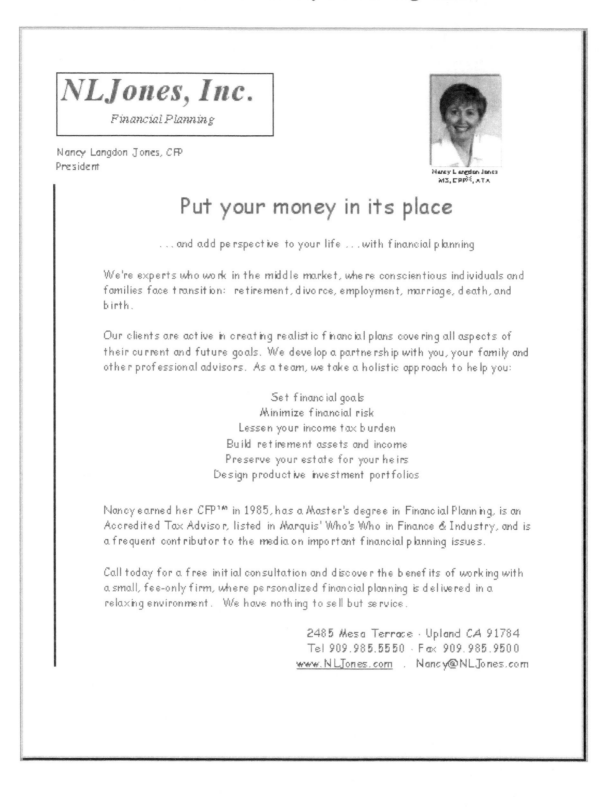

NLJones, Inc.
Financial Planning

Nancy Langdon Jones, CFP
President

Nancy Langdon Jones
MS, CFP®, ATA

Put your money in its place

...and add perspective to your life ...with financial planning

We're experts who work in the middle market, where conscientious individuals and families face transition: retirement, divorce, employment, marriage, death, and birth.

Our clients are active in creating realistic financial plans covering all aspects of their current and future goals. We develop a partnership with you, your family and other professional advisors. As a team, we take a holistic approach to help you:

Set financial goals
Minimize financial risk
Lessen your income tax burden
Build retirement assets and income
Preserve your estate for your heirs
Design productive investment portfolios

Nancy earned her CFP™ in 1985, has a Master's degree in Financial Planning, is an Accredited Tax Advisor, listed in Marquis' Who's Who in Finance & Industry, and is a frequent contributor to the media on important financial planning issues.

Call today for a free initial consultation and discover the benefits of working with a small, fee-only firm, where personalized financial planning is delivered in a relaxing environment. We have nothing to sell but service.

2485 Mesa Terrace · Upland CA 91784
Tel 909.985.5550 · Fax 909.985.9500
www.NLJones.com . Nancy@NLJones.com

APPENDIX G: The Paperless Office

The Paperless Office
By Gary Stauffer

Each day, US workers generate 2.7 billion new sheets of paper. We all need it to do our work, but paper accumulates quickly, and no one knows this better than those in the financial services industry. Keeping up with all the paper is more than a full time job. You need to keep the paper you generate such as: buy/sell orders, applications, illustrations, presentations, correspondence and meeting notes. Additionally, you must keep incoming paper such as: appraisals, fund/investment statements, transaction confirmations, correspondence, applications, quarterly statements, commission statements, newsletters, reference materials, 401k information, tax returns, wills and trusts and medical records.

For a financial planner with 450 to 500 clients, you could be looking easily at 75,000 new sheets of paper each year... paper that you can't throw away, paper that has vital information you may need at some point in the future.

The amount of paper keeps growing, and businesses are paying the price for it. Paper files are often hard to find. Records may not be in their proper folder, or they may be "borrowed" and then lost on somebody's desk. Studies show that professionals often lose up to 500 hours a year looking for documents.

The Costs of Paper Based Files

Information industry estimates show that a typical worker in a typical department will take 12 minutes to process a document. Nine of these 12 minutes are spent searching for, retrieving and refiling the document. The other three minutes are spent processing it.

Coopers and Lybrand study shows that the average office:

- Makes 19 copies of each document
- Spends $250 recreating each lost document
- Loses 1 out of 20 office documents
- Spends $20 on labor for filing each document
- Spends $120 searching for a missing file
- 1 file cabinet cost $25,000 to fill and $2,000 to maintain

Now consider that the number of paper documents flowing through businesses has increased from 2.7 billion in 1996 to an estimated 30 billion in 2001. Along with the increased flow of paper come higher expenses and lower profit margins.

The 2000 survey report from the Seattle based firm of Moss Adams, points out that the average financial planner's office is eaten up by inefficiencies and excessive overhead.

Through the survey, Moss Adams gained insight into the obstacles that planners encounter:

- "Time Management"
- "Keeping Up with Technology"
- "Capacity to Serve Clients"
- "Improving Efficiency"

6 Key Areas of Your Operation to Consider:

1) How much time is lost searching for client files and/or client information?
2) How many billable hours are lost because information is not easily available?
3) How much time is lost copying, mailing and faxing documents?
4) How much is spent on storage space?
5) What would happen to your information should a disaster strike?
6) What's the cumulative impact of 1-5 on profitability and quality of client service?

A Paperless Document Imaging Solution Offers You The Following:

- The power to recapture lost billable hours
- Reduces your overhead expenses
- Improves the level of service you provide to your clients
- Increases profitability
- Time saved can be devoted to cultivating new clients

Going Paperless: What Is Document Imaging?

Document Imaging is the conversion of paper documents into electronic images on your computer. Once on your desktop or network computer(s), these documents can be retrieved effortlessly in seconds. Everyone knows the frustration of not being able to find a file when you need it most. Traditional methods of storing paper and electronic records require a great deal of effort to manage, distribute and find those documents. As the number of files grows, the time and effort required to manage them also increases. Document imaging revolutionizes the management of information and provides the means to rapidly find, retrieve and share all documents in your system.

7 Key Requirements of a Paperless Solution for Financial Services

- Scanning, importing and OCR input tools
- Methods for archiving and storing documents
- Conform to compliance requirements
- Indexing system to organize documents
- Retrieval tools to find documents
- Flexible document security controls
- Disaster recovery

Document Imaging builds on the strong points of paper documents. Files are scanned or electronically converted and a high-resolution photocopy is stored on a hard drive or optical disk (CD or DVD). No longer just ink on a page, document text is "read" by Optical Character Recognition (OCR) technology. A system should allow you to retrieve files by 1) searching for any word or phase in the text, 2) folder location, or 3) index card information. Which documents people can read and what actions they can perform on those documents depend on the user's security rights, which should be controlled by the document imaging system.

The Benefits of Going Paperless

Instant retrieval recovers lost productivity - Imaging lets you find documents quickly, without leaving your desk. Paper and microfilm are slower because users must go to storage rooms and filing cabinets to search for information manually.

Ability to simultaneously share documents - Imaging makes it easy to share documents electronically with colleagues and clients over a network, on CD or through the Web. Paper documents usually require photocopying to be shared and microfilm requires conversion to paper.

Secure, simple digital archiving - Your files are maintained in a secure, unalterable state that can be backed-up to WORM (Write Once Read Many) CD-ROM technology.

Reduce storage space costs - By converting paper to digital images, you eliminate the need to store the paper. You will be able to eliminate not only the filing cabinets in your office, but boxes of files that may be stored off-site or taking up valuable office space. A single CD-ROM can hold up to 10,000 documents, the equivalent of a 4-drawer filing cabinet.

Reclaim billable hours - Instead of searching for information, your time is now better spent meeting the needs of your current clients and having the time to make new ones.

Increased profitability and satisfied clients - Your firm should be able to minimize over-head cost while maximizing productivity and efficiency.

Eliminate document loss and misfiling - OCR technology allows you to never lose a document again, simply by reading and indexing each word in every document.

Improved security vs. paper filing - With paper files, the only security control you have is to lock the filing cabinet. Document imaging provides you the ability to restrict access to sensitive documents, and even black out portions of a document that others may not be permitted to see.

Disaster recovery - With paper files, once they are gone, they are gone for good. With document imaging you can quickly recover from any disaster, as all of your document images, index cards and vital information are easily stored on and recoverable from, CD-ROMS.

Essential Software Features

Organization and Daily Use
Look for a systems ability to organize files in the same manner as your manual system. It should be able to maintain separate files for clients, staff, OSJ files, pending applications, and reference information.

Intuitive Visual Interface and Store in Native Format
You need the system to maintain separate folders and documents for each different account that your client may have. A good system allows you to store electronic documents, such as word processing, spreadsheet files and financial plans in their native formats.

Easy File Viewing
A system must allow you to easily view your documents with a wide variety of viewing options. Open the document for wide screen to see a single page of the document clearly and legibly. Or, open the document with the thumbnail view to see all of the pages in the document.

Add to an Existing Document
Adding pages to an existing client document is important. The program should simply open a document, click scan and instruct the software where to place the pages: the first page, the last page or somewhere in the middle.

Quick Shortcuts to Files
Using a document imaging system for active files eliminates the clutter on desks and floors and eliminates the need to leave your desk to get information form the files. Establish working files for each staff member and then drag the client's folder that you are working on into the staff member's folder. For client reviews, you can easily setup a review folder and drag the client's file there, so that all information is readily available to you and your client.

Add Working Comments
Use sticky notes within the document imaging system to write yourself notes regarding what needs to be done on a particular case or reminders of what information you are looking for.

Easy to Move Documents
When papers are misfiled manually, it is nearly impossible to find them again, especially when you need them. Within a document imaging system, you can find any document by searching on words within the document. If a document is misfiled, you can simply drag the document to the proper folder – without the need for creating additional paper.

Print Directly to Your Files

You can establish planning files for your clients that include the actual proposals, research and illustrations that you created through other software programs. There is no need to print a paper copy for your files, because you can simply "print" the reports directly to your document imaging system and the file for that client.

OSJ Files

You can maintain your entire OSJ and compliance file information directly in your document management system. You can use custom stamps directly in the document imaging system to indicate that the OSJ for your office has reviewed the materials.

Index Templates

Index templates allow you to quickly and effectively cross reference information, as well as provide another means for narrowing down your document searches. Index templates should be customizable to meet your specific needs.

OCR

Optical Character Recognition, OCR, will enable you to find any document based on a single word, phase or combination of words contained therein. OCR reads every word in your documents and indexes them automatically – so when it comes time to retrieve those documents, the documents are found quickly and easily.

Retrieval

Intelligent search capabilities like OCR and Indexes allow documents to be retrieved instantly. This eliminates long, time-consuming manual searches for information through a filing cabinet or pile of papers. OCR turns the words on paper documents into a database of invaluable information at your fingertips created without the excessive data entry. A properly sized document imaging system eliminates your need to physically go to old record locations or offsite storage facilities.

Distribution

With your documents electronically filed in your computer, you can simply e-mail or fax any information directly from your computer to your broker/dealer, fund company, compliance officer, administrator or client without having to leave your desk. If you need a hardcopy of the information, you can simply print the files to your printer. You can share files within your office, simultaneously and without the need to generate photocopies. This enables two or more people to work on the same file from the comfort of their office at the same time…something that you can't do with paper. If you are heading out of the office for a client meeting, there is no need to take a hardcopy file with you. You can take all of the information you need, including the entire history of the client, on your notebook computer, a CD-ROM or access the information directly from your own secured Internet document site.

Security

Security must control who has access to your files, and what content they can view, and what functions they can perform. It should permit you to add annotations, including highlighting, stamps, and sticky notes to your documents, or you can blackout portions of a document to prevent unauthorized access to sensitive and confidential information. Additional security features allow people to view documents, but images can never be altered from their original state. And to protect you against any possible disaster, complete CD-ROM backups of your entire digital archive, including images, indexes and the databases can be stored off-site, with duplicate copies made available at your local office.

Audit Trail

Audit trails monitor who did what, with what document, on what day and time. Not only should audit trails lock your information in time, they can provide a detailed history on any document stored on the system. You have complete control over your documents, something that is near impossible to duplicate in the world of paper.

Compliance

It is important to meet the requirements for maintaining paperless files as set-forth by the NASD, SEC and IRS. To have an approved database you must set the information in time. This means that the date and time that the image was digitally created on your system is recorded and cannot be changed. This is why many state laws dictate that the media must be unalterable.

NASD/SEC Compliance Issues

- You must be able to retrieve your books and records on demand.
- You images and database must be stored on acceptable media.
- You must maintain your books and records in unalterable format.
- A copy of your records must be maintained by a third party, independent from your operation, and they must be readily available to auditors, when requested.
- You must be able to store your documents on WORM media, (i.e. CD-ROM, DVD) or you must deploy Audit Trail tracking that clearly identifies the original dates that all images were captured on your system.

IRS Compliance Issues

The IRS will accept an optical image as evidence as long as the law allows it in the state where it was produced. Code Section 6001 says that the IRS accepts imaged documents as legal records given:

- Records can be scanned or electronically converted.
- A complete and accurate transfer of records can be made.
- System has reasonable controls to ensure integrity, accuracy and reliability.
- System has reasonable controls to prevent and detect unauthorized creation of, addition to, alteration of or deletion of records.
- System has reasonable controls to prevent and detect records deterioration.
- There's an indexing system that assists with finding records.
- System has the ability to print copies.

- System must be able to cross-reference with other record-keeping systems and software.
- System has documentation on how the software works and how it is set up.
- The IRS district director may periodically test the storage system.
- If the system fails, the taxpayer must have paper originals or micrographic backup.

Scanners

The quality of your scanner and the image capturing software it interfaces with will play a major role in the effectiveness of your ability to find information. Without a quality scanner, your images will not OCR correctly, making you documents harder to find when you need them most. Times Roman is the most widely used font in today's offices. However, if you were to scan a Times Roman font-based document with a 200 dpi scanner, less than 75% of the words would be correctly identifiable. This could mean lost documents. When looking at scanners, there are several factors that you should take into consideration.

Duplex - If the majority of the documents that you receive are double-sided, a duplex scanner is a necessity. This will reduce the amount of time required to scan new documents into your imaging system.

DPI - This means dots per inch, and relates to the quality of the image stored on your computer. The lower the number, the lower the resolution, and the harder it will be to OCR and retrieve documents. To ensure better OCR efficiency, the minimum scanner setting should be 300dpi.

ADF - Automatic Document Feeder. Like a copier, the ADF allows you to stack several pieces of paper on the scanner at a single time, rather than feeding one piece of paper at a time.

Speed - The faster the speed, the higher the price tag. However, you must weigh the speed of the scanner with the volume of documents received on a daily, weekly and monthly basis. While a slower scanner may be a lower frontend investment, it could cost you more in personnel time.

Paper Sizes - Make sure that you get a scanner that can handle the majority of your office's paper sizes that you will be dealing with. Most scanners can handle 8½ x 11 and 14 x 11. If you use or store wide ledger sheets (11 x 17) or smaller statement or check size pieces of paper, your scanner must be able to accommodate them.

Backup and Archival

Backups of your imaging system should include more than just images. They should also contain all database and index information. Tape backups are effective for backing up large blocks of information from a computer, but publishing your data to a CD-ROM provides greater flexibility and a more effective means of quickly recovering lost data. All compliance rules and regulations from NASD to the SEC to the IRS dictate that images must be maintained in their original state and must be unalterable. Only CD-ROM and WORM (also including DVD, but it is currently cost prohibitive) provide a guarantee that these rules and regulations are followed. An important issue regarding

CD-ROM and WORM backup is to make sure that the information is completely useable once it is stored on the media. Storing encrypted TIFF images and text on a CD-ROM does not provide good usability. The better choice is to publish a CD that includes the associated images, text files, database and most importantly a viewer, thus making the CD-ROM a completely accessible medium.

Open Architecture

With the multitude of software applications used in the office environment today, you need a document imaging system that has the ability to easily talk to and share information with your other software systems, especially your business-critical applications.

Implementation Guidelines

Careful planning is one of the most important elements of a successful implementation project. Some planning needs to be done before the first dollar is spent on the project. A project has a much better chance of success if someone has documented, in detail, the project scope, system requirements, schedule, business case and technical aspects before you begin. As obvious as it may sound, these first steps are frequently not accomplished until the project has already started…and then it may be too late.

Clearly Identify Your Goals and Objectives.
- What do you expect a document imaging system to do for you?
- What problems are you looking to solve?
- How do you plan on using the system?
- Do you want/need the document imaging system to interface with current business-critical applications?

Needs Analysis
- How many people will need access to the files?
- How many people will be scanning in paper?
- Do you have a network in place now?
- Do you require new computers?
- Do you require computer upgrades?
- How many scanners will be required?
- What capabilities will you need?
- Where does the majority of your paper originate?
- What is the weekly amount of new paper coming into your office?
- Do you need Audit Trial or CD Publishing?
- What are the retention schedules for the documents you store?
- Determine the size requirements for your system by counting the number of filing cabinets and storage boxes you have now, as well as the number of new pieces of paper that come into your office on a daily, weekly and annual basis.

Document Distribution
- Do you need to fax or e-mail documents?

- Do you have offices in various locations that require copies of your records?
- Do you need to take your documents out of the office?

File Structure and Indexes
- How do you look up information?
- What type of information will be stored in the system?
- What type of cross-reference information do you need?
- How many different indexes do you need?

Daily Procedures
- Who will perform the scanning operations?
- What types of information are to be scanned?
- What are the workflow procedures?
- What should be done with the paper after it is scanned?

How to Proceed from Day One?

Conversion from Microfiche or other Imaging System
- Who will do the conversion?
- How long will it take?
- How much will it cost?

Back File Conversion
- 100% or partial?
- Determine what archived records need to be converted.
- How many archived records do you need to convert?
- Who will perform the conversion?
- How long do you need to retain these records?
- Does your office ever refer to these records? How often?
- How long will it take to complete the process?

Day-Forward
- Only scan records from this day forward?
- What if you need old documents in storage?
- What types of information should be scanned?
- Who will perform the scanning?

On-Demand Day-Forward
- Back Files are scanned in only when required.
- The amount of back-files decrease over time.

Gary may be reached at:
Phone: 714-573-7608
Email: gstauffer@sbcglobal.net

Thanks for the Help From

MY FRIENDS

INDEX

ABOUT THE AUTHOR

In the early eighties, Nancy was a dissatisfied Realtor having serious concerns with the proliferation of "creative financing" among lenders. When the College for Financial Planning presented a program for Realtors about a new profession called "financial planning", she was intrigued and enrolled in the Certified Financial Planner (CFP) course in September of 1983.

Six months into the CFP program, she left real estate to begin her full time career in financial planning. Her instructors agreed that the only way to thrive as a financial planner was to sell commissioned products. For several years she was affiliated with a broker-dealer and prepared tax returns on her own. When she learned that she could actually write financial plans for a fee, she established an independent practice to prove that selling on commissions was not a prerequisite to success.

She applied for a position as **adjunct faculty with the College for Financial Planning (1986-1994)** and taught every course in the CFP program while earning her **Masters in Financial Planning** and the designation **Accredited Tax Advisor** from the same institution.

Writing financial plans on retainer for other planners and preparing income tax returns for clients helped cash flow as she struggled to build her sole proprietorship. Naively she entered into a partnership in 1994, which became the **December, 1995 cover story for the Dow Jones Investment Advisor Magazine**, entitled "Can This Partnership Survive?" It didn't.

Starting over for the fourth time, she began working with a turnkey investment management firm, placing assets under management. She volunteered for the **CFP Board Item Writing Committee (1994-1998)**, and wrote multiple-choice questions for the series exams. That led to participation writing Case Study questions, questions for the CFP Comprehensive exam, and in 1999, appointment to the **North American Securities Administrators Association Investment Advisor Competency Exam Advisor Council**.

From 1997 through 1999 she wrote a **monthly consumer column on Financial Planning for the publication "Debt-Free and Prosperous Living"™**

In 1995 she began posting on **Financial Planning Interactive**, and shortly thereafter was asked to help moderate their **"Getting Started" discussion boards**. Today she spends hours every month corresponding with individuals asking for guidance in making a career move to financial planning. After answering the same questions repeatedly, she realized the need for a comprehensive publication on the topic of how an individual can get started as a financial planner.

Today she continues as **Moderator on Financial Planning Interactive**. In 1999 and again in 2000 she was a **panelist for the Los Angeles Times' Investment Strategies Conference**, and was the **Industry Speaker for the North American Securities Administrators Association's 1999 National Conference**. In 2002 Nancy was named one of the **Most Influential People in the Profession** by readers of Financial Planning™, and is an **American Business Women's Association 2003 Top Ten**.

She is listed in Marquis' **Who's Who of Finance in Industry, Who's Who of American Women, Who's Who in America,** and **Who's Who in the World**, and is widely quoted in the financial press.

As President of NLJones, Inc., Nancy and her staff of three run a successful fee-only financial planning practice and manage assets for about sixty families.

Nancy is married to professional actor/director Claude Earl Jones and resides in Upland, California.